An intense
and
haunting
memoir
of childhood
love and loss

John
McGAHERN

Memoir

ff

'Ireland's greatest
living novelist'
*Observer*

ff

# WISH YOU WERE HERE

South Bank Centre London
Queen Elizabeth Hall
Purcell Room

## London's year-round literature festival

| 10 Sept | **PHILIP PULLMAN + TOM PAULIN** on *Paradise Lost* |
| 15 Sept | **CAROL ANN DUFFY** in a world premiere of *Rapture*, set to the music of Eliana Tomkins |
| 27 Sept | **ANTONY BEEVOR** |
| 4 Oct | **CHINUA ACHEBE + CARYL PHILLIPS** |
| 10 Oct | **BRET EASTON ELLIS** |
| 22 Oct | **JAMAICA KINCAID** in *Wanderlust*: a weekend of travel writing (22+23 Oct) including John Banville, Patrick McGrath, Caroline Moorehead, Robert MacFarlane + Rory Stewart |
| 2 Nov | **MARGARET ATWOOD, JEANETTE WINTERSON + KAREN ARMSTRONG** on Myths |
| 9 Nov | **WOLE SOYINKA** in Remember Saro-Wiwa |
| 22 Nov | **GEORGE SZIRTES** gives the T.S. Eliot lecture |
| 29 Nov | **SALMAN RUSHDIE** |
| 13 Dec | **LIONEL SHRIVER** |

Box Office: 0870 190 0901   For more information and booking: www.rfh.org.uk

# GRANTA

## GRANTA 91, AUTUMN 2005
www.granta.com

EDITOR  *Ian Jack*
DEPUTY EDITOR  *Matt Weiland*
MANAGING EDITOR  *Fatema Ahmed*
ASSOCIATE EDITOR  *Liz Jobey*
EDITORIAL ASSISTANT  *Helen Gordon*

CONTRIBUTING EDITORS  *Diana Athill, Sophie Harrison, Gail Lynch, Blake Morrison, John Ryle, Sukhdev Sandhu, Lucretia Stewart*

ASSOCIATE PUBLISHER  *Sally Lewis*
FINANCE  *Geoffrey Gordon, Morgan Graver*
SALES  *Frances Hollingdale*
PUBLICITY  *Louise Campbell*
SUBSCRIPTIONS  *John Kirkby, Julie Codling*
PUBLISHING ASSISTANT  *Mark Williams*
ADVERTISING MANAGER  *Kate Rochester*
PRODUCTION ASSOCIATE  *Sarah Wasley*
PROOFS  *Gillian Kemp*

PUBLISHER  *Rea S. Hederman*

Granta, 2–3 Hanover Yard, Noel Road, London N1 8BE
Tel 020 7704 9776 Fax 020 7704 0474
email for editorial: editorial@granta.com

Granta US, 1755 Broadway, 5th Floor, New York, NY 10019-3780, USA

TO SUBSCRIBE call 020 7704 0470 or e-mail subs@granta.com
A one-year subscription (four issues) costs £27.95 (UK), £35.95 (rest of Europe) and £42.95 (rest of the world).

Granta is printed and bound in Italy by Legoprint. The paper used in this publication meets the minimum requirements of American National Standard for Information Sciences—Permanence of Paper for Printed Library Materials, ANSI Z39.48-1984.

Design: Slab Media
Front cover photograph: Corbis
Back cover photographs: Robin Grierson

ISBN 0-903141-80-9

by Brian Friel
until 13 October

a new play
by Howard Brenton
30 September –
4 February

by Henrik Ibsen
in a new version
by Samuel Adamson
from 21 October

adapted by
Helen Edmundson
from a novel
by Jamila Gavin
from 2 November

by George S Kaufman
and Moss Hart
from 5 December

**A new play by David Edgar**
A comedy of misunderstanding soon
becomes a chilling drama about
multicultural Britain
**12 September – 22 October**

Freely adapted from Gogol's
*The Government Inspector*
**A comedy by David Farr**
**until 5 October**

TheTravelex
£10 Season
National
Theatre

# September 2005 – January 2006

# Motley Notes

Generalizations about the national psyche—supposing there is one—must always be treated with suspicion. In 1997, the great crowds who mourned the death of the Princess of Wales with their tears, flowers and candles were taken as evidence that British behaviour had utterly changed. We were at last in touch with our feelings, prepared to show them, to hug strangers, to weep and tear our hair. We would never be the same again. Eight years later, in July this year, our alleged conversion to the open emotions of (say) Brazil had been forgotten. The traditional strengths of stoicism, resilience and understatement hadn't, after all, died with the princess in her Paris car crash. They were merely sleeping, to spring awake when three terrorist bombs went off in London tube trains and a fourth on a London bus, killing (as I write—the toll may rise) fifty-six people and injuring hundreds of others. London's response to the bombs showed what Londoners were made of; we would be cheerful, we would not be cowed, we would carry on as usual. We showed 'the spirit of London', the same spirit of our citizen forebears during their bombing by the Luftwaffe—'the Blitz'—in 1940 and 1941.

How such conclusions are reached, from what evidence, it is always difficult to know, but on July 7 they were reached very quickly, perhaps with the understanding that the wish can be father to the fact. Speeches by politicians, messages to websites, pieces to camera by television reporters, columnists in the next day's newspapers—all of them spoke of the calm and quiet resolution of Londoners. One commentator daringly ascribed it to the domestic, unthreatening scale of London's architecture; many others saw it exemplified by the sight of hundreds of thousands of Londoners walking quietly home that evening in the complete absence of buses and tubes (and those crowded pavements of one-way human traffic certainly were a striking sight, unknown even in the Blitz, though caused by pure necessity rather than feelings of communal solidarity).

For the sociological record, my own very commonplace experience was this. That morning I got to the bus stop much later than usual, around 10.30. For that time of day there was a surprisingly big crowd—the orderly London bus queue disintegrated years ago—and very few buses, all of them full. My mobile phone wouldn't work. I got a taxi and the driver pushed his window back and asked me if I had heard the news, and I thought for a second that the Queen must have died, and then he told me about the bombs—three or four buses hit, an unknown number of tubes, no casualty figures, lots of rumour. 'I'd fucking hang the fuckers, no questions asked,' he said. 'I'd fucking hang them, whoever did it.' Even for a man in an England football shirt, he was an exceptional swearer and ranter and I was glad to step out of his cab. In the office, people were listening to the radio and looking at the BBC website. On a landline—the mobile phone networks were still jammed—I checked that my wife and children were safe at work and in school. They had no reason to be on the number 30 bus or on the Piccadilly or Circle Lines, but we use all of them sometimes and their routes and stations are very close; King's Cross under a mile away. And then I worked as usual and in the evening walked home to watch the continuous news on television, following the same pattern the next day. Many kind emails arrived hoping that we were safe and well. It was only then, perhaps, that I understood that seen from far away (Tel Aviv, Delhi, New York) I was at the centre rather than the fringe of a global drama. On Friday night, my wife told me of the passenger on the number 30 who, before he got impatient with the bus's slow progress and got off, had noticed a young man next to him who kept fiddling with something in his backpack. I had a nightmare in which I saw a similar thing but couldn't leave the bus. Then, in Saturday's newspaper, I read an account of one policeman's experience working underground in the narrow tunnel of the Piccadilly line, in the carriage where so many had died. Blood, oppressive heat, a multitude of body parts (the blast had nowhere to go). When the policeman reached the surface after his day's brave work he said that he had felt 'lonelier than I thought was possible'. I nearly cried at that, and for most of the day I felt sad and fearful, 'unhinged' might be the word. The attack on London had inevitably come; others would follow—would they ever end?—and, much though I like London (my home for thirty-five adult years), there are safer places to live.

The mood passed. The next day, Sunday, I took a friend from Chicago who is interested in railways to have a look at the civil engineering works at St Pancras station, where the new fast line to Paris will start, stopping on its way at the site for the London Olympics in 2012, which were announced the day before the bombs. We walked around new embankments and looked at the cranes and the earth-movers. A forgotten swathe of London, once occupied by freight yards and more recently by crack addicts, is being redeveloped and spruced up. This is London as an advertising agency might see it—confident, multicultural, new and yet old, the fancy Victorian gothic of the old terminus surviving among undecorated concrete and glass. Then, more or less by accident, my friend and I got to King's Cross. Outside the station, relatives had pinned up pictures of men and women who could only be described as 'missing' because they were not yet confirmed dead. There were flowers, messages of support, and television crews. It was a hot, sunny day. As we stood on the pavement across the road, I realized that no more than a hundred feet or so under my feet, men were still working in the tunnel to retrieve pieces of the bomb, and of the tissue and bone of the people, the ex-people, whose friends and relatives hoped against hope were still alive.

How can we bear such a thought, such proximity? I don't know, but we do. Later in the day my children passed though King's Cross on the Victoria tube and were interested to see that the train slowed at the station but didn't stop. Nothing much more was said about it.

In this, there is nothing special about London. New York, Madrid, Jerusalem, Baghdad; people there have suffered equal (or far greater) terrors and carried on. That London has a special spirit must be a myth. But myths can be helpful—their point isn't their trueness—and to imagine that you are part of some resilient tradition—that you are resilient simply because of where you live— may help rather than harm you, so long as you don't buy it completely, remembering that you are only flesh and blood.

Ian Jack

The myth came out of the last months of 1940. Just like this year's terrorist attack, the German bombing of London had been long awaited, and with an even greater fatalism. As the historian and anthropologist Tom Harrisson wrote thirty-five years later, 'The idea that attack from overhead would become the final, totally devastating stage in coming wars grew [to] near-obsession—comparable, say, to the one-time belief of strict Christian sects in a burning hell for the unredeemed.' The first big raid occurred on 'Black Saturday', September 7, a fine day towards the end of a fine summer. Another writer, Ritchie Calder, watched it from his garden on the Surrey Downs 'with a detachment which surprised and rather shocked me'—until the sight of London, apparently on fire from end to end, filled him with 'dread and horror'. As more German planes came in from the coast, the family (they had been playing cricket) took a break for tea. 'How silly that sounds! How callous and inconsequential! Yet how much in keeping with the strange unreality of it all!'

Calder wrote that in a small book, *The Lesson of London*, published in 1941 as one of a series called the Searchlight Books, which were edited by T. R. Fyvel and George Orwell and also included Orwell's famous essay 'The Lion and the Unicorn: Socialism and the English Genius.' Calder's book is very good—a mixture of eyewitness reporting from ruined east London and a castigation of poor planning by the authorities—and in it he notes that 'the old standards of courage disappeared in the common and unconscious heroism of ordinary individuals', often meaning people who did no more than continue to come to work. Very early on in the war the celebration of quiet 'ordinariness' became a dominant theme—the thinking British patriot's weapon of choice—which was a kind of miracle given that Britain then was a most class-conscious country with the largest empire the world had ever seen, and quite literally pompous. But it was lucky in its writers, its radio-producers and its film-makers, men such as Harrisson, Calder, Orwell, and Humphrey Jennings who had in the 1930s made journeys from backgrounds of relative privilege to discover and document the working class. Their commitment to a certain demotic idea of Britain, at war or at peace, gave British propaganda (or at least Britain's advertisements for its cause) the ring of modest truth, and an appeal to the egalitarian instincts of Roosevelt's America.

The key contribution was made by Humphrey Jennings and another documentary director, Harry Watt, in a ten-minute film called for foreign audiences, *London Can Take It*, and for British audiences, *Britain Can Take It* (presumably to prevent resentment of the capital in other British cities which were also being bombed). As Kevin Jackson writes in his biography of Jennings, the film was 'perhaps the most influential work he ever made—one of the few films that have played some small part in changing the course of history'. It was shot in September, 1940, soon after the night bombing started and when the outcome of both the Blitz and the war was far from clear. The British army had been evacuated from Dunkirk only months before; France was occupied; the Soviet Union and the United States still non-combatants. In Britain, a terrorized population and defeat were strong possibilities, though not ones countenanced by *London Can Take It*. The film showed ordinary people coping—old people asleep in air-raid shelters, a woman kicking broken glass aside as she collects milk from the doorstep, commuters continuing to commute across the rubble—as on the soundtrack the American journalist and broadcaster, Quentin Reynolds, delivers his fiercely optimistic commentary. 'I am a neutral reporter. I have watched the people of London live and die... I can assure you, there is no panic, no fear, no despair in London town.'

It was finished in ten days, and Reynolds took it immediately to the United States, where a special screening was arranged for Roosevelt. Soon afterwards—by October 25—it had taken enough at the American box office to be judged 'a wild success' by the British Ministry of Information. 'The Spirit of the Blitz' had been born.

The film was not untrue to its subject; many diaries and records from the period attest to a remarkably matter-of-fact reaction to being bombed. But like any piece of art it was highly selective in its truths: no body parts, no grief in a city where, between September 1940 and May 1941, about 20,000 civilians died from the detonation of 18,800 tons of high explosives dropped from above.

Other British towns did not react so stoically. After severe raids on Plymouth and Clydebank, smaller targets than London where the effects of bombing were more obvious, many in their populations (from bombed-out homes and otherwise) took to camping in the nearby hills. And it is also fair to wonder how long London would have continued to 'take it' had the bombing gone on at the rate of the first few months. A film called 'Dresden Can Take It' would seem unlikely, though 'Fallujah Can Take It' must never be ruled out.

About a mile away from my house there is a cemetery, the Abney Park Cemetery, which was laid out by a private company in the nineteenth century to accommodate the growing numbers of the London dead who failed to qualify for burial in the graveyards of Anglican parish churches—that is, for Jews, Atheists, Nonconformists, and I imagine Muslims too, had any of their bereaved come knocking. It has some large and well-tended memorials, including those to the Booth family, who founded the Salvation Army, but mostly it is overgrown and tumbledown. Nicely so: it looks like a wood rather than a cemetery, with rambling paths though the trees, crazily tipped gravestones, and cracked monuments in the shrubbery.

One neglected memorial—and quite hard to find—was erected by the Metropolitan Borough of Stoke Newington to those people in the borough who died in the wartime bombing. A lot of the lead has been picked from the stone, but it's still possible to read the inscription. DEATH IS BUT CROSSING THE WORLD AS FRIENDS DO THE SEAS, THEY LIVE IN ONE ANOTHER STILL. Underneath, the dead are listed beneath the names of the streets they lived and died in. The street that suffered most grievously was Coronation Avenue, where on October 13, 1940, a bomb (more probably a stick of bombs) landed and killed ninety-five people. The names suggest it was quite a Jewish street: two Coopersteins, three Edelsteins, one Katz, two Danzigers, two Krakowskys, etc. Perhaps one of them was the man described by Ritchie Calder in his chapter, 'The Courage of London': 'the little German Jew who looked up at a dog fight over the East End, his tattered beard quivering with excitement, and cried, "Our Spitfire boys are wunderbar."'

I've never seen flowers at this memorial, or any other sign of care. It all seems so long ago. What most remains is a folk memory of that time, the stoicism that has been so beautifully enshrined in films and literature.                                    *Ian Jack*

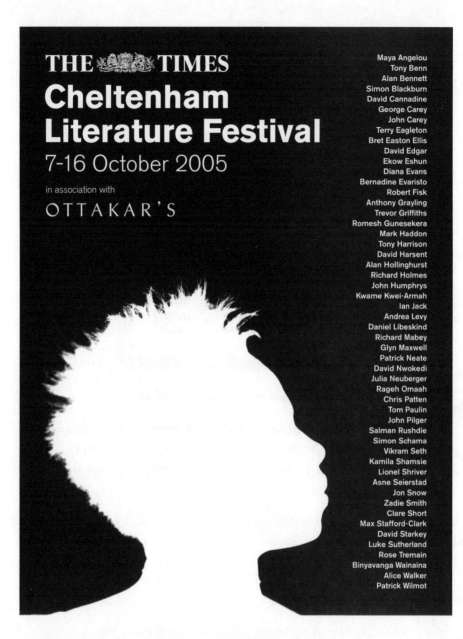

THE TIMES
**Cheltenham
Literature Festival**
7-16 October 2005

in association with

OTTAKAR'S

Maya Angelou
Tony Benn
Alan Bennett
Simon Blackburn
David Cannadine
George Carey
John Carey
Terry Eagleton
Bret Easton Ellis
David Edgar
Ekow Eshun
Diana Evans
Bernadine Evaristo
Robert Fisk
Anthony Grayling
Trevor Griffiths
Romesh Gunesekera
Mark Haddon
Tony Harrison
David Harsent
Alan Hollinghurst
Richard Holmes
John Humphrys
Kwame Kwei-Armah
Ian Jack
Andrea Levy
Daniel Libeskind
Richard Mabey
Glyn Maxwell
Patrick Neate
David Nwokedi
Julia Neuberger
Rageh Omaah
Chris Patten
Tom Paulin
John Pilger
Salman Rushdie
Simon Schama
Vikram Seth
Kamila Shamsie
Lionel Shriver
Asne Seierstad
Jon Snow
Zadie Smith
Clare Short
Max Stafford-Clark
David Starkey
Luke Sutherland
Rose Tremain
Binyavanga Wainaina
Alice Walker
Patrick Wilmot

**Bookings: 01242 227979**
www.cheltenhamfestivals.org.uk

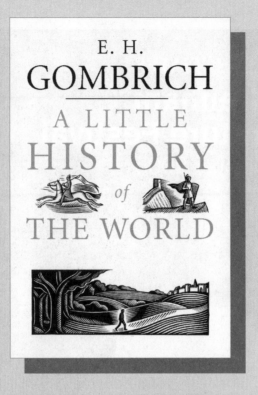

GRANTA

# WISH YOU WERE HERE
## Simon Gray

A seaside diary of the past and present,
Barbados, 2004

Simon Gray at Hayling Island, 1937

# A prayer answered

Here I am, sitting at my table with my pad, the usual table at the usual hotel in Barbados. It's mid-morning now, pigeons hopping about in the sun, little birds with yellow chests settling on the rim of my fruit punch, in front of me the sea in Caribbean blue and green, and from it the occasional purr and cough of small boats, the roar of a speedboat, brief and violent, and behind me the clatter of waiters laying tables while they talk to each other in incomprehensible Bajan—everything very much as you hope it will be when you're in London during Christmas, longing to be here.

So at least that's another Christmas gone, thank God. For me it has become the worst season, the season when people I love die, beginning with my mother, over thirty years ago, then a long gap, and then almost every other year, sometimes on consecutive years, for the past decade—last year on the day after Boxing Day, it was Ian Hamilton, this year on Boxing Day Alan Bates—no, technically by the calendar, that's wrong, Alan, who died three weeks ago, died in 2003, which is now last year, and Ian, who died one year and three weeks ago, died in 2002, which is now two years ago—but on Boxing Day and the day after Boxing Day respectively, in the Christmas season—

# A self-prohibition

My plan is to sit here and get down some thoughts and memories of Alan, but I don't think I can start today, not on the first day, with the pigeons hopping, and the little birds with yellow chests etc., one of which is now sharing my drink. Best let it happen when it happens, tomorrow perhaps, or later in the week, let it sneak up. Today the thing is just to be here, to be back here at the usual table, my yellow pad in front of me, free to go wherever—although I think I must make a pact with myself to lay off the subject of my age, and my physical deterioration, it's really time I outgrew all that, it's not becoming in a man nearing seventy. Now I see those words actually on the page, 'nearing seventy', I find myself gaping at them, I can't think what it is that's nearing seventy, apart from my body, but the most significant parts of my body, the parts whose ageing have a significant bearing on my life expectancy, are hidden from my view: the liver (mistreated for nearly fifty years), the lungs (for over sixty years), the heart, the intestines, bladder and bowels are all concealed from view, their condition reported on a couple of times a year in the form of figures printed out from blood tests which my doctor faxes through to me and which I study with attentive ignorance, looking for asterisks—if he puts an asterisk by a number it means that the number is either too high or too low. These days the number to do with the prostate is too high, but I'm not to be surprised by this, I'm told, because although I have a tumour nesting or nestling there, it might still be nesting or nestling while I die of something else, or a combination of something elses, or in an accident, or unlawfully, at the hands of another—in other words, one way or another, it's there for life. As am I, I suppose. But my point, if I have a point, is that while I am decaying within and without, and quite right too, it's nature's way, after all, the way of all flesh, I am most of the time unaware of the decay, though there are the hints, of course, the days when the bladder seems to fill even as I'm emptying it, the wheeze and double whistle in the chest, the faintness that follows climbing stairs.

## Birth of the jouncer

On the other hand the self itself, my only self, seems to be exactly what it was when I first discovered it at some months old, sitting harnessed in my pram in the garden at Mallows, in Hayling Island. It was a large pram, handed down from an earlier period, capacious, highly sprung, almost brakeless, easily mobile, and I used to be left in it alone for half an hour or so every afternoon. One afternoon I began to shake and buck in my harness, and the pram jolted forward. As I grasped the connection between the movement of my body and the movement of the pram, something in me sprang to life—a self-birth is how I remember it now, with pride and astonishment still. The pram moved maybe only a few inches the first time, but eventually the inches became feet, and then yards, and then quite a few yards, until at last somebody, Mummy? Daddy? Nanny? noticed that the pram when they returned to it was not quite where they were sure they had left it. But how was he doing it, and if not he, who then and why? The next day they planted the pram in the usual spot, withdrew to a distance and witnessed first its swaying, then its juddering, then its slow, unsteady progress along the path, accompanied by a ghastly keening sound from within that reminded them more of a dog than of a baby human. The explanation was so simple that it concealed the real mysteries—of the self, of the will, of the power of solitude, and of the elemental need to make a keening noise when shaking and bouncing one's pram up or down the garden path. Jouncing was the word they used for this eerie combination of causes and effects. I was a jouncer, therefore.

## My battle with the waves

So. To the left of the hotel, if you are facing the sea, there is a small cove with a shed in it. From this shed a pipe stretches into the sea and pumps water out into something or other behind the shed, a cistern, I think, though I've never seen it. The shed and the pipe and the cistern, if there is a cistern, belong to McGill University, in Montreal, their Marine Science Department. My father went to McGill, which is why I always read the sign carefully, though I know it by heart, when I clamber around the little cove to the public beach next to it. I've taken to swimming there because the hotel beach has developed a high ridge close to shore. When you walk out to sea the ground gives under you, and you have to fling yourself forward and swim before you intend to. I like to have a cigarette as I wade out, smoking and contemplating the various mysteries of life. Where does the sea come from? Why does nature exist? What's that scuttling over my feet?—and it's no fun, plus it's very unsightly, to be caught by a wave with a cigarette between your lips, wasteful too, but the worst part is getting out. It's difficult to get a grip on the ridge, which consists of sand and pebbles, your foot slides down the slope, you topple back into the sea, start again, trying to get out between the incoming waves, which bide their time and then, when you've convinced yourself there isn't one, erupt under you as you place your foot halfway up the ridge again. The year before last a visiting friend of ours, Bumma, got caught by a brute of a wave, she was virtually alone on the beach, there was no one to help her as she was tumbled and rolled around, sucked back by the undertow, then before she could regain her footing, rolled and tumbled forward. She was lucky not to have drowned, really, in what would have been a foot or so of water. I kept thinking of her when I was trying to get out the other afternoon, and suddenly hit upon a scheme, a rather daring scheme, basically derived from judo, or ju-jitsu. You use the force opposing

19

you to your advantage—i.e. when a man throws a punch at you, you duck, catch his arm and pull him forward using his own impetus as a lever, then step out of the way as he flows past you and crashes to the ground, where you can kick him at your leisure. I've seen this done often on screen, most notably by a one-armed Spencer Tracy, in *Bad Day at Black Rock*, when he annihilates the brutish two-armed Ernest Borgnine by employing exactly the method I've described, though being Spencer Tracy he doesn't kick him when he's down, he lets him get up to throw another haymaker. Spencer has to go through the whole process three times, his trilby remaining on his head, by the way, throughout. It's a very exhilarating scene, and now I've got the film recorded I can, and sometimes do, play it over and over again. So? Oh, yes, conquering the ridge. My plan was to *use* the waves to carry me over the ridge by surfing them. I am actually rather good at surfing, can do it without a board, and lo! there I was on the other side of the ridge, the beach a mere few feet away, all I had to do was scramble to my feet and take a step or two—I'd made it to my knees when the wave I'd surfed in on surged back, taking me with it and peppering my legs and stomach with pebbles, sharp stones and what felt like fragments of broken glass, and then, like Bumma, I was rolled, tumbled, etc., but unlike Bumma I was watched from the shore by a dozen or so guests at the adjoining hotel, lolling on their beach beds and certainly smiling, in some cases laughing as if I were a floor show. This went on for several minutes. Once or twice I struck out to sea, a dignified, classy crawl, as if I were engaged in a complicated exercise I'd designed for myself, a sort of combat course. I suspect I would still be there, either being rolled around with sand and stone and sea, like a maritime version of Wordsworth's Lucy, or right out in deep water, pretending that that's where I prefer to be, or drowned, if my wife Victoria hadn't come looking for me, sized up the situation in a blink, walked into the water and stretched out her hand, which I took as if intending to shake, but allowed myself to be drawn by it up to safety. Extraordinary how much power, I almost wrote brute power, is contained in her slight and graceful form. I've long accepted that she's stronger than me physically as well as morally, but then she's much younger, hasn't got a paunch, doesn't smoke, so she jolly well ought to be able to haul me out of the sea.

# A glimpse of a lost civilization

Anyway, the above should make it clear why I now go to the left of the hotel, past the cove with the McGill marine science shed in it, and scramble on to the public beach which has only a small ridge, and furthermore soft pebble-and-shard-free sand—altogether a much better swimming beach, in fact, and much more fun, as the local people swim from it, you see them in large groups, almost like congregations, which they may well be, outings from the nearby churches, of which there are dozens, of all known and some (to me) unknown denominations—portly matrons in one-piece swimming suits with vivid sunsets stamped on them, supple young men, sinuous girls, middle-aged men with angry, Rastafarian locks, families dunking naked babies into the water, and here and there the English, sitting stiffly on boulders and tree-stumps if they're middle-aged, or sprawling on the sand with tattoos on their arms and bottles of Banks beer in their hands if they're young, offensive to the eye, let's face it, as offensive as I am in my drooping trunks, pendulous this and puckered that—but I don't have to see myself, do I? And within seconds I'm in the sea, splashing along, ducking through the waves, spouting water out of my mouth, something like a whale.

This morning a boat arrived, full of schoolgirls on an outing, about thirty of them, between nine and fifteen, I suppose, all wearing traditional brown uniforms, their hair in pigtails, children of a sort I haven't seen in England since my own childhood. They leapt squealing and laughing off the boat into the water, carrying their shoes and socks in their hands, and scampered on to the beach. A young woman, presumably the teacher, got off last, her skirt hiked up. She splashed after them, calling out instructions which she really didn't expect them to follow, but at least reminded them that she was there. They poured up the beach and into the changing rooms in the small park, a sort of compound, that also has a cafe, benches, swings, little shops. A few minutes later they poured out again, into the sea, heads bobbing, screams, shrieks of laughter, splashing each other, ducking each other, an absolute rough-house of girls at play, but not a swear word to be heard, nothing bad-tempered, ill-natured, brutish about these children, and it struck me with a pang that such a sight and such sounds would be impossible in the England of today, and will soon be just a folk-memory among the elderly, for what authority would dare to allow thirty children to go on a trip to the beach, to plunge into the sea, with only one teacher to supervise them? Indeed, what authority could muster thirty children who would play freely and joyfully, without bawling out obscenities and threats at each other, and at the teacher, probably. When you live in a barbarous country, it's educative, if painful, to spend a little time in a civilized one, to remember what we once were, to think what's become of us.

## From infant genius to infant pervert

But what was admired in the Hayling Island garden in daylight, indeed interpreted as the early manifestation of an original mind, possibly of genius, became regarded as something other, possibly a perversion, when practised at night in an unmoving bed. The bouncing and jouncing and above all the weird canine keening could be heard all over the house, and all through the night, and persisted through my teens and twenties, actually until I got married at the age of twenty-nine—it was worse than snoring because it seemed entirely wilful, even though I was unconscious, or could be assumed to be, with my face buried in the pillow, and my body sliding and humping. But if my face was buried in the pillow how come I was so audible? And how come, at least in my earliest years, I didn't suffocate? I could have been an early example of what used to be called cot death but is now frequently, after confidently delivered though hopelessly flawed medical evidence, misdiagnosed as murder (a number of mothers wrongfully jailed, families destroyed, children snatched from their homes and placed with foster-parents or in institutions, irretrievably—irretrievably? well, yes, we know we might have made a mistake, say the social services and government ministers responsible, but it's too late now to correct it, for the children's sake they must stay fostered or institutionalized, besides no smoke without fire, even if we're the ones who lit it you can't expect us to put it out, we're comfortable with what we've done and compassionate and caring with it.) So with the hypothesis that I died in my cot because my face was sunk into my pillow while jouncing, and then with a time-jump of those sixty-seven years, it's easy to see how the course of our lives might have run differently, Mummy's would have run in jail, Daddy would either have remarried or sacrificed himself to clearing Mummy's name, Nigel would have been fostered or institutionalized, and I, well, I would have been dead, of course, officially the victim of infanticide (unless they could pin it on the nanny) but in fact the victim of a jouncing habit that led to pillow-suffocation—but what pillow? Surely babies don't have pillows. If they lie flat on their stomachs—a clear impossibility, actually, given that babies' stomachs are round, inflated—I've just been upstairs and tried it on the hotel bed, I lay with my cheek, right cheek as I'm right-hand-side person, pressed flat against the mattress, it felt so easy and natural that I began to slip away for a moment, the great soft belly of me cushioning the middle of my body, in fact becoming a functional asset instead of the pendulous embarrassment it is when I'm upright and in company, and not only when I'm in company, I'm embarrassed by it when I'm on my own, sometimes I stand still in the middle of my study and try to suck it in—I'll try now, I'm in the bar but nobody's really looking—no, nothing stirred except the ghosts in my chest, the effort has left me short of breath, so let me go back to it as it was when I lay down a few minutes earlier—how did I describe it? as a cushion for the middle of my body—so must a baby's be, when it's not full of wind, so must mine have been when I was a windless baby. But just now, when I lay on the bed, I felt no impulse to jounce and bounce and fill the hotel with my keening.

## A peaceful and reasonable man goes sleepless

Daddy needed his sleep. When we moved from Hayling Island to London, into 47 Oakeley Gardens, in Chelsea, he had to be up and off to his path lab early in the morning. He also needed energy for his romantic enterprises later in the day. Furthermore he liked his sleep, not only was he relaxed and nourished by it, but was addicted to it as a kind of pleasure, or was it vice? liked to be in bed early, stay in it until the last possible minute—he took his breakfast in it, along with his post and the newspapers, and he was very uxorious, a very uxorious philanderer, so what with one vice and another, one pleasure and another, you can see that he spent quite a lot of his day, as well as most of his night, in bed, and when he was in bed at night he liked his sleep, drowsy, toasty in Mummy's arms, she in his, *zzzzz*—and I disturbed all that, the sound of my bed jumping up and down, my child's voice keening, clattered and sliced into his slumber, their slumber, and drove him quite wild with rage, though he tried, being by nature a reasonable and peaceful man, to bring the rage under control and to devise reasonable and peaceful solutions to my problem, though it wasn't in fact my problem, after all I wasn't waking myself up, in fact I was probably jouncing and keening myself into deeper and deeper layers of the unconscious, into sweet and holy spaces or places. Or perhaps not, who knows where you go when you're asleep, whether you're jouncing and keening or as still as a corpse?

## Another use for a hairbrush

His first solution was to ask me, and then, a few nights later, after I'd evidently though not consciously turned down his request, to command me, to sleep on my back. I remember lying rigidly, eyes closed, trying to lower myself into sleep by an act of will, a kind of reverse levitation. My next introduction to consciousness was when he rolled me back on to my back with whispered imprecations, dark words I couldn't understand that for all their intensity were designed to be inaudible to Mummy in their bedroom next door, and perhaps to me, too. Whatever they were, their meaning was inescapable. He believed, even though reason and peaceableness must have argued against it, that I was doing it on purpose and that I was a deliberate and premeditating jouncer. Well, possibly I was. I certainly came to believe that I was, and fought against the deep, corrupt desire to roll on to my side, then on to my stomach. One turbulent night he ran into my room and unleashed a powerful but soft, because unshod, kick at my ribs. From the next room came Mummy's, my Mummy's alarmed and imploring response—'James! James darling!'—to his disowning me, so to speak, with 'Will you shut up, you little bastard!' That he should have come to this! He got his foot out of the blanket, threw it over me, and left the room, a little click, a solicitous little click of the closing door, as if being careful not to wake the sleeping child. I heard their voices murmuring away, mainly hers, consoling—I'd recognize the tone now, though I didn't then—she knew her James, he wasn't a man to kick his sleeping nine-year-old, even with a naked foot, for the pleasure of it, this was a James who had been driven to desperate measures, a James beside himself. James, peaceable and reasonable and at one with himself again, devised a practical scheme to prevent me rolling on to my stomach in my sleep. A hairbrush tied through one of the buttonholes on my pyjama top.

# Trouble with pyjamas

One went to bed in suits, in those days, a thickish jacket and a thickish pair of trousers, particularly thick at the waist because of the thick cord that went through it, the ends of which one tied in a burly bow at the front, navel height. It's a wonder, really, that we didn't wear shoes in bed—oh and the gap at the front of the trousers that wasn't a gap but folds of cloth that you somehow had to pull apart, a fumbling and desperate business when you were in urgent need—sometimes it was simpler to pull the trousers down and pee over the top, the dangers of this procedure being manifest in smells and stains that mother drew to your attention, 'Really, must you be so lazy!' and one couldn't explain the difficulties to the mother, how in the cold it was like a tight little knot that tucked itself tightly into somewhere between one's legs, one's numbed fingers needed time to locate it, and then it had to be plucked at and coaxed and stretched like a piece of sensitive elastic, and this after one had fumbled through all the folds of cloth to locate the naked groin, let alone the tightly infolded little knot—how much easier to pull the trousers down so one could actually see where it was, and if one bent one's knees and pushed one's groin or would that be loins? forward, one could mainly miss the crotch in one's pyjama bottoms, it would only be the last little bit, the dribble that sometimes, inexplicably, becomes a spurt before becoming a treacherous dribble again, dribbling down into the crotch and causing that stain.

# Sounds from the next room

So I went to bed with the hairbrush dangling from the buttonhole in the pyjama top, lay rigidly on my back, eyes closed, and woke to Daddy's brawling hands, rolling me back on my back, pulling my pyjama jacket into position—it had become twisted around to the side so that the buttons ran from my armpit down. The hairbush lay away from my body, pointlessly attached. On some occasions, worse occasions, the pyjama jacket was completely discarded, lay on the floor even. These were the signs, were they not, of a deliberate, wilful determination to sleep on my stomach and jounce keening through the night, in complete disregard of the father's need for replenishing sleep? I think that during those nights, many, many nights, I became quite simply the enemy, as a screeching cat or a perpetually barking dog becomes the enemy, first the enemy to sleep, then the enemy to self—in this case to my father's self. I expect he wanted to kill me, from time to time, as he lay beside his wife in the darkness, listening to my night life expressing itself in what, now I come to think of it, must have sounded like an infant parody of the sexual act, the bouncing bed, the twanging springs, the animal keening, at a consistent, monotonous level of a climax impending but never achieved—an eerie parody of his own noises after lunch, say, in the bed in the flat of his secretary, little Mrs Rolls, or in the bed next door, where his wife my mother lay beside him but around whose body his arms—ah, but that was love, I heard it, not in the dead of night but as I lay awake before breakfast, the hairbrush replaced and resting on my stomach. I listened to the real thing, the noises of love, not keenings but murmurs, grunts, laughs, little cries suppressed but still trembling into screams choked off—

## Autistic?

Is it possible to become autistic, or do you have to start off that way? Well, I believe that all day I've been something that corresponds to my understanding of the word autistic—it's as if I've had no inner context at all, no points of reference, a sort of blankness and not a comfortable one—I'm quite unhappy in this, but don't want to talk to anyone about it, not even Victoria, to whom I tell everything, almost everything, certainly more than she actually needs to know. And yet this is something that she probably does need to know, that her husband has plodded beside her to bar, restaurant and beach, indeed swum beside her in the sea, sat opposite her at the lunch and dinner table, and internally there's been no flicker of life at all, his mind a tabula rasa, slightly soiled.

## A good deed punished

Can I, in all conscience, keep my table at the bar while I have lunch at a table in the restaurant? Yesterday I decided I couldn't, and surrendered my bar table to a lanky north country couple, he has buck teeth that fix his mouth in a permanent grin of seeming good-nature, she is blonde, with a handsome, beaky face and long legs made longer by high-heeled sandals. Both wear sunglasses which don't suit them, they make his face seem all teeth, and to hers they give a hooded effect, like a bird of prey. They accepted the table gratefully, as if with full knowledge of the ancient tradition, that it was mine by right, and their tenure was at my convenience. When I returned from lunch they vacated it immediately, with a flourish and some jokes about having been honoured, etc. So that was okay. Today at lunch time when they came to the bar I repeated the offer. When I came back after lunch they were sitting with their heads bowed, stubbornly unaware of my hovering presence. I thought I'd give them a few minutes. When I came back they were just as they had been, heads bowed. Victoria took me for a walk to calm me down, and I was calm when we came back, until I saw that they were still there, heads bowed. Victoria took me for a swim, and when we got back, there, with bowed heads, etc. I walked around the table at a slight distance, and though their heads were still, I could see their hands moving and hear little clicking sounds, like false teeth. I moved closer to make absolutely sure, and yes, it was true, they were playing Scrabble, sitting at my table, the buggers, playing Scrabble— So here I am now, looking down at them from our balcony, I notice that she has a long straight back, and he too sits very upright, both of their postures speak of intense concentration, which is I suppose needed when playing a game for halfwits, you have to keep the other half of your wits at bay, if they joined up you'd surely knock the board and the pieces of the alphabet to the ground—not that I've ever actually played Scrabble, I have no patience with indoor games that involve spelling or knowledge or indeed thought or intelligence of any kind—but the fact is, as I look down at them with scowly eyes, I suspect that they make a more attractive, more elegant spectacle at my table than I do, when I sit there writing, my jaw jutting out, cigarette on the go, a study in ill temper and bad living.

## Like father

It's not true that I've never played games that require thought or knowledge. I used to play chess *en famille*, not with Mummy, of course, she thought it was strictly a man's sport, unlike hockey or cricket, at both of which she'd excelled, along with the standing broad jump and the high jump, but chess, she said, demanded the male mind to grasp its intricacies, she couldn't hope even to set the board, the pieces themselves made her female, or was it feminine? mind reel, they were so sinister, but she used to stand smoking in admiration whenever a combination of the males in the household were bent in archetypal male postures over it—elbows on knees, chins in palms, foreheads furrowed, rather like Thurber's version of Rodin's *Le Penseur*. When Nigel and I played, our games usually climaxed in our rolling around the floor, with our hands around each other's throats, kneeing, punching, kicking, sobbing (me), shouting (him) until she had to come in at a run and separate us with her own more authoritative violence, precisely aimed kicks and clips. So mainly we played alternately with Daddy, who was, Mummy told us, very good at chess, his natural game, because it required thinking. And he seemed to be very good, beating us within a few moves, again and again. At first I accepted this as quite right and proper, in the natural order of things—I think at the beginning I'd have been quite fearful if I'd won, I mean if I could beat him what manner of father was he? How could he be trusted to look after us, bring us up?— but eventually the gorge began to rise, and feelings stirred in me similar to the ones that stirred when Nigel won—no doubt all explicably atavistic, ape junior wanting to overthrow ape senior— his honest, pleasant, thoughtful face as he mowed me down in game after game infuriated me, the gentle peer over the rims of his spectacles, the Scots undercurrent underneath the Canadian accent which ran below the English one, 'Mate, I think, old boy.' 'What, you've won again!' came the cry from the passing Mummy, and if I said something primitively filial—'Any fool can beat me'—the triumphant, 'Oh, don't be such a poor loser, the world hates a poor loser.' I tried cheating, nudging a piece into a different position when he was reloading his pipe or tamping it down though I'm sure I never gave myself any real advantage and I couldn't work out the consequences properly, probably putting myself into worse positions—I don't know why I did it—perhaps just the thought that cheating gave me a kind of psychological edge, I could do things that would never cross his mind—and then I began to study the board with real concentration, practice moves on my own, in fact began to get a remote glimmering of how to think a move or two ahead, of what could be predicted, or at least sensibly guessed at. I got better, our games got longer, he was making his way through two bowls of a pipe rather than half a bowl. There came an evening, a twilight in Halifax, Nova Scotia—the twilight of a God—I had him! I don't know how it came about, all I saw clearly, as clearly as I've ever seen anything, was that if I moved my knight, bishop, whatever, he would be checkmated. 'Mate, Daddy, mate I believe,' I would say, and keep the tremble out of my voice. 'What!' she would cry, 'You've beaten your father!' or with luck, 'You've beaten your own father!'—there would be accusation in it, bewilderment and loss—'I'm just going to have a pee,' I said. I remember it quite well, peeing, washing my hands, looking at my face in the mirror, a boy on the threshold, a boy who beat his Daddy, his own Daddy—I went in, sat down, 'Whose move is it?' though I knew perfectly well it was mine. He was relaxed back in his chair, feet crossed at the ankles, eyes miles away. 'Oh, yours, I think.' I bent to the board, made to pick up the assassinating piece, and saw that it was a square or so away from where I had left it. Furthermore, his queen wasn't where I'd last seen her. I lifted mine eyes unto the Father. He was still in his trance, lost to the trivialities of the chessboard that is life. 'Cheaters never prosper,' I might have said, Mummy-style, but I didn't—it never occurred to me to say anything—I moved my piece, in due course lost the game. 'Well done, Daddy!' I said, losing gracefully for once. 'It was closer than you realized,' he said. 'There was a moment there when you nearly had me.' But I had had him, hadn't I?

## James Davidson Seagull

It's a most beautiful day, the small boats are humming across the absolutely still Caribbean, a couple of waterskiers are criss-crossing each other in complicated patterns, oh, one's just come a cropper, a young woman, a second ago all poise and grace as she rode on her skis, arms stretched out, head back, hair flowing, the next a grotesque flurry of up-turned legs, the skis sticking out of the water like a compass—she's all right, she's waving to the driver, a slim guy in an orange shirt with Rastafarian locks and shades, he's circling around to her—meanwhile a gang of little birds are hopping about my drink, a Virgin Sea Breeze (cranberry and grapefruit). One has hopped on to the rim of the glass, jerking its head now one way and

now the other, seeing what's in front of it out of the corner of its eye—
I think I have to go on doing what I'm doing, to give it a chance to
dip its beak—no, well yes, that is he dipped his beak two or three
times without making it to the liquid, gave a couple of panic-stricken
twists of his head, flew off—I wonder what sort of bird it is, dun-
yellow chested, dark grey plumage—smaller than a sparrow—a kind
of marten, I suppose, it has a blue band around its left leg, just above
the claw—strangely large claws, parrot-like, out of proportion to its
body—the band looks as if it's made of rubber or plastic, put there
by an ornithologist, I suppose, who wants to keep tabs on its
movement—yesterday Victoria pointed out a dove with three blue
bands, two on one leg, one on the other, making one imagine it'd been
specially tagged, like a criminal. I wish I knew more about birds, most
of all I'd like to know how much consciousness they have, or is
everything they do programmed, I think I once read, like computers?
They often look, when they're on the ground, as if they've been wound
up, hopping stiltedly this way and that, but in flight they're a different
matter, actually not very different with these small birds, martens and
sparrows, they zigzag in spasms, as if in response to abrupt electronic
impulses, but seagulls now—my father said once, when we were all
sitting on the beach in Hayling Island, 'I wish I were a seagull'—what
made it surprising was that it was apropos of nothing, a sudden
utterance, as if his soul spoke. 'But why,' Mummy asked, 'why would
you want to be a seagull, James? Is it because they fly so beautifully?'
James said yes, he supposed it was that, the way they swooped and
soared, the freedom and majesty of the flying, the ease of it, just
cresting on the winds, their wings spread—also they can be quite
vicious, attack people, he said, as if it were a continuation of the
thought rather than a qualification, so perhaps he was interested in
that aspect of them too, he envied them their temperaments as well
as their flying skills—I remembered that conversation a few years ago,
when we were visiting Nigel and Barbara at their summer home in
Pictou, Nova Scotia. We went most afternoons—in appalling weather,
grey skies, squally rain, an edgy wind—to a very long, dark-sanded
beach, on which there were washed-up tree trunks that the gulls
squatted on, shrieking angrily—a couple of times when I came out of
the sea, cold and frankly rather miserable, two or three of them rose
from their logs, soared upwards, dropped, or rather lurched down on

me until they got to face level just a foot or so in front of me, then up they'd go, soaring, and back they'd come, jolting at me and shrieking their shrieks—the second time it happened I broke into a run, lumbering across the ridges of sand, shouting swear words at them. We thought they were probably protecting something, their eggs, their nests, but really they gave the impression that they didn't like humans, or more particularly me, as I was the only human going into and out of the sea, their sea—and it was noticeable that Victoria, sitting dry and fully dressed on one of the tree trunks, was never abused. When we told Nigel about it he said, yes, some people had actually been attacked at the beginning of the summer, a man's scalp had been pierced and a woman had had her eye plucked out—can he have said that? Eye plucked out? Well, Nigel being Nigel wouldn't have said it if it weren't true, but on the other hand I wouldn't have gone back to the beach, possibly gone to any beach in Nova Scotia ever again, if I'd believed that a gull had plucked out a woman's eye— so conceivably I've made it up, but attribute it to Nigel as a way of transforming it into a fact. But I still don't believe it.

## Pan, at the next table

Anyway, now I'm alone again, the bar is empty again—I'd just written that—the bar is empty again—when lo! an elderly man, by which I mean older than myself, with a nose so bulbous and knotted and veined that if he's not an alcoholic he should sue it—there he is at the table next to mine, he has chosen it out of all the empty tables, there are ten of them, I've counted, just to sit beside me, attracted by the long shapelessness of my own nose, perhaps, or just by a muddled desire to be a nuisance. He's carrying an object the size and shape of a large book that I didn't at first notice which he fiddled with for a few moments, and then, just as I turned away, he pressed a knob and a man's voice, plus music, both crackly, burst forth, yes, a radio, the old bugger's got a radio, and he's sitting there, holding the radio to his mouth, like a sandwich. He's got very bushy eyebrows, by the way, thickets, actually, and a beard, also thickety, but just sticking out from the base of his chin—it's the head of Pan, and he's holding the radio to his mouth no longer like a sandwich, but like a flute, but with hideous, unflutish noises emanating from it—he's conversing with Sam, the very neat and handsome young waiter, the one with the

Eddie Murphy face, which he is bending to Pan's lips, so that he can hear him behind the music. No need—Pan's voice is loud, boisterous, slurred, he's requesting tea—'Lots of good, strong tea, to wash the alcohol out,' he says, following his words with a coarse chuckle. Sam gives him a polite, blank look. 'I drink lots and lots of alcohol, that's why I drink tea now, always a pot or two at this time of the morning. Sluices it out. The alcohol.' Sam nods gravely, goes off. Probably, like most of the waiters in this hotel, he's teetotal. Pan goes on chuckling to himself, changes the channel on the station, is trying to catch my eye, which I keep resolutely fixed on the page as I write this sentence, which will be my last until he's gone, or his radio's off.

The radio is off. He is drinking his tea, and smoking a large cigar. Clouds of his smoke are drifting over me, making me feel queasy. Nevertheless I've picked up my pen, feeling it important to get this down—that there is a very coarse-looking man in swimming trunks and straw hat sitting smoking a cigar, trying to catch the eye of an elderly, not particularly refined-looking man in swimming trunks and a straw hat who is, in fact, smoking a cigarette and writing about him, and one day when the elderly writing man is back in London he might take out this pad from his drawer in his desk, leaf through it, come across this account, ponder it, and wonder if the old *roué* of a Pan with his stinking cigar and nose like a rotting fig is dead— he's blowing the smoke in my direction, quite deliberately, he's picked up the radio, he's turning it on again, and he's leering at me, I can feel it—Christ! He's got up, he's coming my way, coming straight at my table, at me, I'll keep my head bowed, keep scribbl—

—he spoke pleasantly through his nose into my ear. This hotel, he said, was one of the nicest he'd ever been to, the staff were so charming, he said, and the guests, the great thing about them, he said, was that they were all friendly, but never intrusive, never intrusive, he said pleasantly into my ear, his beard scraping my shoulder, as the fumes from his cigar drifted across my face and the radio hummed and spat almost in my armpit. 'Don't you find that?'—a young lady turned up, attractive, with curly dark hair, bangles on her wrists, a silver chain around each ankle, 'Ah, there you are,' she said, 'I knew I'd find you in the bar,' and gave me a smile, as if she'd known she'd find me in it too. 'I've been having tea,' he said. 'And talking to my friend. And waiting for you.' He clamped the cigar in his mouth, put the radio into one of her hands, looped his arm around her waist, lurched her off towards the swimming pool, or perhaps its shrubbery.

# A conspiracy?

Now he's gone it's the most beautiful morning again, and I would be tranquil, I really think I would be, if I weren't convinced, beginning to be convinced, that I'm the victim of a conspiracy. Is it that people can't bear the sight of an elderly sixty-seven etc. sitting at a shady table at the sea's edge on a sunny morning in Barbados, working— or not even working, just writing, and not even writing to any particular purpose, merely moving his hand which happens to be holding his pen across a yellow pad with long pages with lots and lots of lines on it with lots and lots of spaces between that have, naturally, to be filled, what else can I do in life but fill these spaces? But does the sight of me doing it provoke people into feeling that they've got a duty to stop me? I've been doing this very thing on this date, at this table, for eleven years now, every year on January 20 at this hour, this very minute, in fact, I could be seen at this very table, in this very chair—nonsense, not this very chair, every couple of years they change the chairs for chairs of a different style, progressively more uncomfortable, when I started out the chair was a miracle of comfort, a firm, weatherproof armchair, more elevated than you'd expect in an armchair, that seemed to settle you over the table into a natural writing position, but also allowed you to collapse backwards for thought, vacancy, erotic meditation, then a slight adjustment, almost unconscious, and one was at it again, the shifts between inertia and activity unnoticed by myself—recumbent, erect, active, a full page, recumbent, erect, active, a full page etc. This year we still have last year's chairs, wrought iron, gardeny sort of chairs, with thin white cushions that keep you in a stiff, upright position, oddly unsupported, and you can't help seeing your hand, the pen, the movement across the page, every single word you write as you're writing it.

# Alan at last

And what I'm writing now is the title of a film, *Women in Love*. Presumably from some half thought to do with Alan, who starred in it with Oliver Reed—I wonder if it was any good, I can't remember whether I liked it even—well, I haven't seen it for ages, doubt if I'll ever see it again, or any film with Alan in it—such a disturbing part of modern life, you can find yourself watching a film you saw and loved in your childhood, all the Laurel and Hardys, for instance, or take one of my favourite films, *Shane*, some of its scenes I have watched about thirty times over the last fifty years, I was seventeen, in my last year at school, when it came out in London, so yes, fifty years—nobody in the film is much over forty except perhaps the villainous rancher, and the old chap, played by Buchanan, is it? Edgar Buchanan, whose homestead is burnt down—although now I think about it, nobody apart from Brandon de Wilde, who plays the son of Van Heflin and Jean Arthur is much under forty either, which is surely unusual for a film, even of that period, but you see them there still, is my point, Brandon de Wilde, Jean Arthur, Van Heflin, Elisha Cook Jr, Ben Johnson, Jack Palance creaking about in black, and of course Alan Ladd, blond in blond, or light-brown buckskin. And there's the great scene, the open-air party, the settlers celebrating what can it have been? Thanksgiving, I suppose, Shane dancing with Van Heflin's wife, a curiously stately dance that ends with a bow and a curtsy, Van Heflin leaning on a fence, watching them, seeing the attractiveness, the almost rightness of them as a couple, Shane's tenderness and delicacy, his wife's dignified submissiveness—and later, when Van Heflin prepares to risk almost certain death to defend his family and their future, he tells his wife that if he fails he knows she will be well looked after, as will their son, Shane will be a better protector than himself. How pathetic, sentimental and dull it would seem to an audience of these days, a story about good people who struggle to live honourably, with its assumption that a man who has lived badly, like the professional gun-fighter Shane, is willing to sacrifice himself so that people he has come to love will have what he yearns for, that their lives count for more than his—even Wilson, the dead-souled killer played by Jack Palance, sticks to a code, or the appearance of a code—he doesn't draw his gun until the helpless Elisha Cook Jr, provoked by Jack Palance's smiling, low-voiced contempt for his southern sense of honour, reaches for his gun—to my mind one of the most terrible moments in cinema—the rain beats down, Palance stands sheltered from it on the saloon porch, Elisha Cook Jr stands not many yards from him, drenched, his boots mired in mud, his gun only just out of its holster, still pointing down—Palance's gun drawn so quickly one can hardly see the movement, pointing directly at Elisha Cook Jr's chest—the long pause is the rest of Elisha Cook Jr's life, Palance smiling, Cook's eyes bulging—then the shot, Cook hurled backwards from the impact, spread out in the mud. This is awful violence, violence with meaning, it makes us know and feel what an act of murder is—in fact, there are only two killings in the film, that one and Wilson's by Shane in the saloon in almost identical fashion, but this time it's Shane who does the taunting, and Wilson whose guns are incompletely drawn—Wilson hurtling backwards, his guns a quarter up and firing uselessly, his thin limbs sticking out in all directions, and then the old boss sitting at the end of the bar, shot as he raises his rifle—and of course the boy watching from underneath the swing doors, his arm around his dog, spots the third assassin on the landing above, about to shoot, cries a warning, Shane swivels, shoots, kills the assassin—so four killings in the film not two—and is wounded himself. Then the arrogant, no, flashy, it's actually a flashy twirl of the gun before he drops it in its holster, steps out of the saloon—'You got him, didn't you Shane? You shot Wilson!' 'Yes. That was Wilson. He was fast. Fast on the draw,' this said to the boy in a trance. Then Shane riding off into the darkness, hunched sideways from the pain of his wound, the child crying out for him to come back, music swelling, child's voice echoing—and so forth. Well, not so forth. Credits, and The End naturally. But still, think of all that now, from now, in these days of cinematic trash, when the foul and vacuous *Lord of the Rings*, with its interminable set-pieces, one set-piece after another, of hideous mass slaughter, is voted by the nation as the nation's favourite film, and you find yourself asking, what kind of nation is this? What kind of nation? But what I was actually thinking about, what I started all this from was not *Shane*, its plot and its people, but the fact that they're all dead, all the actors, including the ten-year-old Brandon de Wilde, killed in a car-crash in his twenties, and the contradiction that never existed before the invention of movies, of people who are long dead being visibly alive, you can see them breathe, there they are, the characters and the actors, both with futures of life and death unknown to them in the two stories they're in. I'll go on watching *Shane* until nature prevents me, but I think I shall always avoid seeing

Alan on the screen, or at least avoid watching him, I've already seen him a few times when channel-hopping, a glimpse of him in a bowler hat, an eyebrow raised, smiling quizzically—

## His dependability

We were here at this time last year, when he phoned to say he'd been diagnosed with cancer of the pancreas and the liver. His voice was robust, cheerful, just as it was when he was talking about the usual sort of stuff we talk about, a new role, a new film, a new illness— he'd had a lot of unexplained illnesses recently—he'd had a hip operation, his stomach had been bad, his knee hurt, sometimes shortness of breath—but he'd taken them in his stride, little spells in hospital, a long one for the hip because the operation had gone slightly wrong (botched, he wondered) but he had been unremittingly robust, cheerful, the sense of the comedy of it all pervading—the comedy of getting older, of people's reactions to his illnesses, the expressions they adopted, the tones they assumed—so was his tone when he was talking now—then—a year ago, about his cancer of the pancreas and liver. The trouble was, he said, that he'd known from all the other illnesses that there was something more, something more wrong with him than a dodgy stomach, a difficult knee, occasional shortness of breath, something else had been going on all the time (and actually he'd thought so all the time) but he'd been in New York, playing in *Fortune's Fool*, a complete triumph, he'd been the toast of Manhattan—funny, if you change that only slightly to in Manhattan he'd been toast, a phrase I loved when it first turned up in the sort of movies I used to love: 'Make a move and you're toast!'—well, he wasn't toast in Manhattan, he was the toast of Manhattan, winning all the acting awards—and the thing was, it was his show in more than the star's normal sense, as he'd done the play first in Chichester, where it really hadn't been much good, a plodding and ponderous fable, badly lit and erratically acted by the supporting cast, although he himself, at the ebullient centre, had been Alan enough to give the evening a charge—but really, it had floundered along, and he'd been depressed by the impoverished lighting, the helter-skelter staging—but on the other hand his son Ben had been in it, for Alan a great thing, perhaps the greatest thing, to be on the stage with his son, it justified the enterprise, it justified going on with the enterprise, it justified the long struggle to take it to New York, to play it in first for a long period outside New York. Things were changed and then changed again, the staging was still all over the place, but his co-star Frank Langella was sympathetic and great fun, his director was old but sympathetic and great fun, and Ben was having a great time, learning more and more as he got better and better, and Alan knew, he just knew, that by the time they got to New York it would be a triumph, and so it was, a triumph, he was the toast etc. And yet the things that were wrong with him got worse, the knee, the stomach, the fatigue, whenever he went on stage he was exhausted, couldn't understand, went to a New York doctor who did a series of tests, gave him some pills that settled his stomach, but said: 'When you get back to London you've got to have all this checked out. Don't leave it.' So when he got back to London he left it, didn't have anything checked out but his hip, and even with all the complications of that, he didn't have himself checked for anything serious. 'But why not?' I asked, after a dinner, as we went to his car, a large car, built for cross-country driving, that sort of thing. 'You keep saying you feel awful, you think there's something really wrong with you, so why the hell don't you!' He said he would. We had the conversation several times, with the same firm conclusion— he would, yes, he really would. Well, of course he was a diabetic, had been for nearly twenty years or so, and partly assumed that his diabetes might be behind it all—he was used to being very insouciant about his diabetes, rolling up his shirt in a restaurant, crouching slightly so the syringe couldn't be seen as he plunged it into the side of his midriff, pulling it out, slipping it back into his pocket—the whole business completed in a matter of seconds—but really behind the diabetes he now knew there was another illness, showing itself in different guises and glimpses—but he was in all respects such a sturdy man, his body sturdy, the will and spirit within it sturdy, the whole of him rooted in a sure sense of himself and his place in the world—it was this that made him so complete a presence on the stage and screen, and yet gave him freedom and brio in his acting—though he was so quick from one thing to another, from tenderness to savagery, from contemptuous wit to unfathomable pain, the centre always held, Alan was always there, however dangerous or defeated his mood, the final dot of him was intact, so that audiences, thrilled and sometimes nearly unnerved, felt finally safe in his company—I suppose that's what they loved about him, really, that he could take them into anarchy or despair without loosening them from their trust in his kindness—it was visible in his eyes, even at their iciest you could feel it there, and you knew that you could depend on it, an essential part of his kindness was its dependability.

## How he dealt with the lights

Also his dependability was practical, you could count on him in a tricky situation, on the stage as in life—I remember him making his entrance as Butley, hungover, a wreck, lurching to his desk to turn on the lamp that was scripted not to come on, had never come on before, not in the dress rehearsals, not in the two weeks of performances in Oxford, not in the four or five previews, but at the Criterion, on the night of July 14, 1971, the official opening night with a full house and all the critics in, it came on. Harold Pinter and I, director and writer, standing at the back of the stalls, looked at each other aghast, then looked towards Alan, who, we supposed, would be looking aghast at the lamp. He scarcely gave it a glance as he Butleyed to the other desk, and the lamp which was scripted to come on and therefore, I assumed, now wouldn't, not only came on, it came on while Alan was still reaching for its switch, but went off again the instant he touched it. I'm no longer clear about what Alan did next, actually I don't think I was clear at the time, whatever it was it couldn't have made any logical sense, but it made complete emotional sense and sense therefore to the audience, who laughed in sympathy with Butley's evident frustrations, even though they seemed to be mysteriously, even magically created. But my real memory of the incident is not what Alan did, nor my momentary panic, but my underlying confidence that whatever he did it would be the right, the perfect thing, partly because he was so right and perfect in the part, so founded and centred in it that his any action became the right action by virtue of its being his, and partly just because he was Alan, in whom one had a perfect and complete trust, on and off the stage.

## His laughter etc.

There was a scene in rehearsals that he was unsure of—he hadn't got the feel of it, his tone was wrong, something he couldn't quite catch in the meaning of the lines—each time he got through the scene he would turn enquiringly to the director, who looked at him with a blank, though friendly smile, then turned his attention to something else. Finally Alan asked him—could he please have a comment straight out, whatever struck the director would be welcomed, however trivial, he just needed a note, any note, he badly needed a note on how he was doing this scene. The next time he did the scene, he turned eagerly towards the director, who almost succeeded in failing to catch Alan's eye, but couldn't avoid his eyebrows, fiercely raised in interrogation. He stood for a minute, broodingly, as if sorting through note after note in his head, then swiftly raised his right thumb, then turned away to the other actors. Alan, telling this story, one of his favourites for illustrating the general uselessness of directors, would bend so far forward with laughter that his forehead would actually touch his knees, and he would actually have to mop the tears of laughter out of his eyes, 'Oh dear!' he would say, 'Oh God!' and as like as not he'd jerk his thumb up again, and the laughter would start again—any meal with Alan would contain as much laughter as speech. But when I think about it, what could the director say that would have been more eloquent than a raised thumb—obviously what he meant by it was that Alan's acting of the scene was true and honest and right, words which would also apply to the way he tried to live his life, and why not a raised thumb to that, too, especially if it would have caused him to laugh so much that his forehead met his knee—it was his merriness, I think, that marked him out from anybody else I've known—his laughter made you feel instantly better. A generous, forthcoming laugh that demanded company, so that sometimes you laughed not because you found it, whatever it was, particularly funny, but because Alan's laugh had somehow got into you, yours fed on his and his on yours so you ended up like children, clutching at each other, the initiating cause often forgotten—'But why did we, what were we—? Oh—oh yes!' and like as not, off again. It's terrible to think I shall never hear it again, and that it's nowhere to be heard—his laughter on screen is not the same thing at all, of course, being an organized and probably in some cases frequently rehearsed laugh, although what you do get on screen, in his eyes, is the mischief and the appetite, the exuberance—

# His Claudius

—in Zeffirelli's *Hamlet* is the most sensual, the most appetitive, the most louchely endearing—during an early scene when he's trying to lecture and cajole Hamlet out of his woe, etc. a servant on the other side of the room brings in a tray with a flask of wine and some goblets on it, Alan's Claudius, attempting to be doleful, measured, earnest, catches sight of the tray, scampers across the room, fills the goblets to the brim, turns to Gertrude with lascivious delight—his wine in his fist, his woman before him, his crown on his head, what more could a man want? except to be rid of the spoilsport, killjoy nephew—you can see too, for once, what's in it for her, what fun she has with him in bed, what a rollicking place he's turned the court into, a playground—it's as if Falstaff had come to Elsinore, where he'd been tracked down by a poisoned Hal—Alan would have been a great Falstaff, the wit, the relish in life, the sexiness that would have embraced Hal as well as Mistress Quickly, I used to nag him to do it, and he would pretend to ponder it, but really his vanity got in the way. The problem was the fat, he couldn't bear to play a fat man, however nimble tongued and quick of wit, however gorgeous in his pomp, broken in his fall—really, he still saw himself, until quite late in his career, too late in his career, as a leading man, romantic— to his inner eye lean and svelte and dashing when in truth he was big-boned, stocky, a heavy mover though his energy also made him quick when he wanted to be—but his natural tempo was slow, his natural walk an amble—his energy distracted the attention from his shape, as did the marvellous eyes, the handsome mouth, the line of the cheeks, and the exuberant head of hair—but it grew on a round head, set on a bullish neck, and physically he was a peasant, a Derbyshire peasant, and his hands were agricultural. His consciousness of his body made him shy of exposing it professionally, though he famously exposed all of it in the film of *Women in Love*, but that was when he was young and besides the camera and the editor could redefine, above all select. Later, and especially on the stage, he was careful—in a play of mine, *Melon*, for instance, he hid behind the furniture when stripping down to his underwear, and pretty well stayed there, almost crouching, until the end of the scene—his no-nonsense, let's get on with it exchanges with the girl he was about to fuck seeming more like bombardo—bombardo? Is there such a word? I must have meant bravado, or did I mean bombast? Well, both of them combined give my meaning—his bombardo perversely made him more attractive, it created a tension between his desire and an innate modesty, possibly prudishness, that made him irresistible, so the girl, instead of being swept along by the force of his brute male assertiveness, succumbed to his sweetly boyish bombardo. I tried once or twice, out of a sense of duty to my own text, to get him out into the open, but he invariably said it was no good, wherever he went he seemed to end up behind the desk or the chair, and added that he wasn't a young man any more, there was too much of him, he was bloody well going to keep most of it to himself, they were already seeing more of him than was good for them—or him. But as I say, the truth of it is that though he was in fact bulky, he never seemed it—his intelligence transformed him, gave the illusion of his being light-footed, mercurial—sometimes you scarcely noticed the movements that carried him from one side of the stage to the other, as if his mind and the meaning of his lines had taken him there without help from his body, but in repose he was a massive presence, nothing to do with his height or weight, but of density, really, the bulk of him somehow compacted, concentrated in the audience's concentration—Alan alone on stage at the end of a play, motionless, was volcanic. He was also beautiful, I think, in the way that no artefact can be beautiful, because he was breathing, dying.

## His inadequacies as a hater

He was a great mimic, a great creative mimic—in the course of an evening he could give you a whole novel full of characters, waiters in restaurants, agents, publicists, the nurses and doctors during his last weeks in the hospital, and earlier, in his palmy days, his mother-in-law, whom he adored, and not simply for the comedy she provided him with—and that was it, every character was suffused with his own delight in their being, so that they were always presented in all their vivid absurdity without malice, with a kind of love, and a gratitude for giving him so much pleasure in their creation. Correspondingly, he was not much of a hater, although capable of explosions of anger and contempt, mostly against directors, but he would usually append a coda of forgiveness and the suggestion that it was probably his own fault really. Once, though, when he was coming to the end of his chemotherapy, he went abruptly, without warning, into a low, muttering but precisely articulated monologue of loathing for a famous director. He went on for quite a long time, and when he finished he sat in silence, his head lowered. I waited for a burst of laughter or the fabulous smile, but neither came. 'There,' he said eventually, 'There. I've said it at last. And I don't feel any better for it.' I think he was in part speaking about his illness, about which he scarcely said a bad word, seeming to accept it as a mysterious visitation that probably made sense if one understood the real order of things, rather than as a betrayal of his body, or as an outrage against perfectly reasonable expectations. Shortly after he'd been moved back into the London Clinic for the last time, he said that if he was going to die soon, it was all right: 'I've had a very good life. I've done everything I want, really. Yes, it would be all right.'

## Was his a good life?

For Alan, the birth of his twin sons, Benedick and Tristan, was life's greatest gift, its blessing. Tristan died in a freak accident in Tokyo at the age of seventeen. At his funeral Alan spoke of his memories of the twins' growing up, of the differences and similarities in their natures, of the promises for both the future had seemed to offer, he spoke calmly and gently, seeming almost at ease until suddenly, mid-sentence, he stopped, his face seemed to fall apart, his mouth hung open, his eyes started, as he gaped into the horror of where he was and why he was speaking. He blinked, looked towards Benedick, gathered himself and went on. I've always thought that giving that address was the bravest and noblest thing I've seen a man do. Two years later his wife, Victoria, wasted to the bone with grief and bewilderment, drifted to Italy, to a hotel where she, Alan and the twins had gone one summer. For her it was a place of special memories, memories of herself as a young mother in her prime, of her dashing film star husband, of her beautiful sons who were also *enfants savages*. She arrived at the front desk so enfeebled that the receptionist immediately phoned for an ambulance. She was taken off to hospital where she died the next day, of malnutrition, dehydration, extreme self-neglect, in fact. But how had she managed the journey? How had she found the strength even to contemplate it, let alone complete it? In his funeral address Alan spoke of her with such tenderness and understanding that he sounded at moments almost parental—the truth is, I think, that he was born to be a father, not a husband, and his marriage was really a sort of flawed adoption. He was honest and sad about the ways in which he'd failed her, but then she was always, in a friend's phrase, a reluctant incarnation, and I doubt if anyone could have given her what she needed in life, or even known what it was. His own death—his own death—

## He is spoon-fed

He looked like Galileo, have I said this before? The rim of white beard, his hair growing back to a thick white stubble on his skull, his marvellous blue eyes as clear as they were in his youth, all his natural exuberance distilled into a different sort of energy, to be released after a few moments of rest, but the range of expressions as great as ever, with a new one, sweet and sly as he lay on the bed, his head propped up, studying you, or from his favourite position, a small armchair facing the bed, where he sat in his hospital gown, his feet planted, with the air of a benevolent emperor. He was, in fact, imperial in his dying, deeply happy with what had come to him at the end, his Tony Award on Broadway, his knighthood, all that was his due had come at last. He received his friends until nearly the end, sitting in this chair by the bed, a rug over his lap, full of delight and above all attention. He wanted to hear everything that was going on in our lives, gave sympathy and advice where things were bad, and shared in any pleasures and successes. He was Alan as I'd always known him, the very best of best friends, the one you phoned up immediately when you were in need, the one you hoped would phone you up when he was. Ben came from New York to lodge with him in his room for the final few weeks, sleeping on a camp bed so that he was available at night, tending him like a nurse and son, spooning food into his mouth when he resisted eating, getting him to swallow by cajoling and teasing—Alan adored this reversal of roles, describing how he'd used similar tactics when spoon-feeding Ben and Tristan, and then going into imitations of his father, at the end of his life, assuming a quavering and tetchy tone: 'Take it away, it's disgusting, disgusting, I can't eat it, who are these people anyway, call themselves nurses, call themselves doctors!' and then spluttering with laughter, Ben laughing too as he slipped another spoonful down. They touched each other a lot, Ben patting Alan's head, Alan stroking Ben's cheek, as if they were the same age. Mates.

# His last days

I used to have the taxi stop on the Marylebone Road, at the top of Marylebone High Street, and walk the hundred yards or so to Harley Street and the London Clinic. I'd do it slowly, spinning it out, smoking two cigarettes, and then often have one more on the steps of the Clinic, where there would usually be someone smoking—either one of the hospital porters, or a relative or, like me, friend of a patient, and once or twice a patient, I think. We all had pretty well the same manner of smoking, it was a cigarette that mattered, that we couldn't get enough of, but couldn't linger over, short, greedy puffs, then a decisive step on to the pavement, drop the butt, a quick stamp, a decisive step back and into the clinic—then the lift up to the third floor, or was it the second? anyway, to the cancer floor—along the corridor, not bothering to stop at the reception desk because the nurses know you by now and there's his door—the first thing I did on returning to the pavement was to light up, connecting myself immediately to the man I'd left on the pavement smoking, as if the visit itself were in parenthesis, that linked up to the parentheses of the previous visits, so that the visits now seem to be a continuum, a main sentence all of its own. I would smoke my way through to Marylebone High Street by the back route, and sit at a pub that had chairs and tables outside, even though we were in December, Christmas nearer with every visit— I would sit at a table with a Diet Coke and concentrate on anything but Alan, or find a blankness sometimes so successfully that I'd forget what I was doing there, smoking, with a Diet Coke, outside a pub in the cold, and I'd get the next taxi that came along, hailing it from my table. The truth is that, whatever joy there was in seeing Alan, it was also unbearable—that stretch from the top of Marylebone High Street to the top of Harley Street—whenever we pass it in a taxi I look out of the window and measure it with my eye, but even as I register how short it is, I feel the lurch of dread in my stomach and hope I never have to walk it again, never have to stand on those steps again—and there's another thing that comes back to me, that as I approached the clinic I used to look up to the window of Alan's room, imagine him sitting in his chair or lying on his bed, and then imagine myself as I would be in a few moments, in that room that seemed to me from the outside, looking up at its window, so self-contained and far away that I could never be in it.

## He and Toto find peace

So that's how it was all the days in December, leading up to Christmas—Alan dying in the London Clinic, and our dog, Toto, going mad in Holland Park—I could hear her screams as I came down the street towards the house—not, I suppose, technically screams, but shrill, joined-up yaps that had the effect of screams in that they shredded the nerves and made one think of cruelty, pain and ambulances—such a small dog, and in repose such a pretty one, with alert, intelligent eyes, and affectionate. We'd originally given her as a birthday present to my granddaughters. Victoria had picked her up at the kennels on her way to London from Suffolk at 3 p.m. on September 11—in fact, she was drawing up outside the kennel doors as the news about the Twin Towers came through on her car radio— so in a sense Toto is a 9/11 baby, about whom songs could be written therefore, but her condition that Christmas was actually the result of something far more momentous in her world, an hysterical pregnancy which coincided, perhaps not coincidentally, with her being transferred from one home to another. She gave birth to a small stuffed bear, which she protected with extraordinary savagery from predators like Victoria and myself. When she wasn't crouched snarling over it, she was drooling over it and cuddling it, and then would suddenly rampage around the house screaming the screams I used to hear on coming home from the London Clinic. So the two experiences are intermingled—no, they're not—as I've said, Alan's dying is a long, separate event, and Toto's madness is a long separate event that happened at the same time, parallel with it, one home and one away. The worst was Christmas, Alan in his coma, Toto in a frenzy because somehow her stuffed bear of a baby had vanished and she decided that she had delivered herself of all the presents under the Christmas tree, and crouched, snarling among them—this meant that no one could approach the tree without being threatened—a mad dog is a mad dog, however charming to look at and sweet her nature, and her shows of teeth, saliva dripping from her muzzle, were terrifying among the pink and gold and silver and scarlet packages—when she went on one of her looping, screaming runs, we tried to gather up the presents, but either she would be back before we'd done, or if we shut her out she would patrol the hall screaming—so when it came down to it there was nothing we could do but leave them under the tree and let her embed herself. Eventually the stuffed bear was found on a high shelf in the kitchen and was placed on the floor some way from the presents. Toto ran to it, buried her face in it, licked it, stroked it and rolled it about, then carried it gently down to the basement, and put it to bed—and so, apart from sudden rushes upstairs to check briefly on her other family, under the tree, and other rushes through the flap and screaming circuits of the garden—which led to a petition from some of the neighbours asking us to confine her to the house, her garden screams were too distressing, and set their own dogs off—the situation held through to Boxing Day. We saw Alan a few hours before he died, when we took Ben some food, as the visitors' cafeteria was closed over the festive season, indeed the Clinic gave off the feeling that it had closed down, the only occupants the ill and the dying—he was still, his arms lying straight outside the blankets, his eyes closed, his chest moving irregularly—we could hear his breathing, shallow suckings in and expulsions after long intervals—he was obviously near the end, and looked ready for it, neat and noble, only the breathing disorderly. Ben, white and staring, looked as close to death as Alan—but then he hadn't eaten for a long time, nothing was open in the neighbourhood, not even the pubs. We stayed until Ben had eaten, said goodbye to Alan with a kiss on his forehead, and came home to Toto, running this way and that, screaming. In the New Year we got canine Prozac from the vet. It calmed her down somewhat, and she began to treat the bear as a toy rather than as a baby, knocking it about, throwing it into the air and catching it until she discarded it altogether—it still lies in her basket in the basement, but she scarcely ever goes down there, now that she sleeps in different spots all over the house in the daytime, and on our bed at night.

# Departures

Oh, I saw Pan this afternoon, sitting in the reception with his suitcases, waiting for the taxi for the airport. He looked subdued, no cigar, his hands folded in his lap. He was dressed in a blue blazer, cream-coloured slacks and sturdy brown shoes, for London or Manchester, wherever. His nose seemed to fit in better when he was wearing his usual togs, it could go almost unnoticed in the Garrick Club or the MCC. The young woman with bangles and chains was attending him, but not departing with him. She was wearing beach clothes and hotel slippers, and kept going to the desk to ask about his taxi: 'Mr Prynne's got to be at the airport by three, at the latest.' There's something solemn and poignant about these departures in the lobby, the piled-up luggage, the cold-weather clothes, somebody at the desk worrying about the taxi and the flight—flamboyant Pan with a cigar becomes passive Mr Prynne staring down at his mottled hands. I wonder if Pan and the young woman are lovers, and Mr Prynne is going home to the wife and children, grandchildren. Well, the day after tomorrow it will be our turn, Victoria's and mine, to sit beside our luggage in the lobby, waiting to be returned to the fitful fever, all that, and people who are staying on will observe us and try not to think that one day soon—                                       □

## The Cambridge Companion to Modern Irish Culture
**Edited by Joe Cleary and Claire Connolly**
'... stimulating introduction ... well written and lucid ...'.
Irish Times
'... useful and authoritative ... rish in broad brushstrokes ...'.
Times Literary Supplement
**£45.00** | HB | 418pp
**£16.99** | PB

## The Cambridge Companion to American Modernism
**Edited by Walter Kalaidjian.**
An authoritative overview of the achievements of American
literary modernism in its social and cultural contexts.
**£45.00** | HB | 358pp
**£16.99** | PB

## The Cambridge Companion to the Literature of the First World War
**Edited by Vincent Sherry**
A collection of new essays on First World War literature and
its contexts.
**£45.00** | HB | 344pp
**£16.99** | PB

## The Cambridge Companion to W. H. Auden
**Edited by Stan Smith**
A comprehensive and authoritative guide to Auden's work.
**£45.00** | HB | 288pp
**£15.99** | PB

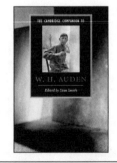

GRANTA

# WHEN SKATEBOARDS WILL BE FREE

## Saïd Sayrafiezadeh

Saïd Sayrafiezadeh

My mother and father believe that the United States is destined one day to be engulfed in a socialist revolution. All revolutions are bloody, but this one, they say, will be the bloodiest of them all. The workers (which includes me and which also includes you) will at some point decide to put down the tools of our trade, pour into the streets, shoot the police, take over City Hall, and usher in a new epoch—the final epoch—of peace and equality. This revolution is not only inevitable, it is imminent. It is not only imminent, it is quite imminent. And when the time comes my mother and father will lead it.

For now, though, things are calm and my father is sitting across from me at Colbeh, an Iranian restaurant in the Garment District, on West Thirty-ninth Street near Sixth Avenue. It is a nice restaurant, with carpeting and soft, romantic lighting and white linen tablecloths. On each table there is a tiny vase with a single daisy so precise in detail that it is impossible to discern whether it is real or fake. It is late spring and the restaurant door has been propped open to allow a breeze to blow over us, the patrons. Conversations and traffic sounds drift in from the street.

The waitress appears. 'Good evening,' she says.

'Good evening,' my father says, and looks briefly at her tits.

The waitress is Chinese. She is young and pretty, though her skin looks as if it has been drained of pigment from too many nocturnal shifts within the confines of the restaurant. She speaks softly and with a heavy accent, forcing us to lean in to decipher her words.

'May I start you off with something to drink?' she asks.

My father and I lean in.

'May I start you off with something to drink,' my father repeats to himself, mulling the sentence over for a moment, as if it's a question he wasn't expecting. Then he asks grandly, 'What kind of house wine do you have?'

'We have Chardonnay,' the waitress says softly. 'We have—'

'Chardonnay! Chardonnay sounds good!' He looks at me. 'Does Chardonnay sound good? If I order some Chardonnay will you have a glass with me?'

'Sure, Pop.'

'Say, do you hear? The birthday boy will have a glass of Chardonnay with me. Therefore I think we are going to need more than just a single wine glass.' My father grins at the waitress as if he has said something clever. The waitress smiles back, but it's apparent she doesn't know what's she's smiling about, and it's apparent my father doesn't know that she doesn't know. His grin widens.

'Let us begin then,' my father says, 'with a carafe of Chardonnay.' And the waitress disappears.

My father has brought me to Colbeh to celebrate my thirtieth birthday. My thirtieth birthday was five months ago. We were supposed to get together then, but an important event arose suddenly: a forum. President Clinton had just finished bombing Iraq for four days under Operation Desert Fox, and in response the Socialist Workers Party had organized 'Imperialist Militarism from the Middle East to the Indian Subcontinent: Washington's War Abroad— Extension of Growing Attacks on Workers at Home'. Open to the public.

'We will have to reschedule,' my father had said to me over the phone. The gravity of his voice implied that the upcoming meeting would have a significant impact on world events.

Although my father and I both live in New York City, I have not seen him for a year. Before that I had not seen him for two years. Before that it had been a year and a half. Once I saw him twice in a single month, but that was balanced by going nearly eighteen years without ever seeing him, a marathon stretch that began with him abandoning my mother and me when I was nine months old.

'He went off to fight for a world socialist revolution,' my mother would say stiff-lipped and teary-eyed, as if she were a widow from a 1950s Hollywood film about the Second World War. The logic behind my mother's explanation was that once this socialist revolution had been achieved my father—her husband—would be resurrected and returned to us. We never stated this belief aloud, it was unnamed and liquid, but we both subscribed to it silently, like a well-kept secret between friends. And thus, since the night of my father's departure, my mother began to save herself for him, denying herself a sexual or even a personal life, never bothering to find either another husband for herself or a surrogate father for me. She remained, however, a committed member of the Socialist Workers Party and pursued the revolution with a ruthlessness and a zeal that bordered on the religious. She attended Socialist Workers Party meetings twice a week, as well as endless streams of petitionings, book sales, newspaper sales, rummage sales, conferences, conventions. If the answer was revolution, then she would do everything in her power to make it solid.

The waitress places a carafe of Chardonnay in front of us. My father looks at her ass as she walks away. Then he looks at the carafe of Chardonnay. Then he looks at me.

'This is white,' he says to me.

'It's Chardonnay,' I say.

'It's white.'

'Chardonnay is white.'

'I wanted red.'

'Chardonnay isn't red.'

'Never?'

'I don't think so.'

'Shit,' he says softly to himself.

In the spring of 1979, a few months after the Iranian Revolution and ten years after I had been born, my father moved back to Iran. He had come to the United States on a math scholarship when he was eighteen and attended the University of Minnesota, where he met my mother, a Jewish girl from Mount Vernon, New York. Because of my father's outspoken criticism of the Shah he was unable to return to Iran for twenty-five years. The very real possibility that SAVAK, the Shah's secret police, would toss him in a torture chamber the moment he stepped from the plane prevented him from doing so. But in December 1978 two million Iranians had marched in the street, the soldiers had refused to fire on them, the Shah was running for his life, and my father was packing his bags.

He called my mother the night before he left. I was in bed with the lights off when the phone rang. Our phone never rang and the sound startled me out of the early stages of sleep. My mother and I lived in a small, one-bedroom apartment. I slept in the bedroom and my mother slept in the living room on a twin bed that doubled, without alteration of any sort, as a couch in the daylight hours, as well as a desk for placing papers and books. I could hear every word that my mother said, and by the voice she was using I knew immediately that it was my father on the other end. It was a confident voice with a touch of breeziness, the kind of voice that impresses employers at a job interview. There was no other time in her life that she used that voice. With me it was doom and gloom. She would let me know, for instance, when she was behind on the rent, or when she thought she was about to be laid off, or when the price of bread had gone up. She also cried almost every day over various things that included, but were not restricted to, the general condition of black people in the United States, the unending struggle of Fidel Castro against imperialism, the death of a young Puerto Rican boy at the hands of the police. And then she would become enraged at the seemingly carefree uninterest of the wealthy. When we walked through a well-to-do neighbourhood she would point to a large home with a manicured lawn and she would say to me, her voice dripping with contempt, 'Look at them. The rich asses.' And I would look at them, their car in the driveway, maybe two cars, and I would despise them for having and I would despise myself for not having, and I would pretend that I did not want what I saw.

On one occasion I mustered the courage to ask my mother to buy me a skateboard (they were all the rage at the time) and she took me to Sears to have a look. In the middle of the sports department was a bin filled with skateboards in bright bubblegum colours. A sign read $10.99.

'Once the revolution comes,' my mother said to me, 'everyone will have a skateboard, because all skateboards will be free.' Then she took me by the hand and led me out of the store. I pictured a world of long rolling grassy hills, where it was always summertime and boys skateboarded up and down the slopes.

One Christmas a tree was donated to us by a local charity.

'When the revolution comes everyone will have a Christmas tree,' my mother said.

'Will we have them year-round then?' I asked.

'When the revolution comes no one will want a Christmas tree because no one will believe in God.'

Then we spent the afternoon decorating our tree together, stringing popcorn and kumquats, hanging lights from the branches, and when we were done we cut a moon out of cardboard, wrapped it in aluminum foil and placed it on the top.

The difference between our family and other poor families was that my mother actively chose to be poor. She was highly literate and she had a college degree, but after my father left she took the first secretarial job she could find and never looked for other employment again. My mother made no effort to disguise our impoverishment; it was a testament to how needed the revolution was and to how deserving we would be when it finally arrived. She found ingenious ways to celebrate our poverty and announce it triumphantly to the world. In the wintertime she would wrap her chapped fingers with masking tape even though Band-Aids and hand lotion were well within her budget. When we were in a doctor's office she would deftly fill her bag with magazines. In order to avoid paying fines on overdue library books, she would pull my hood tightly over my head and instruct me to simply place the books on the counter and walk right back outside. Later she would brag to Party members of how good an accomplice I was becoming. If I ever questioned such dishonesty she would reply haughtily, 'Any crime against society is a good crime.' While even the poorest boys in my school were dressed in suits and ties for our elementary-school graduation, I crossed the stage in slacks and a turtleneck. Every single item in our apartment had either been purchased second-hand or had been donated by acquaintances who had taken pity on us. And if something broke, a lamp say, it stayed broken until someone could be found to fix it.

On the phone that night with my father, however, my mother's voice was full of aplomb. 'Yes,' she said, 'yes, of course. The workers and peasants of Iran have been struggling for one century.'

Then my father's response.

'Imperialism's boot,' my mother said.

My father's response.

Her response.

His response.

Her response.

They chatted like this for a while. She even chuckled. She never chuckled.

'So and so's such a good *comrade*,' my mother said, using the designated term for a fellow member of the Socialist Workers Party. ('They're not *friends*,' she reminded me many times, 'and they're not *co-workers*. They're *comrades*.')

I listened to hear mention of me. But there was none. And then they wound it up. She said goodbye. There was something good-natured in her goodbye. It wasn't a grave goodbye, it wasn't a lugubrious goodbye that implied permanent separation, it was a so-long-see-you-around-sometime goodbye. Then she hung up the phone.

And then she sobbed.

Great sobs. Shakespearean. Racking her body, constricting her breath. Her wails shook our tiny apartment and the other tiny apartments in our building. They shook me in my bedroom in the dark, pretending to be asleep.

When morning came I played dumb when she broke the news to me. In the alley I tossed a tennis ball against the wall. I pretended I was Reggie Jackson throwing the ball, and that the wall was Reggie Jackson hitting the ball and each hit was a home run.

It made no difference to our day-to-day lives if my father lived in the United States or Iran. It made no difference to us if he was dead or alive, really. We never saw him when he was here, nor did we ever plan to see him. He never sent us money, or letters, or gifts, and the one time he called each year (on my birthday), the exchange between us was so formal, so polite, the conversation of a doctor and his patient, that I could not wait to rid myself of the phone.

'Be good,' he would say before we hung up. It was always the last thing he said.

Despite years of this chronic absence, my father's abrupt departure from the country brought my mother's and my private fantasy life to a rude and abrupt end. There was no getting around the fact any more that he was not planning to return to us—ever.

In response to this, my mother took to removing the telephone from its hook each night, making us as unreachable as my father. After she had put me to bed she would set the receiver on the floor. In the dark the dial tone would sound as if it were a strange animal, its long, steady beep filling up the quiet apartment. I would listen to it and stare off into the black. After a good amount of time had passed a male voice would appear, pleasant but urgent, like a messenger bringing news that could potentially be troubling: 'There appears to be a receiver off the hook. If you'd like to make a call, please hang up and try your call again.'

There was something embarrassing about the recorded voice assuming that the receiver must have been displaced by oversight. As if it only needed to make you aware of such an oversight and the situation would of course be remedied immediately. Three times the man would repeat this—'There appears to be a receiver off the hook…'—and three times my mother would ignore him. After his third try he would give up and let a shrill beep take his place. Despite knowing the pattern, I was always startled by the sound. Incessant and slightly chemical, as if alerting us to a fire. My heart pounded along with its rhythm. Fire. Fire. Fire. On and on it went, threatening to continue unabated until the morning. Fire. Fire. Fire. It crept over me and beneath my sheets. Had my mother developed some type of immunity and now I was the only one who could hear it?

Then the sound would stop abruptly, so abruptly that it continued roaming through my head. Eventually silence would drift in, take over, permanent silence, inner and outer. It was as if the phone had exhausted itself trying to get placed back on the hook. It had tried its best, but there was no more it could do. If we could not be budged it could not budge us. My mother and I were on our own. We were floating on a raft in the ocean. It was night and the waves were gently rocking us up and down and from side to side, and all we could do was hope that the raft would not spring a leak, or the water spill over the edge. There was no one anywhere in the world who could save us now. The black silence covered us, a silence so encompassing that I found myself desiring the return of the phone's harsh grating cry. Then I would drift off to sleep.

'Have you been following the coal strike in Utah?' my father asks me.

'No, Pop,' I say, 'I haven't been following that. Actually, I haven't even heard about it.'

'The capitalist media is trying to keep it out of the news, of course,' my father says, without bitterness. Then he unzips his knapsack and pulls out a copy of the weekly newspaper of the Socialist Workers Party, the *Militant*, and hands it to me. 'This is the only publication in which you'll be able to find out the truth.'

The front-page headline reads, MINERS SAY NO TO COAL BOSSES. Beneath it is a photo of a group of miners standing on a picket line, laughing.

'Very interesting,' he says, 'the way things have developed.' His accent causes him to stress the wrong syllable, so rather than say 'deVELoped', it comes out as 'develOPED'. 'We are saying that this is one of the most important strikes in the last ten years.'

'Ten years,' I say.

'Ten years,' he says. 'We have been supporting the struggle to organize industrial...' He goes on, but I've stopped listening, stuck on my father's generous use of the pronoun 'we'. I had known 'we' throughout my childhood. When comrades talked about what they thought, they always spoke in terms of 'we'.

'We believe that the American government needs to get its hands off El Salvador...' 'We argue that the only hope for the working class is...' 'We say end imperialist war through class war.'

It was comforting, such inclusiveness. *What I believe may be marginal*, the subtext went, *you may think that I am isolated, you may think my ideas bizarre and freakish, but I am actually attached to a vast contingent of people who think and say the exact same things that I think and say.*

One early Sunday morning when I was eight years old I helped hand out campaign brochures for Buddy Beck, who was running for Lieutenant Governor on the Socialist Workers Party ticket. My mother and I and a half-dozen comrades stood in the freezing cold outside of a supermarket in Bedford-Stuyvesant. The supermarket had been selected because it catered to some of the poorest constituency of New York City, those who would be most receptive to overthrowing the system. Damaged groceries from other supermarkets were shipped to this supermarket to be sold at reduced prices. If you could not afford the food in this store then you could not afford it anywhere and the next step for you was the soup kitchen.

I liked Buddy Beck. He had big, strong arms and when I saw him at meetings he would lift me on to his shoulders and carry me around. 'Look at the little comrade,' he would say to the other comrades. And the other comrades would ask, 'Saïd, are you going to give the capitalists hell when you grow up?' And then Buddy would answer, 'He's already giving them hell.' And everyone would laugh and I'd feel proud. One spring weekend Buddy had driven me to his parents' farm in the country and let me help him plant seeds. I had never been on a farm before and the soil and the grass and the sunshine all entered me and enticed me and perhaps that is where

I began to draw an association between revolution and long rolling grassy hills and summertime.

For hours I stood in front of the automatic doors of the supermarket holding out the brochures for black people to take from my hand, and for hours black people passed by without taking them.

'Is there a picture of Mr Beck?' one elderly woman asked me.

I opened the brochure. Inside was a photograph of Buddy at a debate with a Democrat, a Republican and a Libertarian. The four men were seated at a table with microphones in front of them. Three of the men were clean shaven and dressed in suits and ties, while the fourth man wore a full beard and a striped sweater and was in the middle of bringing his point home, his mouth open, his hand gesturing.

I pointed to the fourth man. 'That's Buddy Beck,' I said.

The woman chuckled and said loud enough so others could hear, 'I wouldn't vote for that man.'

From time to time I would step inside the store so I could warm myself. Through the window I was able to watch my mother. She was standing near a pile of shopping carts that had been pushed carelessly together without regard and in her mittened hand she was holding up a copy of the *Militant*. When a person came near her she would take a few quick steps toward them and begin to expound on the top articles in that week's issue. Her body language was such that it looked as if she was considering taking a stroll along beside the person, and the person, acutely aware of her proximity, would quicken their pace, leaving my mother behind. The whole interaction took only seconds. She had at most ten or fifteen words to make her pitch.

'US imperialist troops out of Nicaragua and El Salvador. End the...'

'US imperialist troops out of...'

'US imperialist troops out of Nicaragua and El Salvador. End the illegal embargo against Cuba and...'

People approached her, she stepped forward, she began to speak, they passed her, she stopped, she waited for the next person. If there was a long enough lull she would pound her hands vigorously against the arms of the plaid wool coat that she had purchased at the Salvation Army and she would squat up and down to invigorate the muscles of her legs. Then someone would approach and she would right herself quickly.

'US imperialist...'

I observed all of this action through the supermarket window and I willed the passers-by to buy the *Militant* from my mother. Maybe this person will, I thought. Maybe that other person will. I willed a thousand *Militants* to be bought, ten thousand, one million. I willed the patrons of the supermarket to join the Socialist Workers Party, to become comrades, to become us, to fight for the revolution.

*I am one of you*, the proud, sad expression on my mother's face seemed to say. *I understand you, your misery. While other white people have either ignored you or derided you, I have come out on a Sunday morning to stand in the cold in front of your supermarket to help you.*

And one by one the endless stream of poor blacks passed by without so much as a second glance.

We were destined to be on the outside, my mother and I. But it didn't matter because we were we. We would always have we and that was warm and soft. There might not be one million behind us now, but we had each other, and we had the other comrades and we had Trotsky and Lenin and Marx and the Russian Revolution, and we had the right ideas, and we knew that one day we would triumph.

'What's this for?' a little black girl my age asked me. She was dressed for church in a pretty pink dress and a matching flowery pink hat.

'It's for socialism,' I said.

'Oh,' she said, as if she had been expecting to hear that. And then she took the brochure from me and very carefully folded it in half and then in half again and elegantly placed it inside her purse.

'Now I have something to put in my new purse,' she said.

My father wants me to buy a copy of the *Militant*. I don't want to buy it.

'I guess I should buy this,' I say.

'Now your perspective will be broadened,' he says happily.

I take out my wallet and remove a dollar.

'The coal strike is in an anthracite region. Do you know what anthracite is?' He takes my dollar and then he lowers his voice and leans towards me conspiratorially. 'On the surface this strike is about wages and the right to organize. But what is it really about?'

'I don't know, Pop.'

He takes a breath and says with great conviction: 'It is about human dignity.' Each word is emphasized. Then he pauses and looks me dead in the eye as if anticipating that human dignity might be a subject of some controversy for me and that he is prepared to defend it. I think briefly about responding, 'I'm actually opposed to human dignity, Pop.'

'We're having our subscription-fund drive now. Maybe you want to think about buying a subscription. We have a twelve-issue introductory rate.'

'How much is that, Pop?'

'Five dollars.'

'I guess I should buy that.'

My father takes four more dollars from me, pulls an empty envelope out of his knapsack, marks down my name on it, and then places my money inside.

The waitress arrives at our table. 'Would you like to hear tonight's specials?'

My father quickly zips up his knapsack and says, 'I'm afraid there's been a mistake.'

'Mistake?'

'Yes, a mistake.' My father looks at the troublesome carafe of Chardonnay hoping the waitress will intuit the problem. 'What I really meant to ask for,' then he laughs shyly, a little-boy laugh, 'what I really wanted was red wine.'

'Oh?'

'I am very sorry,' my father says with genuine feeling.

'Red wine?'

'Would you by any chance have Zinfandel?'

And the waitress swiftly removes the carafe of Chardonnay.

One of the benchmarks for being a good member of the Socialist Workers Party is the willingness to open your home to comrades who might be travelling to New York City to help out with a campaign, or to give a speech, or to teach a class. Communists should have no sentimental attachment to homes—they provide shelter—and like everything else they are good only as long as they are useful. On one such occasion, when I was four years old, my mother allowed a man to stay with us for a few days while he helped to renovate the Party headquarters.

'After the revolution people will be able to live wherever they want to live,' my mother told me. 'Private property will be a thing of the past.'

Such hospitality would no doubt have been looked upon favourably by my father. Perhaps my mother thought that someone might even mention to him in passing, offhandedly, 'Martha has let so-and-so comrade stay with her.' And that my father upon hearing the good news would realize how committed and dedicated a revolutionary my mother was and that he could no longer live without her. In the dead of some night she would find my father standing outside our front door, his face wet with tears, his hands clenched, asking, imploring, to be let back in her life.

Our house guest had a wide, friendly face and a huge head of red hair that made him look to my four-year-old eyes something akin to a lumberjack. I told him so and it made him shake with deep laughter. On the first evening, in order to repay my mother for the kindness she had shown in opening her home to him (although such sacrifice was of course done selflessly) he repaired a lamp of ours that had been broken for a very long time.

I watched him repair it.

'First I'm going to make sure it's unplugged,' he said to me patiently.

I was even allowed to hand him some of the tools, but my hands were so small that the tools clattered to the floor in the middle of the exchange. My mother and the guest found this delightful.

When the man was finished tinkering he turned the switch and the room was filled with light.

'Look! How wonderful,' my mother said.

On the second evening we all sat down together for dinner. This was unusual for me as no man had ever eaten with us before. I was awed by the enormous amount that he was able to consume. He was also very gracious and he would ask for the salt politely and pass the butter if you needed it and he complimented my mother's cooking and said that I was such a good boy.

On the third and last evening the man offered to babysit me so that my mother would be able to attend a forum the Party was having on Trotsky and the Fourth International.

No. My mother couldn't possibly ask that of the man.

It was no bother for him.

Was he sure?

Sure he was sure.

She'd be home by eleven.

Take your time.

Very nice of you.

And then my mother kissed me on the head, told me to behave, picked up her bag and closed the door behind her, shutting me inside, alone with a man whom she did not know except insofar as he was a revolutionary—and therefore a friend. A comrade.

I was happy to play with the stranger. I became a monster chasing him around the living room.

'I'm so afraid,' the man said, fleeing from me, then cowering behind a chair. I was gleeful at his feigned terror.

My mother was blocks away now, descending the steps to the subway, fumbling in her bag for the token, dropping it in the turnstile, pushing through, looking down the empty tracks, wondering how long the train would take.

'The hideous monster is coming to get me.'

My giggles filled the apartment as the subway arrived, as my mother entered, took a seat, folded her legs, took out something to read, rocked on the train as it hurtled underground towards Manhattan.

Then the man became the monster and did what my mother could not do so easily, stooping down to pick me up and swing me over his shoulder. His power thrilled me.

'The monster has caught you. The monster has caught you.'

'The monster has caught me.' Laughing. Laughing.

And then my mother's stop arrived, and she exited the subway and walked outside and around the corner on to Broadway and up the stairs to the Socialist Workers Party headquarters and greeted everyone and made sure to comment on how the renovation showed the power of the communist movement in America and got a cup of coffee and took her seat.

And meanwhile the man's hands were tickling me under my arms, and then beneath my shirt, and then on my calves.

'You're laughing too much,' the man said playfully. And his mock entreaties of course made me laugh even more.

His hands travelled up towards my knees, then past my knees.
'Stop laughing. No more laughing.'
I squealed in his grasp.
'If you keep laughing you're going to make yourself sick.'
Then on my thighs, then higher.
And as I squirmed to free myself from his strong arms, and as my mother took her seat and patiently waited for the speaker to approach the podium, the comrade put his hands in my pants and gently ran his fingers over and around my dick and balls sending a shockwave coursing through my four-year-old body.

'Comrades, thank you all for coming,' the speaker intoned, adjusting the microphone. And my mother, having had the presence of mind to have brought a pad and pen, removed them from her purse and began to take notes. 'Trotsky and the Fourth International,' she wrote in large letters at the top.

'You're sick,' the man said with playful banter. 'You've made yourself sick. The doctor is now going to have to perform an important operation.'

Then he unzipped his pants.

The waitress appears at our table. She has a tremulous look on her face and in her hand she is gripping the very same carafe filled to the brim with Chardonnay.

'I am sorry,' she says to my father, 'but we are unable to exchange this.'

My father leans in and stares at her as the words register, and then snickers as if he has just been let in on a good joke.

'I am sorry,' the waitress repeats hopefully, 'because the bottle was opened, you understand, the bartender won't be able to re-sell this.'

'Re-sell,' my father luxuriates in the word.

The waitress smiles a reasonable smile, a no-hard-feelings smile. My father looks toward me thoughtfully as if I might intercede, then he nods his head once, twice, tucks his chin against his chest as if he were about to take a nap—then quickly looks up at the waitress.

'Bring the manager,' my father says.

The waitress looks nonplussed. The manager? It has suddenly, unexpectedly come to this. She hesitates for a moment and then hurries off, carafe in hand, the Chardonnay sloshing dangerously, violently in its container. My father looks at her ass and then at me.

'Do you see?' he says to me, his eyes flashing in anger as if I've participated in committing a crime. Then with great sympathy he reverses: 'They put her in a bad situation.' Then to himself, sadly: 'What is it to them?'

There's a dead, awkward silence after this. We watch a couple being seated a few tables away. My father fingers the daisy in the vase and asks, 'Is this real?' We adjust and readjust the silverware.

'Do you know about the history of this Garment District?' my father finally says as an ice-breaker.

'Not really,' I say.

'Women,' he says. 'Poor women.'

The Socialist Workers Party headquarters happens to be located in the heart of the Garment District, only a few blocks from where my father and I now sit. Years before the headquarters occupied an entire building on Charles Street overlooking the Hudson River in Greenwich Village, where the party churned out books, pamphlets and the *Militant*. In the late 1980s the party managed to raise 125,000 dollars and commission eighty artists from twenty countries to paint a giant mural covering the side of the building, six storeys high. There were colourful portraits of all the major revolutionaries, Malcolm X, Rosa Luxemburg, Eugene Debs, Che Guevara, Marx, Engels, everyone imaginable (except Stalin and Mao), all floating over an enormous printing press dispensing rolls of newsprint with Castro's famous maxim, 'The truth must not only be the truth; it must also be told.'

The mural was a huge achievement for the Socialist Workers Party. It was covered every week in the *Militant* for months prior to its completion, and when it was finally unveiled it was heralded as an accomplishment that had been born of the Nicaraguan Revolution.

But the planners had planned poorly, and less than eight years later the colours were fading and the paint was peeling and the brick wall was discovered to have stress cracks and needed to be completely replaced before the entire building itself was compromised and demolished. So another hundred thousand dollars was raised and the faces of Malcolm and Karl and Che were pulled out brick by brick. This, too, was covered for weeks in the *Militant*, and somehow also celebrated as an accomplishment of sorts until no trace of the mural remained. It was replaced instead by a huge pink-coloured plastic siding.

'Have you read *The History of the Russian Revolution?*' my father asks me.

'I haven't read that, Pop.'

'Trotsky writes about how the revolution began with the seamstresses. Do you have a copy? Next time I'll bring you a copy. Don't start with chapter one. Start with chapter six.' And as if reciting poetry, he says, 'The struggles of the seamstresses are like rising suns for the world to see.'

My father knows nothing about the history of seamstresses, of course. He's never read a book about them, or seen a film, or gone to the library to look up an article. He just knows implicitly. Lack of knowledge, however, is not a deterrent for him. My father will often hold forth on the largest of subjects: the social evolution of human beings since *Homo habilis*, the materialist underpinnings of ancient civilization, the French Revolution. The subjects he chooses are so vast, so breathtaking, that you could fail to realize how hollow the information is that he imparts. Try mentioning, for instance, the artificial divisions imposed on the Arab world after the break-up of the Ottoman Empire and he will stare back at you blankly. But he can speak about imperialist oppression of the Middle East in general terms with great verve and for many hours. It's his job. He is a socialist missionary among proletariat savages and every discussion presents itself as a possible opportunity for conversion. It doesn't matter if he himself knows the intimate details of the topics he expounds on, his concern is with truth. He has heard things said by comrades about the seamstresses who have heard things said by other comrades, and he can understand that they are more than likely correct, that they do not demand a major reordering of the world as he perceives it. Beyond this hearsay, though, he has never ventured independently. Such exploration would be redundant and an egregious waste of time.

My mother's bookcase did indeed contain a copy of *The History of the Russian Revolution*. I never read it though. There were also books by Lenin, Marx and Engels, as well as by leading members of the Socialist Workers Party, Farrell Dobbs, James P. Cannon, Jack

Barnes. Those I never read either. Nor had I read *The Origins of Materialism, The Origin of the Family, Private Property and the State, Empiricism and its Evolution: A Marxist View, The First Five Years of the Communist International, The First Ten Years of American Communism* or *Defense Policies and Principles of the Socialist Workers Party*. I would, however, look at the titles when I played with my toys on the floor and wonder what they meant and what was inside. When I opened them to see if there might be pictures to entertain me, I discovered that the covers, the spines, the pages were still stiff and fresh. The books had never been opened by my mother. The titles were all you needed to know.

The restaurant manager appears. He is Indian. He wears very thick glasses and a white shirt that has remained brilliantly clean and which must indicate to my father how little the man labours. Behind him stands the waitress, who could have been a school girl visiting the principal's office with her father. She is clutching the carafe of Chardonnay by the neck as if it's a chicken she's chosen to strangle for supper. The manager squeezes a managerial smile out of his face. It is obvious he is the one who has issued the dictum and is now prepared to stand behind it in the most diplomatic of ways.

'Because, you understand,' he embarks, 'the bartender had to open the bottle of wine in order to pour…'

'Okay,' my father says, dismissing the finer points of the argument with a wave of his hand, 'then I tell you what we do. This is what we do. I tell you. You bring us the cheque for the wine. We pay for the wine. And then we go.'

It's a deft bargaining strategy on my father's behalf.

'Perhaps you would also care to order dinner?' The manager presses his luck.

My father smiles.

'Would you like to hear the specials?' the waitress offers.

And in response my father calmly reiterates the game plan: 'The cheque. We pay. Then we go.'

Every Friday and Sunday night of every week of my childhood were reserved expressly for the Socialist Workers Party. On Friday nights a forum was held that was open to the public, where Party members or an invited guest would speak about the Vietnam War, abortion rights, affirmative action... Sunday nights were meetings for comrades only which pertained to the management and strategy of the Socialist Workers Party itself. This is not to imply that these were the only evenings of political activity. There were also 'plant-gate sales', which meant selling the *Militant* at the gates of factories and mills during shift changes; 'paste-ups', which entailed illegally pasting posters of upcoming events on walls and lamp posts—done late at night to avoid being spotted by the police; the occasional party to celebrate an accomplishment of some sort; conferences; rallies, etc.

These Friday and Sunday night meetings bored me. I would sit beside my mother not understanding what the speaker was saying and only able to follow the cadence of the voice as if I was watching a film in a foreign language. I became adept at knowing when a speech was reaching its climax or when applause was being elicited or when a comrade's question to the speaker was opening up an entire new path of discussion. I was ill-equipped for these meetings. I once fell off a row of folding chairs while asleep. Another time I inexplicably shouted out 'nay' during a voice vote, embarrassing myself and my mother. My mother would confine me to the back rooms where I would pass the time by playing with various office supplies, paper clips, staplers, once even painting my fingernails and toenails using a bottle of WiteOut. If there were pre-meeting doughnuts I would find them and gorge myself. I also complained heavily to my mother about the late night, interminable subway rides home. So beginning around the age of six, my mother concluded that it was better to leave me home alone while she attended these meetings.

The solitude of home was not preferable to the ennui of the forums and branch meetings. I was frightened by everything, by the plunks and clinks of the building, by the sound of footsteps in the hallway, by the thought that my mother might not return at all this time. Shadows cast by furniture hid lurking men, car headlights reflecting on the walls were flames, sounds of a neighbour's toilet flushing was the doorknob being jiggled, a fly was a cockroach, a cockroach was a rat. My mother had posted the number of the meeting hall by the phone in case of emergency, which served only as a constant flashing reminder that danger was an ever-present possibility and that I would be helpless in the face of it. Everything I did while she was off went toward constructing an alternate reality.

The stories I read were expunged of conflict, the games I invented were of the lightest fare of the happiest people of the brightest colours, the stuff of contemporary Christian plots. The power of these modes of entertainment to distract me was temporary and the only thing that kept the terror in check was our thirteen-inch black and white television set. This was forbidden to me except for special occasions, but in my mother's absence I would linger for hours in front of it, counting among my many friends the Jeffersons, the Bunkers and the Flintstones. Programmes were replaced by hour-long dramas which unsettled me with their darker scenarios. I am speaking about programmes like *The Incredible Hulk* or *Fantasy Island* or *That's Incredible!*, in which I once watched a man, in the interest of science, dive into a swimming pool with twenty-pound weights attached to his wrists and ankles so that researchers could monitor the effects of drowning on a human being. I was petrified by this nightmarish content, but I would forego my bedtime and continue watching. The television set, no matter how terrifying it might become, was always a more palatable alternative than the reality that encircled me, waiting for a moment's silence to rush in.

At some point, however, my mother began to realize the unhealthy aspects of such excessive television watching. It would destroy my mind, she told me, my intellect. It would turn my brain to mush. 'It's a boob tube,' she'd say. I was instructed to read or draw while she was gone. I protested. She insisted. I disobeyed. She demanded. I would open a book and pretend to be engrossed as she readied herself to depart, but as soon as she was out of earshot I would turn the television on. She caught on to this, tiptoeing back up the stairwell and pressing her ear against the door. If I denied my crime she would feel the back of the set as if checking a feverish forehead.

'Why is it hot?'

'The light from the lamp must have made it hot.'

She tried being angry with me, but I could not be swayed by admonishment. She would affect disappointment, hoping that would appeal to my conscience. It did not.

One day she discovered that she could remove the electrical cord from the back of the television set. Now, an hour or two before leaving, she would unplug the cord and hide it. This did not elicit the effect she desired, either. As soon as she had gone I would begin to search for the missing cord. It was not as bad as you might think. The search kept me occupied, I was able to fix my mind on a goal and pursue it with relentless fervour. Everything became about finding the cord. Loneliness, sadness, anger, fright were all submerged. It was an attainable goal, too, the cord was somewhere within the confines of our tiny apartment, and although there were quite a number of places of where it might be, the options nonetheless were finite. I rifled through everything like a seasoned burglar: her underpants drawer, her bra drawer, her diary drawer, her jar of keepsakes. Nothing was sacred. I always found the cord in the end.

Years of treasure hunts went by. Five years, twice, sometimes three times a week. I evolved out of dread at my mother's departures and found myself looking forward to them as opportunities to indulge in the terrible elixir of situation comedy. I would plot my viewing days in advance. If for some reason or other a meeting had been cancelled or rescheduled and my mother stayed home I would lapse into terrible disappointment and frustration. Eventually my mother had removed the cord so many times that it no longer stayed firmly connected to the set, but would, in the middle of a programme, fall straight out of the back. The flood of silent reality would propel me from my chair like a sprinter at the gun. The more I pushed the cord into the set the more compromised it became. In the end I came to some well-reasoned childish conclusion that wetting the end of the cord would cause it to stick firmly in place. So with the electrical cord still plugged into the wall I would put my mouth on the end of it and lick it, then lick it again, then push it into the television set.

Then one Sunday evening when I was about ten years old, I watched in horror as my mother, in the sombre ritual of a robbed priest at mass, unplugged the cord from the socket, removed it from the back of the television set, opened her purse, placed it inside and left for her meeting. I listened to the key turn in the lock and then heard her footsteps in the hallway, down the stairs, clip clip clip, and then gone. The battle was over. My mother had won. The night stretched before me. My defeat was my imprisonment. A life sentence. In an apartment somewhere above a dog barked. The bark was a woman's scream.

The Chardonnay conflict has been resolved amicably. The waitress has arrived at our table holding a carafe of blood-red wine and silently pours it like a defeated soldier being forced to serve the enemy-king. My father watches the glasses fill with Zinfandel with a contrite look on his face, as if to assure her that despite his victory he will not gloat. I imagine my father hungrily fucking her later, full of apology.

'Look how she fills the glasses all the way to the top,' my father says, imagining this to be some sort of an accomplishment by the waitress. The waitress smiles meekly.

'Some people say the glass is half full,' my father presses, 'but when it is wine it should always be filled to the top.'

She reads the specials in an automatic voice, like a bored weather forecaster telling us that there's a chance it might rain tomorrow. The dishes have Persian names. I bury my head in the menu pretending to be considering the full range of options. The foods are all unfamiliar. I feel as if I should know them, that I've been handed a test that I had ample warning of yet still find myself unprepared for. My father listens to the waitress intently, repeats back for clarification, asks if this thing has eggplant, if the other thing is fried. He orders for both of us. He says thank you a lot, smiles, bats his eyelashes. Asks for extra rice and a side of onions, if it's not too much trouble. He takes a long look at her ass when she walks off.

'A toast to your belated birthday,' my father says, and raises his glass.

I raise mine.

'To the young man.'

'I don't feel like a young man,' I say.

'That's the contradiction,' he says. 'I don't feel like an old man.'

Clink.

Then my father spills the red wine down his shirt.

Three blocks from where my mother and I lived was a pizza shop called 'Uncle Charlie's'. It was a losing proposition. Every few years it was sold by one sucker to another. It was a small dim place with a video game and a pinball machine. The pinball machine appealed to a previous generation to which I did not belong. The video game, however, was always crowded with boys eagerly watching the action like gamblers at a cockfight. Some afternoons I would insinuate myself among the older, stronger boys and watch them play. There was a masculinity to what they could accomplish, deftly reaching levels the younger boys could only hope to aspire to, while enduring an inhuman amount of pandemonium as the machine worked to separate the player from the quarter he had inserted.

I was horrible at the game. I never fully understood the rules. I panicked quickly under pressure. I was too deliberate at aiming at the enemy spaceships. I'd exhaust my precious 'smart bombs' almost immediately, like a junkie unable to preserve their stash. As the game progressed, everything moved faster and faster including my own plane. I'd fly through outerspace like a drunk driver, careening from top to bottom. There was relief when it was over, like returning to the waking world from a bad dream. Then I would step back and let the older boys take the reins.

The night my mother left with the television cord, it occurred to me that, unlike a prisoner, I was free to go to Uncle Charlie's if I wanted. I had a dollar bill that I had come by somehow. I withdrew it from my dresser drawer and looked at it. What evidence would there be that I had ever left the apartment? Not a trace. I visualized myself out in the city streets, walking. The thought of it unsettled me. There was something clandestine about the act, something akin to thievery.

Uncle Charlie's was then owned by an overweight Jewish man with black hair and bushy eyebrows whose name was Joel, but whom everyone called Charlie. He was eating a slice of pizza when I entered. (I envied the endless supply of pizza that was afforded him.) The place was empty. The floor had been swept clean, the small tables cleared of debris. The clock on the wall read 8.50. I was prepared for him to ask why I was out so late, but he did not. With uninterest he gave me four quarters for my dollar. I dropped a coin through the slot of the game, there was a loud beep as the box ingested it and then came to life with swirling lights and sounds. The machine beat out its drum-drum music as the enemy spacecraft flew in to attack. I fired at them, bullet after bullet and the spaceships disintegrated on impact. It was satisfying to destroy.

In my mind as I played, I began to play a different game. I imagined my spaceship was a communist spaceship and the enemy spaceships were the spaceships of the capitalists. The stakes of this duel energized me. On level one, I soundly defeated capitalism. And on level two as well. And then on three. As each subsequent level of the video game appeared on the screen, all who I had killed before reappeared to be killed again, and each time there were more of them and they were faster and more resilient, and each time I was up to the task. On and on I went. I thought of the older boys and their video-game athleticism and I wondered what they would think of me now. My left hand ached from gripping the joystick and the tips of the fingers on my right hand pounded away furiously at the yellow button that dispensed my bullets. My weapons were the weapons of Marx, Engels and Trotsky, and the ships that came to kill me were piloted by Rockefeller, Reagan, Carnegie, the 'rich asses', Uncle Charlie himself. Eventually there was no chance whatsoever, the speed of the machine had grown exponentially, and in the middle of an impossible number of capitalist spaceships I went down in flames.

I stood at the machine dazed, spent, watching as it ranked me and invited me to put in my three initials. I had three quarters left. It was 9.20. There was plenty of time remaining in the night. I put another one of my quarters in. I made a careless mistake and was killed on the first screen. It was 9.22. I put another quarter in. I was killed on the second screen. I slapped the side of the machine.

'Hey!' Uncle Charlie cried out.

I put in another quarter. I played with resignation, with defeat. An insult to the machine. 'If I lose, I lose because I do not even care enough about you to try to win.' I lost. I had no more quarters. I looked at the floor for a possible stray. The floor had been swept clean. I was humiliated by my need. I felt sudden rage at the boys who always seemed to be in possession of an endless supply of quarters. The rage was replaced by sadness. It would be a long time before I came by another dollar. I wanted it back. I wanted to undo it. I caught a glimpse of my face in the glass of the machine. I looked gaunt, depraved, my eyes were bloodshot.

As I left I kept my head down to avoid making eye contact with Uncle Charlie. There wasn't a soul on the street. I realized suddenly how odd it was for a little boy to be outside in the streets alone at this time of night. I was like someone who has ventured far out into a driving rainstorm before realizing that it is in fact a hurricane. I took the long, most well-lit way home. I walked slowly, hoping to affect an air of nonchalance that might dissuade a predator. A man approached me from the opposite direction, then passed. I entered my apartment building with great relief and walked the two flights of stairs to my floor. Perhaps my mother's meeting had let out early and she was now home, frightened, irritated, waiting to chastise me for my senselessness. I opened the door and the stillness of the apartment washed over me.

On a shelf in the bookcase my mother kept a little, brown, sugar jar in which she used to store sugar. It was always filled with coins and crumpled-up bills. When I first discovered the jar it seemed miraculous to me. I had always come to associate the jar and the money with my father. Perhaps the jar itself had actually once belonged to him and so I imagined that the money in the jar was his too and that he had given it to my mother as a sort of one time alimony payment when he left. That night I unscrewed the lid and took out a dollar. I felt I was crossing an invisible barrier, but I did not recognize the boy crossing it.

I went out again, this time without deliberation. The novelty of the experience had worn off, it seemed old hat now. It was dark, but I was not frightened by the darkness. Charlie was noisily sipping a Coke through a straw when I entered. He didn't ask how I had come by another dollar. He gave me change. I played hard, I lost quickly. The quarters were gone. The clock read 10.12. There was a pinching in my elbow from the strain of clutching the joystick. I wanted to crush something in my hands. I badly needed to pee and the sensation incited me. I thought briefly about tearing my shirt off, thinking there would be some satisfaction in that. I looked at my shoes. They seemed too large, and my hands too thin.

The short cut to my home was through an alleyway. It was jet black, but as a punishment for having spent and for having lost, I walked through it anyway. There was a recklessness to the act which I deserved. I fantasized about being accosted by the shadows. I had homework to do, but it was too late to do it now. I had wasted the night. I wanted the night back. The only thing that could alleviate this discomfort, that could redeem me, that could let me pee, was to play the video game again. I entered the apartment. The stillness. I did not hesitate, I went straight for the sugar jar. I unscrewed it. The stranger took out a five-dollar bill.

It's nearly midnight when we leave Colbeh. There's a nice mist covering everything, softening the streets and the buildings. It's quiet. We pass an old-fashioned gaslight.

'That is very nice looking,' my father says.

'It's real nice, Pop.'

'When I was a boy in Iran we never had gaslights. Iran went directly from no light to electric lights. That is the kind of thing that happens in a backward country. The Law of Combined and Uneven Development.'

'What's that, Pop?'

'The Law of Combined and Uneven Development. Trotsky talks about it. Two countries, one that exploits and the other that, you know. There are things that develOPED unevenly. But combined. Trotsky talks about it...' He trails off.

We walk in silence. The streets are empty. Cars pass us softly. I think about how ironic it is that someone who stresses the importance of history is so woefully and wilfully ignorant of his own son's. My mother, for instance, never told my father what transpired that night she left me alone with the travelling comrade. It strikes me as a crime tantamount to the crime itself. *The truth must not only be the truth, it must also be told.* It never occurred to my mother that this might be news worth passing on to my father. Or perhaps she thought that such an unseemly development would make our home less inviting were he ever to consider returning. When she called Party headquarters and told them what the comrade had done to me she was told, 'Under capitalism everyone has problems.' And it was left at that. Such an explanation, which my father no doubt would have heartily endorsed, was apparently sufficient for her. It was never mentioned in our home again. Life was miserable, of course, and there was no use fighting against each and every indignity that we encountered. It was up to each of us to bear those personal miseries ourselves, until that glorious day in the future when it would all be resolved once and for all.

My father and I come out on to Eighth Avenue and into the crush of the world. The subway station looms before us. He stops and stands in front of me, the splotch of red wine, now dried, running like a birthmark across his chest. He holds out his hand. We shake like friendly acquaintances. Then he pulls me to him suddenly and hugs me awkwardly, slightly off centre, my chest pressing into his elbow, a vague approximation of an embrace.

'It's been nice walking with you,' he says.

There hadn't been many walks and there wouldn't be many more. Our lives together had not existed. He was my father in fact only, a biological father, but besides the genes there was nothing really, no past, no memory, only our very own personal combined and uneven development.

'Be good,' he says.

The A train is empty except for a few people. I sit across from a black man wearing construction boots and covered in a fine grey dust. He watches me closely as I unfold the *Militant*. Two thoughts of equal import appear in my brain simultaneously. One thought is that I will be hailed by him for being a liberator, one who understands his plight and the plight of all those who labour. The other thought is that he is an informant for the government.

I read an article about some recent developments in Haiti. The reporting is similar to an article I came across about a week earlier in the *New York Times*. I realize that most of the information has been culled from the *Times* and rewritten with a Marxist bent. The word *American* has been replaced throughout with the word *imperialist*. 'The imperialist troops entered the capital...' 'The imperialist government stated that...' Some background history has been added, and some references to the Cuban Revolution. The article concludes by saying that real change can only come about in Haiti if the working class makes change in the form of a socialist revolution. The photograph of angry demonstrators burning tyres in the centre of the street is credited to Getty Images.

The A train stops at West Fourth and the black man stands and exits. I watch him walk away. His trousers are fraying and he has a slight limp, a hitch in his step that causes him to lean to the left. The doors close and the train begins to pull out of the station, passing the man, paused at the foot of the stairs, resting against the railing, summoning his strength before he attempts the ascent. *Socialism will save you.* I look down at the *Militant* and I am suddenly struck by how much it resembles a high-school newspaper. The type is a bit too big, the photos too grainy, and the whole thing is only several pages thick. You can feel an earnestness behind the effort, a diligence that doesn't quite live up to the size of its ideas. It's a newspaper aspiring to be a newspaper aspiring to world revolution.

There is an article about the latest eight-week subscription drive. I study the table that has been provided to show the drive's weekly progress. The goal for the entire United States is to sell 1,000 subscriptions. That is to say that out of a possible 300 million people the Socialist Workers Party hopes to sell 1,000 subscriptions. Out of eight million people in New York City the goal is listed at one hundred, of which seventeen subscriptions have already been sold. There are five more weeks to go. They will make their goal, of course. They always do. There is always the extraordinary distance to reach, the insurmountable odds that can only be overcome by a disciplined, fighting cadre. There are always the articles, every week, that chronicle how many subscriptions have been sold, how many still need to be sold and what it reflects about the overall class-consciousness of workers in the United States. There are the editorials that urge on the comrades to sell and sell. Then there is the blazing headline that heralds a miracle in the eleventh hour. As a little boy I had dreamed of those goals being met. We were always just one more subscription away, one more brochure, one more *Militant*, one more book. All we needed was that one more thing and we would win, the revolution would come. It always resolved itself the same way and in a few weeks there would be another subscription drive and we would begin again.

I realize I have now become the eighteenth subscription for New York City. □

GRANTA

# THE VISITING CHILD
## Karen E. Bender

In their neighbourhood between seven and eight p.m., after her children had fallen asleep and as the streetlights blinked on, Jane Goldman stepped on to her front porch to listen to the faint sound of screaming float from the other houses on her street. The screaming was the sound of children protesting everything: eating, bathing, sharing toys, going to sleep. As the weather had warmed up she stood outside on her porch, smoking a rare cigarette and listening. This was her life now, at forty: she had married a man whom she admired and loved, and after the initial cruelty of early marriage—the fact that they betrayed the other simply by being themselves—they fell into the exhausting momentum that was their lives. They had produced a son, now five years old, and a daughter, now ten months, two beings who hurtled into the world, ruby-lipped, peach-skinned, and who now held them hostage as surely as masked gunmen controlled a bank.

Jane was a freelance editor for technical manuals, a job that she did not love but had drifted into, and her husband, after seeing his business as a high-priced website designer dry up, settled in a job as a consultant. They had moved to a mid-sized city in South Carolina. It was not their first choice and they did not know if they would ever feel at home there but they could afford, finally, a small house as well as a car. They had found their own happiness, weighted by resignation: that they were who they were, that they could never truly know the thoughts of another person, that their love was bruised by the carelessness of their own parents (his mother, her father); that they would wander the world in their dreams with ghostly, intangible lovers, that their children would move from adoration of them to fury, that they and their parents would die in different cities, that they would never accomplish anything that would leave any lasting mark on the world. They had longed for this, from the first lonely moment of their childhoods when they realized they could not marry their fathers or mothers, through the burning romanticism of their teens, to the bustling search of their twenties, and there was the faint regret that this tumult and exhaustion was what they had longed for, and soon it, too, would be gone.

Jane stood on the porch each night, watching the dusk settle on to their quiet street, and she did not go inside immediately. She sat watching the other families move behind the windows, gliding silently in their aquariums of golden light.

Karen E. Bender

One morning soon after, Jane sat cross-legged on the floor of the bathroom at 6 a.m., the baby grappling at her breasts, and watched the line form on the test. She and her husband had not been trying for another child. She pressed her lips to her baby girl's soft head, this one she wanted to love, and she understood, clearly, that she did not feel capable of loving a third child. She had given everything to the others. She kissed the baby's head, grateful for the aura of kindness the baby bestowed on her, for there was now no illusion, as there had been when she was a young woman, that this being inside of her would not become a child; she held the thick, muscular result in her hands. The baby's tiny soft hands made her feel faint. They lived in a part of the country where a third (or fourth or fifth) unexpected child arrived and, with jovial weariness, families 'made room' for them. She looked at the red line and it measured all the moments remaining in her life. Suddenly, she was afraid.

It was time for breakfast. The husband staggered awake after a depressing dream in which a childhood friend had retired early and moved to Tuscany. He was in a surly mood believing that his ideal life had passed him by. The kitchen smelled fetid, as though an animal had crawled into a corner and died. The boy, still grief-stricken over his sister's birth, utilizing their guilt over this to demand endless presents, described his longing for a Slinky that a colleague of his had brought to pre-school. 'I did want it,' he wailed in a monotone. 'I did. I did. I did.' He wanted to wear his Superman shirt with the red cape attached to the shoulders and spent his breakfast leaping out of his seat and trying to shoot his sister with a plastic gun. She, too, already had preferences, and screamed until Jane put her into a purple outfit with floppy bunny ears. They wanted to be anything but human. Her husband could not find anything to put on his lunch sandwich and, with a sort of martyred defiance, slapped margarine on bread. 'What a man does to save money,' he murmured.

'Why don't you just buy your lunch?' she asked.

'Do you know how much that costs?' he said. 'Do you know how much I'm saving this family by eating crap on bread every day?'

'I want a Slinky,' the boy moaned. The baby screamed.

'Will everyone please shut up?' she bellowed.

'Don't say that around the children,' he said.

'I can say what I want.'

'Don't say *shut up*,' said the son, in a ponderous tone.

'Eat your breakfast,' she hissed at him.

'I don't want it,' he wailed, writhing out of his seat and on to the floor, where he curled up under the table as though preparing for a nuclear bomb. She had no sympathy for any of them. She glanced at her husband; their love had been, like all love at the beginning, a mutual and essential misunderstanding, a belief that each could absorb qualities held by the other, that each could save the other from loneliness, that their future held endless promise, that they would not be separated at death. This version of joy was what they had chosen of their own free will.

The baby, not wanting to be outdone, suddenly struck a pose like a fashion model. 'How cute,' said the husband; they all hungered for a moment of beauty. The baby laughed, a glittery sound. The boy wept. The future lay before them, limp and endless. The husband got on his hands and knees by the son. 'Come on,' he said, his voice exquisite with tenderness. 'You're a big boy now.' He pleaded for maturity for about five minutes, and when his voice was about to snap, the boy crawled out and donned a backpack, which made him resemble a miniature college student. He turned around, delighted, so they all applauded.

Their son ran out on to their lawn. There was a sweet green freshness in the morning air. It was a Tuesday; she believed she was six weeks along; there was a bad taste in her mouth, of ash. Behind them was their house, a flimsy tribute to the middle class, but one bad car crash, one growing lump, a few missed paychecks would send them packing. They could not afford to have a heart attack, to lose their minds. It was just spring: daffodils burst out of the cold earth. She and her husband stood, bewildered, watching the children dance in the golden Southern sunlight. She loved them so deeply her skin felt as if it was burning, and she also knew that she could not endure one more.

She called the babysitter, kissed her children goodbye and went to the clinic. She was afraid that he would have tried to convince her to have the third child, that he would have felt himself capable of more love than he actually held. She wept on the way there, for her certainty that she could not have another, for her desire to be good enough for the boy and girl. When she arrived at the clinic, she had stopped weeping. She drove home, sore and cramping, three hours later, down the broad grey lanes bordered by fast-food emporiums, wanting to swerve in and run inside to the high-school girls in bright hats behind the counters so that she could hear them say brightly, *May I help you?*

Sometimes during the day there would be a knock on the door, and it would be their eight-year-old neighbour, Mary Grace. She was the only person who was ever at the door. She was beloved by their son, and for this reason, Jane let her wander into their house at all times. Mary Grace was fiercely competitive in all areas including height, hour of bedtime and the quality of bribe her mother had given her in order for her to get a flu shot. She had thin brown hair, was heavy, ordinary, and her eyes were hooded with the suspicion that her parents would do anything possible to keep from listening to her.

Mary Grace's parents were silent, mysterious types who were very involved in their Baptist church. Jane and her husband tried to guess why the parents never spoke to them and why they never invited the son to their house. Perhaps Mary Grace's father was having an affair. Or the mother was having an affair. Perhaps they never had sex or had bad sex. Perhaps they did not make each other laugh. Perhaps the mother was sad because her daughter was not beautiful, or because she wished she had herself become a ballet dancer, a doctor, a rock star. Perhaps one drank too much. Perhaps he wanted to live in Australia. Perhaps she hated his taste in clothes. Perhaps one of them had cancer. Perhaps they did not want their floors to get dirty. Would they break up or marinate in their sourness for years? Mary Grace's parents did not set up any sort of social life for her. Jane noticed the wife spending most of her free time snipping their front hedges with gardening implements that were large and vicious. Jane saw the husband on his dutiful evening walks around the block, his eyes cast down, his feet lifting in a peculiar way so he seemed to be tiptoeing across ice. Mary Grace scuttled over to Jane's at least once a day, neatly dressed and clean but she always had the demeanour of someone who was starving.

That day, she was grateful for the girl's knock. Jane had returned from the clinic, opened the door to her home slowly, as though she were an intruder. The children noticed nothing; their absorption in their own crises was complete. They saw only that she was their mother and fell towards her ravenously. She was aching and exhausted, but the babysitter couldn't stay. Jane needed a stranger in the kitchen, someone to speak because she could not.

'Let's make a magic potion,' Mary Grace announced. She believed touchingly that she could realize her great dreams in their home. The girl rushed into the kitchen. Her greedy hands rummaged through drawers, plucked juice boxes from cupboards. 'We need to make a magic potion,' she said. 'We need olive oil. Lemonade. Baking soda. Seltzer.'

'Yes,' her son said, gazing at Mary Grace.

Jane brought the items over and Mary Grace poured them carefully into a glass. Her son was now whispering to her, his face intent, and the girl said, rolling her eyes, 'No. It will not make you into a cheetah.' Suddenly, Jane looked at Mary Grace and felt anger flash through her.

'He can become a cheetah if he wants,' Jane broke in.

'Then I want to become a princess,' said Mary Grace.

The baby pushed some magnetic photos off the refrigerator. The children stared out from the photos like prisoners shackled by their parents' desire to have something to love. She brought them some vinegar and mayonnaise and seltzer and watched them stir their concoction. Mary Grace looked up and said, 'My mother's doing her fitness video. She wants to get to her high-school weight.'

'Oh,' said Jane.

'She was going to become a fitness instructor but then she was dating my dad and they knew each other three weeks and then she dropped everything to have me.' She giggled frantically, as though she was not sure what sound to make. Then Mary Grace grasped Jane's forearm. The girl's nails were long and sharp. 'Can we add perfume to make princesses?' she asked.

Jane allowed the girl to hold her arm for a moment, even though Mary Grace's fingernails were painful. 'No,' she said. She patted Mary Grace's hand, carefully, in what she hoped was a reassuring gesture. 'I'm sure she's very glad she has you,' she said and reached up to a cabinet for some baking soda, which forced Mary Grace to release her hand.

'Then she had my brother, like that, *boom*, and then my sister, and she says if she gets back to her high school weight, she'll look seventeen again.' Mary Grace took the baking soda, poured it in and the mixture began to fizz and rise. The children shrieked at the possibilities implied in this and when the potion puttered out looked towards Jane. 'More!' called her son.

'I want a snack now,' Mary Grace said.

Jane opened the refrigerator. She felt more blood slip out of her and sharply took a breath. 'Do you want some carrots?' she asked.

'I want ice cream with hot fudge syrup,' said the girl. 'Please.'

In Boston, where Jane used to live, her husband had a successful business constructing corporate websites, but he most enjoyed helping people create elaborate personal shrines that floated in no place on earth. People wanted all sorts of things on them: personal philosophy, photos both personal and professional, diary fragments, links to other people whom they admired but to whom they had no actual connection. Her husband understood their desire to communicate their best selves with an unknown, invisible public; a shy person, he had forced himself to become sociable and liked convincing people of all the intimate facts they needed to tell strangers about themselves. When she met him, he was exuberant and she was shy, disdainful of websites; she was the only person he had ever met who did not want one for herself. 'Don't you want people to click on and find out all about you?' he asked. 'Your achievements and innermost thoughts?' He was leaning, one arm against a wall, clutching cheap wine in a plastic glass. They were just thirty, old enough to have started to look old.

'No,' she said.

He sensed she was holding back and that made her appear that she concealed something deeply valuable. She admired his shamelessness, the way he could go up to anyone at a party and convince them to create a monument to themselves. They had both stumbled out from families in which they felt they did not belong: she, second of four, he, oldest of three. He had a beautiful, careless mother who had left the family for two years when he was seven; this created in him a sharp and fierce practicality, a need to ingratiate himself and to hoard money. She had been belittled by her father and for years had cultivated the aloofness of the shy who secretly believe themselves more brilliant than others. She excelled at finding low-level but glamorous-sounding jobs in advertising, public relations, script-analysis; when her boss asked more of her than she was willing to give, she got herself fired and complained about it for years. Her husband liked her bounty of imaginary talent, enjoyed complaining at parties about how her true worth was never acknowledged. They drifted like this for longer than was necessary, or even decent, but that was the way all their friends in the city lived.

The economy quickly broke apart their life. People and companies were running out of money to create themselves in an invisible space. She had been working as an editor for a small publisher and that was the first job she lost simply because the company was folding. Their rent was shooting up, they were in their late thirties with a three year old, another on the way, and a paltry sum saved for retirement. It was time to move on.

Her husband came home that evening in a cheerful, determined mood, armed with a new digital camera. He wanted to take pictures of them in the garden and arrange them on a website that would record the children's growth as well as that of the various vegetables and flowers they had recently planted. The routine quality of his new job sometimes filled him with a manic, expansive energy. So many parts of him were unused. The camera had cost $345. 'We can do this every few days,' he said. 'We can tell people about it. They can click on from everywhere and see our garden. We can start a trend!' She wondered how he had been misunderstood at his work that day. He tried, with difficulty, to arrange the children beside the plot of dirt.

She did not want him to take a picture of her. She did not want later to see a picture of her face on this day.

'We need more good pictures of you,' he said, irritation flickering across his face. 'I look too fat,' she said.

'No, you don't,' he said. 'You need a picture with pearls. Holding a rose. Jackie Kennedy. A socialite surrounded by her darling cherubs.' He laughed.

'Oh, come on,' she said. It was a sweet but clichéd world view that he reverted to when he felt uprooted, and it comforted him. He had nurtured it when he was alone and neglected as a child and formed his ideas of happiness, what his family and love should be. He was generally a smart man but he was prone to mythologizing:

her beauty, their children's capacities, their lazy sunny future on an island surrounded by sea.

She had been the daughter of frightened parents who cut up apples in her lunch so she would not choke and drove only on the right side of the road, and she had been drawn to his point of view when they were dating, wanted his assumed confidence to envelop her. She remembered the first time she saw his childhood house, in a suburban tract in Los Angeles—it was a small house that attempted to resemble a Southern mansion, with columns on the porch and a trim rose-bed in the front. There was something in the stalwart embrace of other people's tastes that made Jane envious—not of the house so much as the purity of longing.

She heard the children shriek and there was no such simplicity. Your own family was the death of it.

'Come on,' he said. 'Throw something on. Wash your face.'

She looked at him. 'What's wrong?' he asked.

She did not want to injure his perception of himself as a good person. But now he clutched his pillow as though he were drowning.

Her family stumbled around the barren garden, hair lit up by the late afternoon sun. He was clutching his camera, eager to record the physical growth of their children and vegetables. 'Look at me,' she said, wanting him to see everything.

His face flinched, bewildered. 'You look beautiful,' he said with hope.

The children were in bed, sleeping. She brought blankets to their chins, watched their breath rise in and out. Their eyelids twitched with fervent dreams. The sight of her children sleeping always brought up in her a love that was vast and irreproachable. No one could question this love. She remembered the first time she and her husband hired a babysitter and went to dinner, two months after their boy was born. They had walked the streets, ten minutes from their home. They had hoped they would forget about him, that when they sat down in a restaurant, they would enjoy the same easy joy of self-absorption. But they realized, slowly, that they would never in their lives ever forget about him. The rest of the date they spent in a stunned silence understanding, for the first time, how this love would both reward and entrap them for the rest of their lives.

She sat beside her husband in bed. She was still cramping; she went to the bathroom to urinate and there was still blood. She was relieved as she felt the blood leave her, pretending that it was just another period, but did not want to look too closely at the material that came from her, though the nurse had said it was too early for there to be any form. The names they might have used came to her: Charles, Wendy, Diane. But they were names for nothing now, air. There was no kindness she could offer it now, and that made her feel dry, stunted. She went back to her children's rooms and kissed them again.

She could not sleep. She sat in the darkness, and suddenly she noticed a light go on in her neighbours' house. Their houses were side by side, about ten feet apart, and the neighbours' blinds were usually closed. Tonight she saw that they were open as though they were trying to enjoy the new warmth. The mother had put up curtains, but they were sheer, and Jane could see right into their room.

She saw Mary Grace's mother sitting on her bed. Their bedroom had been decorated with the lukewarm blandness of a hotel room, and was so clean as to deny any human interaction inside it. The mother was heavier than she had imagined; the jumping jacks seemed to have had no effect. She wore a frilly aqua nightie that made her resemble a large, clumsy girl. She was sitting on the edge of the bed and suddenly pulled the nightie over her head. She was watching the husband, who wore bright boxer shorts and no shirt. The curtain lifted in the warm wind. The husband walked over to the wife and she lifted her face for a kiss; the husband pulled her breast as though he was milking a cow. The wife's face was blank.

'I know what you forgot! The detergent!' she exclaimed, in a clear voice. The husband drew back. His shoulders slumped as though he were begging. There was quiet and Jane waited for his answer.

'Sorry,' he said. There was a plaintive quality to this word, his inability to come up with any sort of excuse; it seemed to designate everything about their future. The lights went off.

Jane sat in her quiet room, startled by what she had just seen. She and her husband had not had sex in three weeks. However, when they had, she believed that it was superior to whatever was going on across the way. She was suddenly deeply competitive, wanted to wake him up, to show the neighbours their own prowess in this endeavour. She was comforted by this, her aggressive pity, briefly, but felt herself cramping again. She placed her hand on her stomach; the cramps stopped.

Her husband slept. She stared into the quiet room for a while. The moments left in her life suddenly encased her like a grave; she got out of bed and went downstairs. She told herself she needed to take out the garbage but she just needed to get outside. Opening the door, the night was thick and black and the air was fresh. Usually she locked the night out of their house but now she stepped into it. She threw the bag of trash into the can and stood in front of her house. The cicadas sounded like an enormous machine. The sky was a riot of stars. She glanced around the empty street and began, slowly, to run.

The neighbourhood was beautiful in a sinister way at this hour, flowers and bushes randomly lit by small spotlights, as though each family wanted to illuminate some glorious part of itself. It was ten-thirty and the only discernible human sound was the canned television laughter floating out of windows. The houses looked as though they had been anchored on these neat green plots of land forever. How much longer would her neighbours wake up, shower, eat their cereal, argue, dress their children, weep, prepare dinner, sit by the television, make love, sleep? She ran slowly, the sidewalk damp under her naked feet; she smelled the flowers, the jasmine, honeysuckle, magnolia, sweet and ferocious and dark. No one knew anything about her, and she believed she did not know anything about anyone; she was filled with a loneliness so strong she thought her heart would burst.

She ran one block like this and stopped, breathing hard. Her temples were sweating. She was a middle-aged woman in her pyjamas, running from her house at ten-thirty at night. Looking at her house, the small night light in her son's room cast a lovely blue glow through the window. From here, his room looked enchanted, as if inhabited by fairies. Her breathing slowed, and the night air felt cool in her lungs. She headed back to her house slowly, as though she had just been out for a walk. When she glanced up at the neighbours' bedroom window, she noticed that their blinds were now shut.

Mary Grace knocked on the door at three-thirty the next day. Jane thought she was dressed up early for Halloween, with a short blue accordion-skirt and a T-shirt with a halo made of rhinestones on it, but it was actually a cheerleader outfit. She was going to cheerleader practice for Halo Hoops, the church basketball team. 'I have to go to our basketball game at church,' she said. 'I have ten minutes. That is all.' Jane held open the door and Mary Grace jumped inside and did a twirl.

'Can I marry you, Mary Grace?' her son asked.

'No,' said Mary Grace. 'I'm older than you.' She looked at Jane. 'I'm going to be a superstar singer. I'm going to be in the top five. Wanna hear—' She belted out a few words of a pop song. She was stocky, tuneless and loud. Jane's son was enchanted and requested more. He grabbed Mary Grace's hand and Jane's heart flinched.

'Can we make cookies?' Mary Grace asked. 'Quick?'

They bustled into the kitchen and proceeded to bake. No one came to take the girl to Halo Hoops. The kitchen suddenly smelled like a bakery. Mary Grace stood too close to her. 'Do you like my singing?' she pleaded.

'Sure,' said Jane.

'Me, too,' said the girl. Jane felt Mary Grace's breath on her arm. The girl's breath had the warmth of a dragon or other unnatural beast. The girl's belief in Jane's worth was awful. 'You have pretty hair,' said Mary Grace, reaching up to Jane and touching a strand. The girl had a startlingly gentle touch. Her hand smelled of sweet dough and chocolate.

'Thanks,' said Jane. The boy and the baby stared at Mary Grace. The baby, hanging on Jane's hip, reached out and swatted Mary Grace away. Mary Grace's face tightened, aggrieved.

'Do I have pretty hair?' asked Mary Grace.

The baby yanked Jane's hair. 'Ow!' said Jane grabbing the tiny hand.

'Do I?' asked Mary Grace; it was almost a shout.

Before Jane could answer, her son stepped forward and grabbed Mary Grace's arm. 'Do you want to stay for dinner?' he asked.

Mary Grace recoiled from his touch. Jane saw all of the girl's self-hatred light up her eyes; that she had no other friends besides this five year old, that her parents did not want her at their table. 'No,' she snapped, 'Why do you keep asking me!'

Her son dropped his head, wounded. Jane slapped her hand hard on the table. It made a clear, sharp sound. 'Then just go home!' she yelled at Mary Grace. 'Go home, now!'

The children were suddenly alert. Jane was frozen, ashamed. The girl slowly picked up her jacket and, shoulders slumped, eyes cast downward, trudged to the door, a position already so well-worn it had carved itself into her posture. Her son screamed, 'Stay!' and skidded toward her, arms open, but Mary Grace moved to the door and was gone.

That night Jane sat beside her husband and realized that they had known each other for fifteen years. She wanted to tell her husband something new about herself, something she had never told anyone before. She wanted to tell him a secret that would bring them to a new level of closeness. What else could she tell him? Would he be more grateful for a humiliating moment in her life or a transforming one? Did people love others based on the ways they had similarly debased themselves, or the proud ways they had lifted themselves up?

'What?' he asked, sensing a disturbance.

'I yelled at that girl,' she said. 'She was snippy and I couldn't stand it. She turned around and left.'

'They already hate us,' he said, and returned to his book.

She was suddenly revved up for an argument.

'I'm wasting my life picking up towels,' she said. 'For every ten towels I pick up, you pick up one. I'm sick of it, and they smell like goats.'

Now he looked up. 'I pick up towels,' he said. 'Plenty of them.'

'Not as many as me,' she said.

He jumped out of bed, standing on the balls of his feet, like a boxer who had been secretly preparing for this barrage, and then grabbed a robe and tossed it over himself. 'What do I give up for this family! Look at my leg.' He held it out. 'If I had any time at all to exercise, then I would be able to get in great shape. I could run a marathon! I could make love ten times a day.' The edge in his voice, the raw and bottomless yearning, was so sharply reminiscent of her own father's in her childhood that she felt time as a funnel, as though she'd been emptied into her old home, the same person but just a different size. It made her feel faint. Thirty years later, had they simply recreated the longings of their own parents? They rushed down to the kitchen as they often did during an argument, as though the simple symbols of a domestic life, the plastic-wrapped bread and bananas and stale coffee in the coffee maker, would fool them into believing that they understood how to create a home and provide tender guidance for their children. He sank down into his chair and began to tap his foot nervously, looking anywhere but at her.

They were guideless, marching beside each other into nowhere. He stretched out in his seat, laying his arm on the chair next to him, in a gesture that did not make him look expansive, as it did when he was a young man, but exposed. She could not bear not to tell him any longer; she reached forward and grabbed his arm.

'We would have had a third child,' she said. 'I stopped it.'

He looked up.

'This week,' she said.

She remembered the night that she and her husband had brought their son home from the hospital. They had cupped him in their hands, a person just two days old. When he began to cry, his first human wails rising into their apartment, she and her husband realized that they were supposed to comfort him. They had looked at each other, frightened, and she felt a profound sense of vulnerability and aloneness.

He stared at her. Carefully, he clasped his hands. His eyes were bright; she realized there were tears in them.

'Did you forget about me?' he asked.

His voice was soft and it sounded as though it came directly out of the black night outside. Inside, the kitchen light cast a fraudulent cozy glow over them.

'We couldn't have done it,' she said.

'You didn't want to,' he replied, sharply.

'You didn't either,' she said. 'I know you.'

'Do you?' he asked. 'Look at me. What am I thinking right now?'

She looked into his dark eyes. When they got married, she wanted to know, to own everything about him. 'You're sad,' she said.

'What else?' he asked.

She leaned toward him and looked closer. She and her husband were sitting beside each other, half-dressed, their windows open. She thought she heard a sad laughter in the neighbours' house, carried through the street on a warm and fragrant wind.

Mary Grace was back the next afternoon, washing up at their door as inevitably as the tide. As she stood at the door there was something ancient about her, the way she smiled warily at Jane, scratching her leg and pretending that yesterday had not happened. She was optimistic to the point of delusion; she loved them simply because they opened the door.

'Could we make a lemonade stand?' Mary Grace asked. 'We could sell lemonade for twenty-five cents.'

Jane moved outside. It was a cool day, with drizzly rain. 'I don't know,' said Jane, looking at the sky. But her son ran out of the door, bubbling with joy that she was back. 'Yes!' he yelled. He and Mary Grace arranged themselves around a card table in the front yard, a pitcher of lemonade and some cups between them. Mary Grace clutched an umbrella. Jane watched their small, dignified backs as they regarded the neighbourhood, set in their belief that others would want to drink their lemonade.

She did not have many plastic cups. She thought of Mary Grace's mother sitting on her bed and looking at her husband. She thought she could ask if she had any cups; she would try to talk to her. She did not even have the woman's phone number, but looked it up the phone book and picked up the phone.

'Hello,' said Mary Grace's mother. Her voice sounded high-pitched and young.

'It's Jane Goldman, next door,' she said. 'Mary Grace's over here right now. I just wanted to say hi.' She waited. There was a silence. 'Well, the kids are having a lemonade stand and well, I wondered if you have any plastic cups—'

She heard a deep intake of breath. 'Stop,' said Mary Grace's mother.

'Excuse me?' said Jane.

'She says you keep feeding her.'

'Look,' said Jane, her hands suddenly shaking, 'Look.' She closed her eyes. 'She comes over here because she likes it. You could thank us—'

'She knows that she can get sweets from you. She needs to lose ten pounds. I don't want her to look ugly. Do you?'

'No!' said Jane. 'Maybe she'd stay at your house if you actually talked to her—'

'I'm a good mother,' said Mary Grace's mother. 'I keep her clean.

She minds her manners.' There was the sound of growling. At first Jane thought it was the mother but then realized it was the family dog. 'Stay away from her,' said Mary Grace's mother, her voice rising, 'Stop feeding her—'

Jane banged down the phone. 'Dammit!' she yelled. She heard Mary Grace and her son laughing outside and she knew that it would be the last time the girl would visit their house. It would be his first grief, the loss of a friend; it would tip like a domino against the losses to come. Mary Grace would have her own disappointments with her sour and careless parents and the families would live side by side until this particular race in life was over.

She looked outside. The children sat, stalwart, behind a plastic pitcher. How beautiful her son looked! He looked happier than he had in a long time. The clouds broke apart and sunlight fell upon them. She went outside and bought a cup for a dollar because she had no change. Others bought lemonade, too, with dollars, and the children still had no change, and within an hour they had ten dollars. Huddled under their umbrellas, the children were gleeful at their unexpected riches. 'I will buy billions and billions of toys!' her son screamed. The baby walked around in joyous circles. Everyone—the children, the parents—were visitors on earth; they were here briefly and then would vanish. She stood in the darkening light, staring at the children and wondered how she could be good enough for them.

□

GRANTA

# FAMILY PICTURES
## Robin Grierson

TEXT BY LIZ JOBEY

For most of us 'family pictures' mean the hundreds of snapshots bundled into coloured envelopes and—with a few exceptions rescued for albums, or taped to the fridge door—stuffed to the back of a drawer. We might have one or two formal portraits, taken at a studio, and annual pictures from school, but for the most part they are rarely seen by, or of interest to, anybody outside the family to which they belong. For a professional photographer, however, family pictures inhabit a different, more difficult, area somewhere between the private and the public; and if they are published, questions arise about responsibility, and exploitation; whether you should use your children in this way.

Before his daughter Lottie was born in 1994, Robin Grierson's principal experience of photographing children was taking portraits of his niece and nephew with a larger-format camera. He felt both artistically inspired and a personal responsibility to extend the existing Grierson family album. Once Lottie arrived, it was inevitable he would take pictures of her, and then of her sister Daisy who was born in 1997. By the time their brother Milo was born in 2000, Grierson's collection of family pictures had grown into a separate and significant body of work.

He is well aware of the problems inherent in making this kind of picture public. He tries to photograph truthfully and not to be opportunistic, nor to idealize his children, but to capture the emotion of the experience. 'Photography always reveals truths about the relationship between the photographer and the person being photographed,' he says. 'That is evident, even in most amateur family pictures. The problem is, if you're a professional photographer, you can mess up that purity by trying to dramatize reality in some enterprising way, by exaggerating aesthetically or manipulating technically the essential truths standing there in front of you.'  □

Rebecca and Daisy in Daisy's grandmother's garden, Fishburn, Co. Durham, 1997

Lottie, Milo and Daisy at home, Sydenham, Kent, 2000

Lottie and Daisy, Sydenham, 2000

Uncle Willie, Whamphray, Dumfries, 1997

Daisy, Whamphray, 1997

Robin Grierson, with Lottie (taken by her cousin Josie Grierson), Fishburn, 1998

Robin's father, Dave Grierson and his brother Willie, Whamphray, 2004

Willie and Lottie, Whamphray, 1997

Lottie and Rebecca with Milo, Seasalter, Kent, 2003

Whamphray, 2002

Rebecca and Milo, Lulworth Cove, Dorset, 2001

Sheila Grierson, Sydenham, 1995

Lottie, Hastings, Sussex, 1999

Rebecca, her mother Pauline, and Lottie, Guildford, 1999

Lottie, Seasalter, Kent, 2001

Willie's dog, 'Pup', Whamphray Glen, Dumfries, 2004

Rebecca, Daisy and Lottie, Hastings, Sussex, 1999

Whamphray, 2004

Daisy, Freiburg, Germany, 2004

Whamphray, 2004

Lottie, Baugé, France, 2004

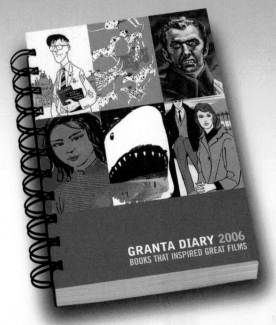

GRANTA

# THE ERROR WORLD
## Simon Garfield

1965 Post Office Tower 3d

# 1.

In 1968 I had a crush on a girl who was frightened of the Post Office Tower. The girl, Melanie Kilim, aged ten, was the sister of my best friend, and even as an eight-year-old I understood this relationship to have the potential of something socially complicated. The crush passed and we went our different ways, but my friendship with her brother endured and I still see a good deal of him. Almost forty years have passed. We each have wives and children, and when I visit his house on a Sunday morning we talk of property prices and knee-joint trouble. It was because of other conversations during these visits that I knew his sister Melanie was still frightened of the Post Office Tower.

One evening in April 2005, when I had just turned forty-five, I called her up about it out of the blue. 'Hi Melanie, this is Gus.' Gus was my school nickname. 'It's been quite a while, but I want to ask you about something I've always wondered about...' Melanie was forthcoming. She said her phobia began soon after the building went up in 1965, transforming and modernizing the London skyline. She thought her fear of it might have something to do with the robotic Daleks in the BBC serial, Dr Who, and with the memory of a man in a neck-brace she once saw in the local greengrocer in Golders Green. I thought it might have a more obvious explanation—something to do with the phallus and sex—but she dismissed this. She wasn't nervous of any other tall buildings, only what she called this 'grey-green monster'. She thought that the tower might suddenly jump out at her. She would turn a corner in Soho or Bloomsbury, and there it would be: 'I think it might attack and strangle me—something to do with the neck again.'

To avoid this possibility, Melanie Kilim told me that she had developed an extraordinary sense of positioning and direction. She said there was no street in the tower's vicinity where she didn't know what she would see when she came around the corner. If this was to be the tower, she knew the perfect diversion. She told me that once, when she was visiting the Middlesex Hospital, only a few hundred yards from the tower, she had worn a blindfold to avoid an otherwise inevitable sighting.

The object that always repelled Melanie had always attracted me. As a boy, I was fascinated by it. It was new. It was statistically engaging. Out of the then generally flat London townscape, it rose astonishingly to 619 feet—the highest structure in London, nearly twice the height of the dome of St Paul's. It weighed 13,000 tons and contained 780 tons of steel. It could handle 100,000 telephone calls simultaneously and boosted radio and television signals, bouncing the waves over the new London high-rises on to the home-county hills. Its two lifts travelled at 1,000 feet a minute, and if you took one to the top you could sit in the revolving restaurant which turned two-and-a-half times every hour, which meant that, if you were a Londoner, you didn't have to wait too long to point to the streets that contained your own home. My father took me up to the top a few months after it opened, and I treasured the green plastic model he bought me at the gift shop. I still have it in a cupboard next to a plastic grouping of the Chimpanzees' Tea Party from London Zoo.

For me, the opening of the tower marked not only the completion of a landmark, but the birth of something equally special—a commemorative postage stamp with a fabulous error on it. I first became aware of this in 1968 when a stamp magazine carried the news that less than one sheet of these errors had been discovered. About 55,500,000 of the stamps had been sold, but only about thirty of them had the mistake. I looked at a photograph of a stamp with the flaw—a printing glitch: it was captioned 1965 POST OFFICE TOWER, OLIVE-GREEN OMITTED. To an eight year old, this was unbelievable. The only thing that was supposed to have been printed in olive-green was the Post Office Tower itself; the surrounding buildings were all there, but in place of the tower there was only white space. I thought then (as I thought again nearly forty years later), 'This would be the perfect stamp for Melanie.'

# 2.

I'd like to think that every schoolboy collected stamps in those days, but I'm sure that even in 1968 it was a hobby that was falling away. What kind of boy was I, to have this love of stamps? Self-description is the hardest art, but some things can be said.

I was, I think, a quiet boy with no evident talents, and my main interest, apart from my basset hound (and until stamps arrived), was procuring sweets from a shop called Lollies. My room was covered with pictures of Chelsea footballers with tight shorts and crinkly hair, but I never had hopes of being a football star myself. I didn't know what I wanted to be; certainly not an astronaut or fireman or anything heroic. I thought I might like to be a pop singer, but I imagined myself quite happy working behind the counter in a sweet shop or post office—perhaps in Hampstead Garden Suburb, the leafiest and most fashionable of London suburbs, where we lived in a very comfortable house among neighbours who also kept pets and had an aversion to noise after 7.30 p.m. Among people, in fact, like my father, a successful solicitor in the City who drove a soft-top Triumph, played golf, smoked cigars, took me sometimes to synagogue on a Saturday morning, and wished me to do better in school. He was a generous man but he didn't like noise or unruliness and I could stir him to rare anger by breaking a window with a tennis ball. My brother was almost five years older, effortlessly skilled at maths and science, and fast enough as a bowler to practise with junior teams at Lord's. I once broke his arm wrestling on the carpet, but usually (both before this event and after) we had little to do with each other. My mother looked after us all, occasionally helping in local old-peoples' homes and entertaining friends with Robert Carrier's *Classic Great Dishes of the World*. This life was all I knew, and it seemed ideal. I remember walking back from school with a fellow pupil called Will Self, who had still to discover drugs or novel writing, and learning that he was about to go on holiday to the Seychelles. I had no idea what or where that was. I hadn't yet experienced abroad; my parents went on foreign trips together, leaving my brother and me in the formidable charge of a Mrs Woolf, who wouldn't let us drink water with our meals because it filled us up. The most daring thing I did was have my hair cut by a man in flares called Paul whose salon was called Unisex, a word the entire neighbourhood found exceptionally unsettling. Stamp collecting, that most quiet and respectful of pastimes, was something that all of my neighbours and parents' friends would have approved of; it offered no evidence of nonconformity, noisy childish rebellion or the budding turmoil of sex. The postage stamp is a silent thing, and an emblem of social order rather than its opposite.

I can't say precisely when I got interested in stamps. As for why, that may be as unknowable as the causes of Melanie Kilim's fear of the Post Office Tower. But by the time I was eight they had me in their grip; in their grip and also, quite soon, slightly ashamed of their grip. I remember feeling sheepish about telling my friends of my interest. The first time I entered my school's annual philatelic competition (which, for the winner, meant a prize on Speech Day, enabling some people in the hall—perhaps my parents—to believe the prize had something to do with academic merit) I was not at all surprised to learn that the other entrants were the sort of boys I looked down on—the friendless, the ungainly. I didn't envy their lives, but I did envy their stamps: one boy, also called Simon, had a small collection of King George V 'Sea Horses', high-denomination stamps that, although postally used and not 'mint', were probably worth a hundred pounds. I think he had been left them in a will, something that as far as I knew would never happen to me. For the school competition one year I put together an elaborate story inspired by the British Wild Flowers set of 1967, describing each of the flowers in turn and where they grew. I think I listed some varieties I had seen in magazines, such as 'missing campion bloom'. The other Simon mounted his Sea Horses on clean album pages, labelled them 'George V Sea Horses, 1913, 2s 6d, 5s, 10s and £1', and won. I think the teacher who judged, probably a collector himself, thought the other Simon's stamps worthy of space in his own collection, whereas he probably had my flowers as full sheets, ordinary and phosphor (the phosphor was an innovation to aid automatic sorting).

I confess that I thought for a minute about stealing the other Simon's stamps. Not because I wanted them, but because I wanted him to be unhappy. The thought quickly passed: I'd be found out, I'd be expelled from school, I'd still feel unsatisfied. It was probably at this point that I came to terms with one of the great universal philatelic truths: no matter what you have in your collection, it isn't enough. You could collect all the Queen Elizabeth issues, but there would be new ones every few weeks, and a gnawing feeling that there were some rare shades or misperforations you didn't yet have. And could you really call yourself a collector if you didn't have something or everything from the Cape of Good Hope and the British Commonwealth? In this way stamps taught me about setting boundaries and limiting one's ambitions—about life, really—but unfortunately this knowledge didn't quell the overriding desire to obtain more stamps.

1966 Technology issue 6d

At school we all put our acquisitions in albums by licking tiny translucent 'hinges' and sticking one bit on the stamp and the other on a page, a process known as mounting, something which instantly reduced the value of mint items by about two thirds. Not that value was ever the thing. I probably entertained the hope that when I was older I would be able to sell my collection and buy a car, but I think that when I bought my first strip of stamps in 1966 (special ones issued to commemorate the Battle of Hastings 900 years before) I knew in my heart that they would probably be worth about the same for years to come, or much less if you separated each of the six stamps from the strip, which I did, and then less still when I mounted them... I know now that 14,865,204 of the ordinary 4d (pre-decimal pence) Hastings stamps were sold, and another 2,643,660 of the phosphor printing, which means that after almost forty years these stamps are worth about the same as I paid for them, and I can't even use them for postage.

Occasionally I would buy cellophaned packs from the newsagents W. H. Smith which cost a few shillings and promised to contain stamps with a catalogue value of £5 or £10. This told even an eight year old that catalogue values were not to be trusted. Some packs came with plastic tweezers and a plastic magnifying glass, so that a beginner could pretend to be a pro, much like a child turning a fake plastic driving wheel in the back of a Ford Consul. But it was laughable to imagine that the magnifying glass would actually discover anything interesting in such a cheap pack of stamps; the tweezers were redundant, too, as you could have handled the stamps with treacle on your fingers and not reduced their value further. The best stamps were the ones that came free on envelopes through the letter box. Franking machines were not yet in every office; secretaries were dispatched to buy 200 stamps at a time, and even the most official mail had a colourful corner. The stamps could be detached from their envelopes with the steam of a kettle or by being placed in warm water and then dried on a newspaper, and they filled a lot of album space.

Then there was this system called 'approvals', the idea being that you sent away for stamps 'on approval' and only once you had received and 'approved' them did you send on the postal order as payment. In theory, I suppose, you could have approved some stamps

and kept them and rejected others and sent them back, haggling with
the dealer about how much was owed; or that, at least, may have
been the implication in the advertisements which appeared regularly
in boys' magazines. But when I sent away for a packet of approvals
I had no idea what that word meant—only that the prospect of
receiving expensive-looking stamps for no outlay was appealing. The
packet I received did not contain especially good stamps, a lot of them
being Victorian issues with heavy cancellations. I think one of them
was a Penny Black, the world's earliest gummed stamp first issued
in 1840, but it was probably a stamp with one or no margins, an
example of which sat proudly at the beginning of every schoolboy's
album, worth hardly anything compared with a three- or four-
margined example. (In the days before perforations, the margin
showed where a stamp had been cut from the sheet, and the
postmaster doing the cutting had no concern for posterity—which
explains why a used strip of six Penny Blacks with excellent margins
recently sold at auction in London for £90,000.) One month after
my free stamps arrived, there was a follow-up letter. 'We are delighted
you have chosen to accept the full card of stamps. The total is £3
15s.' My father sent a cheque, and stopped my pocket money for a
while. I think the stamps are now worth about seventy-five pence.

Eventually, when I was twelve, I discovered the adult world of
stamps and the dealers who had their premises on or near the Strand.
The trips took place on a Saturday afternoon and at first I was
accompanied by Aunt Ruth and her old dachshund, to make sure
that nothing untoward happened to me on the streets of central
London. But soon enough I was wandering by myself through the
market underneath the railway arches by Charing Cross Station and
then to the many stamp shops near the Aldwych and Covent
Garden. At the market I could afford a few space fillers and
commemorative issues that had appeared before I started collecting,
and I bought secondhand magazines for a few pennies each. *Stamp
Magazine* contained articles headlined POSTMARKS, PLACES AND
PEOPLE and INTERNATIONAL REPLY COUPONS — NEW DESIGN! There
were also articles specifically for beginners, explaining the meaning
of philatelic terminology such as '*tête-bêche*' (two or more joined
stamps, with one upside down), and advice on how to look for
priceless stamps on old documents in your grandmother's loft. This

1961 Seventh Commonwealth Parliamentary Conference 1s 3d

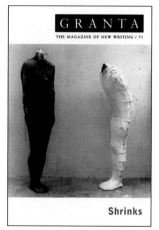

# S ave up to 40%!

Each quarterly issue of *Granta* features a rich variety of stories, in fiction, memoir, reportage and photography —often collected under a theme. Each issue is produced as a high-quality paperback book, because writing this good deserves nothing less. Subscribers get *Granta* delivered to them at home, at a big discount. Why not join them? Or give a subscription to a friend, relative or colleague? (Or, given these low prices, do both!)

## G R A N T A
**'ESSENTIAL READING'**
*Observer*

---

## ORDER FORM

I'D LIKE TO SUBSCRIBE FOR MYSELF FOR:
- ○ 1 year (4 issues) at just £27.95   **30% OFF**
- ○ 2 years (8 issues) at just £51.95   **35% OFF**
- ○ 3 years (12 issues) at just £71.95   **40% OFF**

START THE SUBSCRIPTION WITH ○ this issue ○ next issue

I'D LIKE TO GIVE A SUBSCRIPTION FOR:
- ○ 1 year (4 issues) at just £27.95
- ○ 2 years (8 issues) at just £51.95
- ○ 3 years (12 issues) at just £71.95

START THE SUBSCRIPTION WITH ○ this issue ○ next issue

MY DETAILS (please supply even if ordering a gift): Mr/Ms/Mrs/Miss _____

_____

              Country                       Postcode

GIFT RECIPIENT'S DETAILS (if applicable): Mr/Ms/Mrs/Miss _____

_____

              Country                       Postcode

05JBG91

TOTAL* £_____ paid by ○ £ cheque enclosed (to 'Granta') ○ Visa/Mastercard/AmEx:

card no: __ __ __ __ __ __ __ __ __ __ __ __ __ __ __ __

expires: __ __ / __ __ signature: _____

* POSTAGE. The prices stated include UK postage. For the rest of Europe, please add £8 (per year). For the rest of the world, please add £15 (per year). DATA PROTECTION. Please tick here if you do not want to receive occasional mailings from compatible publishers. ○

➧ **POST** ('Freepost' in the UK) to: Granta, 'Freepost', 2/3 Hanover Yard, Noel Road, London N1 8BR. **PHONE/FAX:** In the UK: FreeCall 0500 004 033 (phone & fax). Outside the UK: tel 44 (0)20 7704 9776, fax 44 (0)20 7704 0474 **EMAIL:** subs@granta.com

would have been fine if grandfather hadn't got there first, and sold anything half-decent to dealers or friends. By the time I began collecting in the 1960s, the world had got wise to the value of stamps. Philately was more than 120 years old, and lofts had long given up their treasures.

# 3.

Men and women began collecting stamps in 1840, the year stamps first appeared, but nobody then could have imagined the cult—the industry—it would become. Sheets of Penny Blacks and Twopenny Blues contained 240 stamps and, to limit forgeries and to enable the tracing of portions of a sheet, each stamp had a letter in the two bottom corners. The rows running down the sheet had the same letter in the left corner, while the right corner progressed alphabetically. The first row went AA, AB, AC and so on, and thirteen rows down it went MA, MB, MC... There were twenty horizontal rows of twelve, so that the last stamp at the bottom right-hand corner was TL. People who got a lot of post thought it would be fun to collect the set.

One of the first mentions of the new hobby appeared in a German magazine in 1845, which noted, much in the manner of comedian Bob Newhart describing Raleigh's attempt to promote tobacco, how the English post office sold 'small square pieces of paper bearing the head of the Queen, and these are stuck on the letter to be franked'. The writer observed that the Queen's head looked very pretty, and that the English 'reveal their strange character by collecting these stamps'. The first collector history is aware of was a woman known only as E. D., who is identified in an advertisement in *The Times* in 1841: 'A young lady, being desirous of covering her dressing room with cancelled postage stamps, has been so far encouraged in her wish by private friends as to have succeeded in collecting 16,000. These, however, being insufficient, she will be greatly obliged, if any good-natured person who may have these (otherwise useless) little articles at their disposal, would assist her in her whimsical project.' There were two addresses to send the stamps, one in Leadenhall Street in the City, one in Hackney. There are no further records of E. D.'s collection, nor are there pictures of her room, which must have been a shade on the dark side with its walls of Penny Blacks,

Twopenny Blues and the new Penny Reds of 1841, and would surely have put E. D. among the ranks of Young British Artists in the next century. The following year, *Punch* noted that 'a new mania has bitten the industriously idle ladies of England. They betray more anxiety to treasure up the Queen's heads than Harry the Eighth did to get rid of them.'

By the mid-Victorian period, stamp collecting had become a small craze among public schoolboys, prefiguring many later crazes—collecting locomotive numbers, Batman cards, Pokemon—which have turned school playgrounds into centres of scholarly pursuit, abstruse to parents. S. F. Cresswell, a master at Tonbridge School in the late 1850s, informed the periodical *Notes and Queries* that a boy had shown him a collection of between 300 and 400 different stamps from all over the world, and wanted to know if there was a guidebook available which listed all known stamps, and a place in London where one might buy and exchange them. Subsequent issues of *Notes and Queries* offered him no help, but Cresswell was only slightly ahead of his time, as we know from the first history of the hobby, a book called *The Stamp Collector* by William Hardy and Edward Bacon, published in 1898. Hardy and Bacon listed the large number of philatelic societies that had sprung up since S. F. Cresswell had first looked for them forty years before. There was the Stamp Exchange Protection Society of Highbury Park, London, the Cambridge University Philatelic Society, and the Suburban Stamp Exchange Club of St Albans, Hertfordshire. There were also societies in Calcutta, Melbourne, Ontario, Baltimore and Bucharest. Hardy and Bacon identified the key moment that always defines the coming of age and validation of any serious collecting hobby: the publication of a catalogue. This told a collector that they were not alone, and it set the boundaries of a collector's ambitions. This moment came in 1862 with *The Stamp Collector's Guide: Being a List of English and Foreign Postage Stamps with 200 Facsimile Drawings* by Frederick Booty, which begins with the observation that 'Some two or three years ago...collectors were to be numbered by units, they are now numbered by hundreds.'

When Hardy and Bacon's book was published, Bacon was a member of the Expert Committee of the Philatelic Society (London) for the Examination of Doubtful Stamps (by the end of the nineteenth century philatelists were already a target for forgers). But some years later he acquired another role in which this expertise was more than usually vital: he became Curator of the Collection of King George V, charged with the growth and care of the most significant and valuable stamp collection in the world. The roots of George V's obsession are no more amenable to reasoned inquiry than mine or Melanie Kilim's, though personal vanity may have played more of a part (few collectors get to appear in their own albums). He was certainly a most determined collector. In February 1908, when he was still the Duke of York, he wrote to a friend about the purchase of some stamps from Barbados: 'Remember, I wish to have *the* best collection & not one of the best collections in Britain, therefore if you think that there are a few more stamps required to make it so don't hesitate to take them...' As king, and when not on tour or at his country residences, he devoted four hours of every day in London to his stamps, and he regularly showed choice items at the big exhibitions, but his zeal was not universally shared by his courtiers. After he spent £1,450 on a mint Two Pence Post Office Mauritius specimen, one of his staff unknowingly asked him whether he had seen that some 'damned fool' had paid so much for a single stamp. When he died, his British Empire collection comprised 350 volumes and it has since been augmented, with slightly less enthusiasm, by his son and granddaughter, George VI and Elizabeth II.

George V's principal inspiration—'the man to beat'—was Thomas Tapling, MP, who amassed almost every stamp in the world between 1840 and 1890, when such a thing was still possible. The Tapling Collection is thought to be the largest private nineteenth-century collection still intact, and many of the rarest specimens are errors— wrong colours and inverted heads. Among the rare Barbados stamps that George V bought was the 1861–1870 One Shilling printed in blue rather than the intended brownish-black. Twelve copies are known, one of them in the Tapling Collection. But Tapling's achievement was greater than a painstaking gathering of wonderful stamps. He also inspired more collectors than anyone else, George V being simply the most famous. The visitors who today pull out examples from Tapling's collection in their sliding cases at the British Library can only marvel at the gems on display, and perhaps feel a little envy. For there will never be another collection like

Tapling's. Unless the British monarchy decides to part with the hundreds of albums stored in the St James's Palace Stamp Room, no single collector could hope to acquire such a magnificent variety of stamps in a lifetime.

How was it done? With money. If the first key moment in the validation of a collecting hobby is the catalogue, then the second is the value of the things collected: their quoted price in the market. Both Tapling and the king bought some of their collection from Stanley Gibbons, the man who became to stamps what Berenson and Duveen are to painting, the founder of what is now the world's oldest stamp company, an institution in the Strand since 1893. Edward Stanley Gibbons began collecting in his early teens, entranced by the romance of the stamps that reached his home town, the port of Plymouth, on mail from overseas. (By the time he began trading out of his father's chemist shop in 1856, more than twenty other countries had also begun issuing postage 'labels'.) His big break came in 1863 when a couple of sailors sold him a large quantity of triangular Cape of Good Hope stamps they had won in a raffle. He bought them all for £5 and with the profits from their resale he greatly expanded his stock. He published his first price list in 1865, three years after Booty's catalogue, and his clientele, including many doctors and barristers, were reported to have been taken aback by his high charges. How was it that a tiny piece of paper decorated with a mechanically-reproduced picture could be worth three guineas when only a few years earlier it could be had from a post office for threepence? And could such a question be answered by the simple statement that, as with gold, value depended on quality, rarity and demand?

Gibbons died in 1913, presumably content that his name was associated throughout the world with exhaustive stock and overwhelming prices. Long after his death his shop in the Strand was infused by the kind of atmosphere you might find in a West End establishment that sold game-shooting guns or fine claret to gentlemen. It was an imposing and patronizing place and when I first went there, in the 1970s, I felt nervous even asking for a new pack of hinges. 'And what can we do for the young master today?' I had a stammer. I wanted to look at their stock, but my stammer overwhelmed me (like many stammerers, I found that the hardest words to say were those beginning 'st', such as stock and stamps). 'Just looking,' was all I would usually manage. I received a warmer welcome in the smaller and more chaotic shops nearby, though the dealers who owned them could never have anticipated a big sale. I hardly ever bought anything, principally because I couldn't afford to but also because I had a sense that I was going to be outsmarted, sold a pup.

Even after five years of collecting and reading, I knew at the age of fifteen that I was lost in a world of experts. I didn't believe I would be deliberately cheated but that I would cheat myself; I would be offered a vast choice of Penny Reds from the 1860s, and I'd be bamboozled, and I'd flee the shop in a shaming panic. Of course, I had my Stanley Gibbons catalogue as guide, but that was too crude a compass to steer me through so many subtleties of shade and printings and plate numbers and postmark cancellations, all of which affected the price.

I needed a simpler approach, and before I got the tube back to Hampstead Garden Suburb I would visit the philatelic counter at the large post office in Trafalgar Square, where they understood and indulged a boy-collector's needs and would sell you a whole sheet or particular sections of a sheet such as the 'traffic light' control strip down the side indicating that all the colours were present and aligned. In my teens I would buy new issues in blocks of four, for no particular reason other than they looked more solid than individual stamps. I write 'no particular reason' and now wonder about it, because perhaps there was a very particular reason: greed. Not desperate avarice (though of course this afflicts collectors as well), rather the ambition to put together an album more desirable than those of one's peers and one which would increase in value over time. There are other convincing reasons to love stamps—an appreciation of their beauty, the thrill of the hunt, the pursuit of completion—but none is so compelling as the profit motive. It exists in every collector I have known. No matter how many people say otherwise, I won't believe that any stamp collector over the age of seven does not have profit somewhere at the back of his mind.

# 4.

For about twenty-five years I forgot about stamps, or at least I neglected to collect them. First came university, then work, then marriage and children, a mortgage. Then, when I was in my early forties, my interest ignited again. I can't pinpoint the cause—perhaps it was an article in the newspapers, or a browse online—but my enthusiasm returned and with it just enough disposable cash to pursue the stamps I could never afford in my childhood. What I wanted was, in a word, errors: the Post Office Tower stamp without the Post Office Tower on it, and much else besides.

When I was younger I could recite a list of the most famous errors better than I could recite 'The Charge of the Light Brigade'. I knew them still. For example:

1961 2 1/2d Post Office Savings stamp missing black and the 3d of the same set missing orange-brown
1961 European Postal Conference 2d missing orange and the 10d missing pale green
1962 National Productivity Year 3d and 1s 3d, both missing light blue
6d Paris Postal Conference Centenary missing green
3d 1963 Red Cross Centenary Congress missing red

These are British stamps that I can understand and, though rare enough, they are sometimes affordable. In the period that interests me—before Britain decimalized its currency (and its stamps) in 1971—well over half of all issues had something glaringly wrong with them. Not the whole issue, of course, but a sheet here and there where the printing machine had run out of ink, or a paper fold had caused the colour to be printed on the gummed side. Even a schoolboy couldn't make many mistakes with stamps like these, and even a person with no interest in stamps could see the appeal. Tens of millions printed and sold, all of them perfect—the perfection of the machine—and here and there a flaw, a beautiful accident, which had escaped the eyes of the inspectorate. Accordingly, stamps with errors will always be more sought after, and dramatically more expensive, than stamps that are perfect. This feature alone makes stamp collecting an exceptional and perverse hobby. No one wants a Picasso with missing bistre. A misshapen Ming vase? A 1930s Mercedes without headlights? There are some coins with errors, and some rare vinyl records with misprints on the labels, but they do not form the cornerstone of a collecting hobby, and they do not make men bankrupt. The first big error appeared on a stamp in 1852, an engraving slip that caused the word PETIMUS to become PATIMUS, thus changing the meaning of the inscription on the British Guiana 1 cent and 4 cent from 'We seek' to 'We suffer'. Ever since, errors have been the most treasured items available, or rather, unavailable. The Swedish *tre skilling banco* yellow of 1857, the only known example that isn't the intended green, was discovered by a fourteen-year-old schoolboy in 1885. It was sold at auction in 1996 for £1.4m—making it pound for pound the most expensive man-made object on earth.

I don't think I mentioned the Post Office Tower error to my father in 1968. It cost several pounds. Several pounds for a stamp! You could send an elephant first-class for that. My father would have been intrigued by the idea that imperfection equalled added value but he would also have doubted it (a chipped glass or an unreliable wristwatch were just things to be endured until you could afford something better). How was he to know that there would never be more than thirty of such stamps? How could he have known that a stamp worth a few pounds in 1968 would be sold at auction in March 2005 for £1,300?

Studying these rare stamps in my schooldays I learned a bit about history and a bit about colour. I knew what bistre was, and agate, and could distinguish new blue from dull blue. But what I really learned about was inflation. The 1966 Technology 6d issue, for example, which should have contained three Minis and a Jaguar, but instead had only the Jaguar against a bright orange background, was on sale in 1967 at the Globe Stamp Co. in William IV Street, just off the Strand, for £95. A year later the price was £130. At that point the precise quantities of the error stamp were unknown but today it is thought that there are just eighteen mint copies. In an auction in March 2005, a collector bought one for £6,110. Of course I would have loved to have owned this stamp just as I would have loved to have owned all the others. But my favourite was five years older.

In 1961, the Seventh Commonwealth Parliamentary Conference was held in Westminster. There were two stamps issued. The 6d value was a horizontal rectangle with a purple background and a gold overlay depicting the roof-beams of Westminster Hall. The 1s 3d stamp was vertical, with a racing-green background, and was split into two halves: on the top was a picture of the Queen printed in dull blue, and beneath it was an engraving of the Palace of Westminster and a mace and sceptre. On the error, there was no Queen. Simple: a white box on a green stamp. In the late 1960s, when I first became aware of it, it was the most beautiful small object I had ever seen, and remains so for me today.

In 2003 it took me a while to tell anyone of my revived passion for stamps. When I eventually disclosed it to my family, my children spoke the same word they use to describe anyone over the age of twenty-five who wears trainers and affects an interest in rap: 'Sad.' My wife took a tolerant interest (in the same way I show interest in her passion for the theatre), though now her questions are invariably focussed on one aspect of it all. I want her to say, 'Tell me about the history, the beauty, the rarity! Tell me about that one!' but mostly she says, 'How much was it?' And so while I, an adult with money, returned to the Strand confidently, I was at the same time more furtive than I'd been as an adolescent.

The area had changed utterly since I'd last viewed it with a collector's eye. Gibbons and The Strand Stamp Centre were still there, but the weekly Saturday market had gone, along with many other traders. Some had retired, some had gone bankrupt, others had decided to work from home and do it all by mail order or the Internet. David Brandon's shop was one of the shops that had disappeared, and I was particularly sad about that because it had opened in 1975, during my first collecting phase, and I had marvelled at the treasures on display. Brandon sold almost everything—GB across all reigns, British Commonwealth, most of the rest of the world, as well as albums and accessories. Then I discovered that Brandon still traded from his home. He advertised in the stamp magazines. Along with his son, Mark, he had developed a new speciality. 'Honesty, Integrity and Confidentiality,' said his advertisement in *Gibbons Stamp Monthly* soon after I had taken up collecting again. 'We believe that these are the three most important words when choosing a dealer to help you build the Great Britain Collection of your desire. Being the world's leading and most active dealers in Important Investment Quality Errors we would be pleased to hear from you, should you care to obtain major pieces such as the items illustrated.' The items illustrated in this first advertisement included the Jaguar with the missing Minis, and a Red Cross stamp without the red cross. Then, in a subsequent issue of the same magazine, I saw that he was selling another twenty major pieces, including a George VI *tête-bêche* 'mis-cut booklet pane'—and a horizontal pair of missing Post Office Towers.

I telephoned and we talked, and then we talked again, and eventually he said that if I was ever in his area, I should call in and see him. I could see no prospect of being accidentally in Guildford, Surrey, but I really wanted to see more of his stock, and so we fixed a date for lunch. He sent me an email: 'Dress casual, have a relaxing time.' The error world was pulling me back in.

## 5.

Brandon's house was on the outskirts of Guildford. It was protected by steel gates and security cameras. His office was lined with shelves of stamp catalogues and a large safe which contained many boxes of breathtaking errors. Brandon is now in his early sixties, a small man in large glasses, but the passionate kernel of him was planted in the 1950s. 'My plan when I was at school was to have one stamp of every country in the catalogue,' he said, 'but that was when the simplified world catalogue was in one volume, not four.' And also, he added, when the smallest English town had a stamp shop and everybody collected. '*Everybody,*' he repeated, because he knew how hard this was to believe. Once a week his mother gave him sixpence to buy stamps from his headmaster's office during break-time, and he also bought from a shop near his home in Barnes in south-west London (he said he could still smell the smoke from the dealer's cigars). He obtained the last stamp to complete his all-world collection in 1960, travelling to Bridger & Kay in the Strand to spend £1 5s on an item from Mafeking. He's been collecting Boer War ever since.

As a young man, Brandon worked as a salesman for Lyons ice cream. His hobby became a part-time career when he began to advertise in *Stamp Collecting Weekly*. 'Occasionally I would advertise something I didn't have. If there was something coming up at auction that I thought I could get for twenty pounds and sell for twenty-two pounds, then I couldn't lose. If I couldn't buy it for less than I'd already sold it for I'd just return the money and say, "Sorry, the item's sold." Of course nowadays you're not supposed to do that.' Then Brandon met a man who advised a merchant bank on alternative investments, who would telephone to ask him to buy stamps with other people's money. He would spend £1,000 to put together a portfolio of, say, classic Canada or Mauritius and make a little profit on the side. Then he bought a shop, an old dry-cleaner's in the middle of London's stamp quarter (he remembers there having been about forty competing dealers within a few hundred yards) and with a prime position directly opposite Gibbons. He is still fond of saying, 'No—actually *they* were opposite *me*.'

In this shop Brandon would spend a portion of every day disappointing people. Men and women would come in with stamp albums, their own or those of the recently deceased, imagining that they contained a fortune. Brandon could usually tell what the stamps were worth by the sort of albums they came in. If they were tatty, he would sometimes pretend to weigh them in his left hand and, without even opening the cover, proclaim: '£20!' Some customers took him seriously and considered the offer with a sigh. Their eyes would brighten a little when Brandon then spent a minute flicking through the pages. If it was better than he had first thought, he might say: '£25!' The cause of the customer's hope (their soon-to-be cancelled hope) often lay in the price lists of the Stanley Gibbons catalogues, but those were top-end selling prices and often included a handling charge. The cheap stamps listed in the catalogue at 20p each were actually worth about a penny when you came to sell them; only the truly rare stamps ever achieve the catalogue price. Every collector learns this lesson early on, and then they have to make a decision. Do they throw it all in as a waste of time and money, or do they persevere?

I persevered. I went to see David Brandon several times, and learned a lot from him about the business of stamps and how he conducts it. For example, all of the expensive items Brandon sells are accompanied by certificates of genuineness, which he signs with two other experts. Forgeries are common. During one of my visits he pointed to a pile of certificates he had just done for a small auction house, and he showed me the card of stamps from Bermuda to which they referred. 'That's repaired, that's re-backed...that's a forgery, that's a forgery, those are all genuine, that's a forgery...' Brandon said he had issued about 33,000 authentications, which leave no room for misinterpretation: 'The Committee is of the opinion that the Great Britain, 1965 (October 8), 3d multicoloured, chalk-surfaced paper, Watermark Multiple Crowns (sideways), Perforation 14x15, olive-yellow (Tower) omitted (SG.679a) unused pair with full original gum...is genuine.' He has put the knowledge he has amassed over fifty years to the service of investors; people who are nervous of sharedealing, or unimpressed with the performance of gold and pensions, give Brandon their money to put into stamps. Perhaps they have read that after a couple of decades of stagnation stamps are now on the up again, and over the last two years auction houses have regularly reported world-record prices for individual items. Unless his investors request a certain country or specialty, Brandon will choose a mixture of stamps from his stock that have a good chance of resale within five to ten years. He chooses things that will always be easy to sell at auction, and items he says he will be happy to buy back himself. Portability is a great asset of stamps. As one of his brochures explains, countries with organized securities markets and the free movement of funds across national borders are still the exception. 'Even when such freedoms are finally established, confidence that they will not be taken away by the next government is always a concern. For individuals with some accumulated wealth, stamps represent a portable vehicle for flight should that become a necessity.'

But what I learned particularly from David Brandon is how good a salesman he is. At the end of each of my visits, I would take a quick look at his error stock. There were all sorts of stamps I had no interest in, and many stamps I loved but couldn't possibly afford. As I flicked through each specimen on its showcard, Brandon would say things like, 'that's a wonderful example...' and, 'that block is unique—as far as I'm aware, the biggest in the world'. Once or twice, I made a point of not bringing my chequebook so that I wouldn't be tempted by a rash purchase. But this cautionary act was irrelevant. 'You can just take it if you like,' Brandon said as I admired a copy of the 65p Nobel Prize stamp from 2001. The normal examples had a small hologram of a boron molecule on them. The error had no hologram, just white space on a white stamp with a little inscription on it. These were purchased from a post office in Kent, and there were eight known copies. While I was admiring it he told me that there are a lot of collectors whose partners have no idea how much they spend on stamps. A lot of people say to him, 'Here's the cheque, please don't send me an invoice, the wife wants a new cooker.'

'Just take it if you like,' Brandon said as I admired the stamp without the hologram, 'and you can send me payment in instalments.' I'd only seen one in a magazine before. I took it.

And then I took it back. After I'd spent a couple of weeks looking at it, I decided I had made a big mistake. The stamp was stunning, and genuinely rare, but by buying I knew I would be letting myself in for tens of thousands of pounds in future expense: not in the price of this stamp itself, which cost several thousand pounds, but in the new collecting direction it would point me towards. Previously, all my major purchases had been pre-decimal, a manageable specialization encompassing only a decade of commemoratives. After 1971, the field opened up into a vast territory dominated by imperforates, and they held no comparable charms. I called David Brandon: 'The bad news is, I think I've made an error of my own.'

'It really isn't done to take things back,' he said. 'But okay, because it's you.'

Of course, I did buy stamps from Brandon—beautiful stamps, though not the rarest. I bought a block of four 5d ships from the 1969 issue which celebrated the new Cunard liner, the *QE2*. They sold more than 67 million; mine are four of the seventy-two known examples where the black is missing, hence no Queen's head, value, hull, or inscription. I also got what is called a 'wild' perforation on a block of Battle of Britain stamps from 1965, where the sheet had somehow got caught up in the perforating machine and the stamps were cut at odd angles. And then, more than thirty-five years after I first saw them, I bought the pair of Post Office Towers missing olive-green. They were lovely—objects of desire that still make my heart beat faster every time I look at them—but the fact is that they were not the 1s 3d 1961 Parliamentary Conference stamp missing the blue and minus the Queen, the stamp I most coveted. I talked to Brandon about it. 'I know what you mean—it's absolutely beautiful,' he said. 'If I had a dozen I could sell them all by the end of the week.' I asked him what my chances were of getting one. 'You never know,' he said. 'I'll have to talk to Mark.' Mark was his son who now lived in Portugal, and also specialized in errors. 'The problem is,' David Brandon continued, 'you could have all the money in the world, and if a stamp isn't available you can't get it.' There were only six known examples of the 1s 3d Parliamentary error, and only four of those in mint condition.

Mark Brandon, when I met him, looked to me more of a businessman than his father, and he was even more interested in errors. As a boy he hadn't been passionate about stamps but he'd still followed his father into the trade, first as an assistant behind the counter at Stanley Gibbons. He graduated from selling albums and tweezers to handling stamps, and one day a customer walked in and said he wanted to look at the modern errors. Brandon sold him a lot, and he began to see their appeal.

We talked over lunch about some of the classic rarities: conversations of longing, on my part to own and on his part to sell. We talked of the 1856 British Guiana one cent magenta that should have been inscribed 'four cent', of which there is only one universally recognized copy, bought in 1980 for $935,000 by the chemical-industry heir, John du Pont, who was later sentenced to thirty years in jail for murdering an Olympic wrestler. Mark said he had once handled this stamp at auction and 'felt like royalty'. We talked of the most celebrated error of all which came about in 1918 when the US Post Office issued a set of three stamps to mark the beginning of its domestic airmail flights. Each of them featured the Curtiss Jenny biplane, but only the twenty-four cent value was printed in two colours, dark blue (the plane) and carmine (the frame). The two colours required that the sheet of a hundred stamps be pulled through the printer twice, and on one occasion the sheet was pulled the wrong way round, so that the biplane appeared upside down. The man who bought the entire sheet over the post office counter knew the value of this great find immediately, and refused all offers until a consortium of businessmen bought it for $15,000 and then sold it immediately to E. H. R. 'Harry' Green, a fat millionaire with a cork leg who would stop his car outside the shops of New York dealers, open the door, and wait for the dealers to come to him. The sheet was long ago split into blocks of fours and singles. In May 2002 a collector bought three of the blocks for $2.5m.

The stamp I so wanted was not remotely in this league. But in what league was it then? A reasonable indication of its value was to be found in a book that Mark Brandon and a pseudonymous co-author, Tom Pierron, first published in 2003: *The Catalogue of*

*Errors*. Its 400 pages and its CD-Rom comprised the first comprehensive guide to Queen Elizabeth II varieties, and the upsurge of interest in (and price of) GB errors may be attributed partly to its publication. To the collector and the trade, it was a wonderful volume which legitimized interest in these relatively modern stamps and also attempted to place a market value on each of them. The value was based on visual appeal as well as rarity: a stamp missing phosphor bands, of which there were only six known, was almost always worth less than a stamp with a missing value or colour of which there were ten. In his introduction, Pierron considers the issue of investment. 'A tactic to consider,' he suggests, 'is buying up as many of a single error as possible and sitting on the copies for a while. Then release them slowly over time to extract the best possible price. It can be a costly and slow process, though.' He calculated the approximate value of certain classic errors over an extended period, based primarily on auctions. I saw that the Parliamentary 1s 3d missing blue was worth £500 in 1980, £900 in 1985, £3,000 in 1990, £4,000 in 1995, £4,500 in 2000 and £6,500 in 2003.

I felt gloomy—there is no other word for it—the sort of gloom that descended the day I saw the Post Office Tower error as a boy and has rarely lifted since. And then I heard early news of an auction and, hope triumphing over experience once more, the sun shone again on my pursuit.

# 6.

David Brandon sometimes mentioned his celebrity clients, including the television antiquarian Arthur Negus ('came into the shop a lot, charming gent'), the pop singer Adam Faith ('a great friend'), Lee Marvin Junior ('looked just like his dad') and the comedian Leslie Crowther ('couldn't stand him'). His biggest and best customer, however, was Sir Gawaine Baillie, a name on very few lips.

I first became aware of Sir Gawaine soon after his death, aged sixty-nine, in December 2003. The obituary in the *Daily Telegraph* recorded his career as a racing driver racing Jaguars and Fords alongside Stirling Moss in the late 1950s; his stewardship of the company he ran for forty years, HPC Engineering; and his inheritance on his mother's death in 1974 of the estate surrounding Leeds Castle in Kent (the castle itself was bequeathed to the nation). What it did not record was his interest in stamps—a large omission since he devoted four hours a day to them and in the process assembled one of the greatest private collections of modern times. Baillie collected Britain and the British Empire and the extent of his collection, when it was eventually revealed, surprised everyone in the world of stamps. It showed a mastery of the British West Indies, the Australian States, British Africa and Rhodesia, British North America, New Zealand and all outposts of the Empire. As for Great Britain itself, Baillie's eye and pocket had secured him Victorian colour trials and plate proofs; mint blocks of Penny Blacks and Twopenny Blues; a unique sheet of the 1880 2s brown; the famous 2d Tyrian Plum, which, following the death of King Edward VII in May 1910, was never issued; and a wide range of QE II errors, including the 1966 Technology 6d—the one where the illustration of cars included the Minis but omitted the Jaguar—which was said to be Sir Gawaine's personal favourite. Because he bought so much so regularly from so many dealers—an estimated thirty of them—each dealer had thought he was Sir Gawaine's main supplier. Nobody had suspected the collection's true size and brilliance. Even his widow was surprised at Sotheby's valuation of £11 million: she had guessed £800,000.

Baillie had also bought from Sotheby's, where he became a friend of Richard Ashton, the head of the stamp department, and soon after he died the auction house made an approach to Lady Baillie. All the big auction houses employ staff who keep track of the changing fortunes of the great collectors. Obituaries are studied carefully; contacts are pursued among divorce lawyers. 'It sounds rather macabre,' Richard Ashton told me, 'but if you don't do it, someone else will.'

Before Sotheby's competed to handle the Baillie sale, Ashton was called in for a probate valuation. 'It didn't matter which book I picked up,' he said, 'every one was a gem.' He told Lady Baillie that Sotheby's was going to show people what a wonderful thing her husband had achieved. The catalogues would be a memorial to him. Lady Baillie said, 'The wider the distribution the better.' Ten sales from the collection were scheduled to take place over two years at Sotheby's in New Bond Street, the first of them over three days, September 29 to October 1 last year, to conclude with Queen Elizabeth GB pre-decimal errors.

When the sale catalogue arrived I spent the rest of the day with it. In the next few days I had learned it by heart. There were so many perfect examples of stamps I had first seen before my bar mitzvah that I drew up a list of things I could sell (the car) or cancel (the summer holiday) or cheaply substitute (state education for private) to make them mine. Of the many fine items, three stood out. A Red Cross block missing red (nineteen examples known), a Post Office Savings Bank missing black (seven known), and the stamp I had thought about for almost forty years—the 1961 1s 3d Green Parliamentary Conference without the blue Queen's head (six known, two of which are damaged). This was Lot 1061, which consisted of a progressive row of three stamps (the first perfect with the blue present, the second with the blue half-gone, the third with the blue gone altogether), and the estimate on it appeared to me to be astonishingly reasonable; the catalogue priced it at between £2,000 and £2,500 plus a buyer's premium of 17.5 per cent. I could handle that. I doubted that anyone could be as determined to buy it as I was.

I signed up for a bidding paddle and turned up for the start of the third day at 10.30 in the morning. There was a lot of other business to be got through before the QE II errors, including many fine blocks of George V Sea Horses, the stamps that had done for me at the school stamp competition. This was a bad omen, and not the only one in the saleroom that morning. Many of the hundred or so other people present had attended the first two days of the sale and I noticed that even they had not become immune to the steep prices that many of the lots were reaching, some of them twice or three times the upper estimate. Several dealers I knew spent much of the morning tutting and shaking their heads. This was a terrible indication.

The two major QE II errors before mine each went very high. The Post Office Savings Bank without black attained £13,000, £4,000 more than the upper estimate, while the European Postal and Telecommunications Conference strip, in which the green dove erroneously turned white, went for £6,000, more than three times the estimate, to a bidder on the phone. And now it was my turn. The bidding began slowly, and I hadn't yet raised my paddle at £4,000. I thought to myself, 'I'm going to be okay.'

I put up my paddle. The auctioneer said, '£5,000, new bidder.' For a moment there was silence. This was going to be a great day for me.

Then a white-haired woman at the very front, seated by a desk, said '£10,500.'

I knew who the woman was. It was Mary Weekes, a stamp agent acting on behalf of anonymous clients. Her bid of £10,500 was the amount she had needed to clear the under-bidder. I may have imagined it, but I think that at that moment a movie cliché happened in the saleroom: there was collective sucking-in of breath. And then the gavel came down and I felt empty inside, like an amateur interloper who has just discovered hidden rules in a professional game. I'd failed to buy my favourite stamp and I might never have the chance again. I thought briefly that I would give up my stamps altogether.

And yet what had I missed and what had I saved?

The answer to the first: a small piece of paper, gummed on one side, produced in 1961 at the printing works of Harrison & Sons of London and High Wycombe, Buckinghamshire, whose machinery had for one second run out of blue ink.

The answer to the second: about £8,000, the price I was prepared to bid up to, roughly three times the estimate.

Rationally, financially, a good outcome but I was morose for a week, and when, at the end of it, I told my wife the reasons for my poor behaviour—you might say an addict's behaviour—I still lacked the courage to disclose the exact sums at stake.

# 7.

One day at lunch with David and Mark Brandon I asked them about forgeries—the forging of error. They said that gold Queen's heads could (and had been) removed from many stamps, including the 1966 Hastings set, with the use of chemicals and ironing, though their removal could be spotted because the original embossing of the paper would usually be removed as well. As for fraudulent changes to the original colour, those could often be detected with a good ultraviolet lamp. The only forgeries I have bought, knowingly at least, are far less sophisticated: the so-called 'Maryland Forgeries' of which very little is known except that were printed in the American state of Maryland. The forger copied all the famous GB missing colour errors—the Post Office Tower, the missing Minis, the Red Cross missing red—but even a ten-year-old wouldn't have been fooled. The perforations were too stubby, the colour weak, the paper thin and far too white. Also, they cost about £3 each from a respectable dealer, who sold them as a novelty item with 'forgery' printed on the back.

The day after I spoke to Melanie Kilim about her fear of the Post Office Tower, I walked to the postbox at the end of my road and sent her a Maryland Forgery of the stamp that omitted the Post Office Tower. I hoped that she would see the joke and enjoy the stamp. In fact, the opposite occurred. She wanted to know the answer to a question that, more calmly expressed, might have been a Zen riddle: if the tower wasn't on the stamp, 'Then where the hell was it?' She said that the stamp gave her palpitations.

I was tempted to reply, 'I know exactly what you mean.'     □

GRANTA

# THE GREAT WALL

## Ismail Kadaré

TRANSLATED FROM THE FRENCH
OF JUSUF VRIONI BY DAVID BELLOS

# Inspector Shung

*Barbarians always go back over in the end.* My deputy sighed as he spoke those words. I guess he was staring into the far distance, where their horses could just be seen.

For my part, I was reflecting on the fact that nowhere in the vast expanse of China—not in its small towns, not in its large cities, not in its capital either, although people there do know more than provincials—nowhere in China can you find a soul who fails to comment, when nomads come over the Wall (even nomads that come as part of an official delegation), that *Barbarians always go back over in the end*, while releasing a sigh of the sort usually sighed in response to events you imagine you'll eventually look back on with fond sadness.

It's been as quiet as the grave around here for decades. That fact does not stop our imperial subjects from imagining an unending brutal conflict, with the Wall on one side and the northern nomads on the other, both forever hurling spears and hot pitch at each other and tearing out eyes, masonry and hair.

But that no longer surprises me very much, when you think that people don't just bedeck the Wall with false laurels of valour but envision the rest of it—its structure, even its height—quite differently from the way it really is. They can't bring themselves to see that though there are places where the Wall is quite high—indeed, sometimes so high that if you look down from the top, as we could do right now from where we're standing, you go quite dizzy—along most of its length, on the other hand, the Wall's dismal state of repair is a pity to behold. Because it has been so long abandoned, because its stones have been taken away by local people, the Wall has shrunk: it barely tops a horse and rider now, and in one sector it's a wall only in name, just lumps of masonry scattered round like the remains of a project that got dropped for God knows what reason. It's in that kind of shape, like a snake you can hardly make out as it slithers through the mud, that the Wall reaches the edge of the Gobi desert—which promptly swallows it up.

My deputy's eyes were blank, like the eyes of someone required to stare into the far distance.

'We now stand in wait of an order,' I said, before he could ask me what we ought to do next. It was obvious that the result of the negotiations with the official delegation of nomads would determine what that order would be—if any decision of the kind ever got taken at all.

We stood in wait of the order all summer long, then until the end of the summer-house season, when the Emperor and his ministers were supposed to be back in the capital. The autumn winds came, then the snow-flecked drizzle of winter, but still no decision reached us.

As always happens in cases of that kind, the order, or rather its reverberation, arrived just when everybody had stopped thinking about it. I call it a reverberation because long before the Imperial mail reached us we learned of the government's decision from the people living in the villages and camps strung out along the line of fortifications. They deserted their homes and resettled themselves in the caves in the nearby hills, as they did every time news reached them, by means entirely mysterious, ahead of our being informed of impending repair work on the Great Wall.

It was probably a wise move on their part, since, by making off to the hills, they would spare themselves the officials' whip, at the very least, not to mention many other punishments of every kind. I've never understood why they constantly take masonry from the Wall to build their hovels and yards, while knowing full well that they always have to bring it back to rebuild the Wall.

The process, so they tell me, has been going on for hundreds of years. Like the skein of wool used to make a scarf—which is then unpicked to knit a sweater, which is then undone to knit another scarf, and so on—the Wall's great stones have made the return trip many times from peasant hovel to Wall and back again. In some places on them you can still see streaks of soot, which predictably fire the fantasies of tourists and foreign plenipotentiaries, who can't imagine that the marks are not traces of some heroic clash, but only smoke-stains from hearths where for many a long year some nameless yokel cooked his thin and tasteless gruel.

So when we heard this afternoon that the peasants had abandoned their dwellings, we guessed that the whole of China had already heard news of the call to rebuild the Wall.

Although they were a symptom of heightened tension, the repair works did not yet add up to war. Unlike armed conflict, rebuilding was such a frequent occurrence that the Great Wall's middle name could have easily been: Rebuilt. In truth, and in general, it was less a wall in any proper sense than an infinite succession of patches. People went so far as to say that it was in just such a manner that the Wall had come into being in the first place—as a repair job on an older wall, which was itself the remaking of another, even older wall, and so on. The suggestion was even made that at the very beginning the original wall stood at the centre of the state; but from one repair to another, it had gradually moved ever closer to the border, where, like a tree that's finally been replanted in the right soil, it grew to such a monstrous size as to terrify the rest of the world. Even people who could not imagine the Wall without the nomads sometimes wondered whether it was their presence that had led to the building of the Wall, or whether it was the Wall rising up all along the border that had conjured up the nomads.

If we had not seen the coming of the barbarian delegation with our own eyes, and then seen it going again, we might have been among the few who attributed this rise in tension (like most previous events of this kind) to the disagreements which frequently flare up inside the country, even at the very centre of the state. Smugly content to know a truth lost in an ocean of lies, we would have spent long evenings constructing hypotheses about what would happen next and about the plots that could have been hatched in the Palace, plots with such secret and intricate workings that even their instigators would have had a hard time explaining them, or attached to jealousies so powerful that people said they could shatter ladies' mirrors at dusk, and so on and so forth.

But it had all happened under our noses: the nomads had come and gone beneath our very feet. We could still remember the many-coloured borders of their tunics and the clip-clop of their horses' hooves—not forgetting the expression *Barbarians always go back over in the end* uttered by my deputy along with his sighs, and his blank stare.

In any other circumstance we could have felt, or at least feigned, a degree of doubt, but this time we realized that there were no grounds at all for such an attitude. However tiresome winter evenings may be, we could find better ways of filling them than fabricating alternative reasons for the state's anxiety apart from the coming of the Barbarians.

A vague apprehension is coming down to us from the Northlands. Right now the issue is not whether this state of heightened tension derives from the existence of a real external threat. From now on, and this is more than obvious, the only real question is whether there really will be war.

The first stonemasons have arrived, but most of them are still on the road. Some people claim that that there are 40,000 of them on their way, others give an even higher figure. This is definitely going to be the most important rebuilding effort of the last few centuries.

*The call of the wild goose awakes the immensity of the void...* Yesterday, as I was looking out over the wastes to the north, this line from a poet whose name I forget came back to me. For some time now, fear of the void has been by far the greatest form of apprehension that I feel... They say the nomads now have a single leader, a successor to Genghis Khan, and that amidst the swirling confusion and dust that is the Barbarians' lot, he is trying to set up a state. For the time being we have no details about the leader except that he is lame. All that has reached us here, even before the man's name, is his limp.

These last few days nomads have been emerging from the mist like flocks of jackdaws and then vanishing again. It's clear that they're keeping an eye on the repair work. I am convinced that the Wall, without which we could not imagine how to survive, is for them an impossible concept, and that it must disturb them as deeply as the northern emptiness troubles us.

# Nomad Kutluk

I've been told to gallop and gallop and never stop watching over it, but it's endless and always the same, stone on stone, stone under stone, stone to the left, stone to the right, all bound in mortar, however much I gallop, the stones never change, always the same, just like that damn snow that was always the same when we chased Toktamish across Siberia at the end of the Year of the Dog, when Timur, our *Khan kuturdilar*, told us: 'Hold on in there, men, because it's only snow , it's only pretending to be cold like a conceited bitch, but just you wait, it'll go soft and wet before long.' But this army of stones is much more harmful, it won't flake or melt, and it's in my way, I don't understand why the Khan doesn't give us the order to attack that pile of rubble and take it down, like we did at Chubukabad when we laid our hands on the Sultan Bayazed Yaldrem and the Khan sent us this *yarlik*: 'Honour to you who have captured Thunder, no matter that you have not yet handcuffed the heavens entire, but that'll come'; and like at Akshehir during the Year of the Tiger, when we buried our prisoners alive, all bent double as in their mothers' womb, and the *Khan kuturdilar* told us: 'If they're innocent, as Qatshi the Magician believes, then mother earth, whose womb is more generous that that of a woman, will give them a second birth.' Oh! those were the good times, but our Khan hasn't sent any more *yarliks* asking us to raze things to the ground, and the chiefs, when they assemble to hold a palaver in the *kurultai*, claim that what people call towns are only coffins we must be careful never to enter, because once you're in you can never get out, that's what they say, but the *yarlik* of destruction keeps on failing to come, all I get is that never-ending order going on again and again just like the accursed stones: 'Nomad, keep watch!'

## Inspector Shung

Repair work is apparently proceeding along the entire north-western stretch of the Wall. Every week parties of masons arrive, gaily flaunting the many-coloured flags and banners from their province (the regions of the Empire compete with each other to send the largest work-detail to the Wall), but nowhere can any troop movements be seen. Nomad look-outs flit across the horizon as before, but because the fog has thickened in the winter season, we often cannot make them out very clearly, neither the rider nor the horse, so that they look less like horsemen than mutilated body-parts from who-knows-which battlefield whipped by wild gusts of wind into a flying swarm.

What is happening is like a puzzle. At first sight you might think it a mere manoeuvre, each camp trying to show its strength by displaying contempt for the other. But if you consider matters with a clear mind, you can see they contain perfectly illogical elements. I believe it is the first time there has ever been such a gap between the Wall and the capital. I had always imagined they were indissolubly connected, and that was not only when I was working in the capital, but even before then, when I was a mere minor official in the remotest valleys of Tibet. I always knew they tugged on each other the way they say the moon does on the tide. What I learned when I came here was that while the Wall is able to move the capital—in other words, that it can draw it towards itself or else push it further away—the capital has no power to shift the Wall. At most, it can try to move away, like a fly trying to avoid the spider's web, or else come right up close so as to nestle in its bosom, like a person quaking with fear; but that's all it can do.

In my view, the Wall's forces of attraction and repulsion are what explain the movements of the capital of China over the last two centuries—its shift to the south of the country, when it went to Nanking, as far away from the Wall as possible, and then its return to the north, to the closest possible location, when it came back to Beijing, which for the third time assumed its role as China's capital city.

I have been wracking my brains these last few days trying to find a more accurate explanation for what is going on at the moment. Sometimes I think the wobble, if I can use that word, results directly from the proximity of the capital. Orders can be countermanded more easily than if the capital were, say, four or five months away— when the second carriage bearing news of the cancellation of the order either fails to catch up with the first carriage or else, because of its speed or its driver's anxiety, tips over, or else the first one crashes, or else they both do, and so on.

Yesterday evening, as we were chatting away (it was one of those exquisitely relaxed conversations such as often arise after time spent hidden from the view of others and which thus seem all the more precious), my deputy declared that if not only the capital, but China herself, were to move, the Wall would not budge an inch. 'And what's more,' he added casually, 'there is proof of what I say.' Indeed, we could both easily recall that in the one thousand or so years that have elapsed since the building of the Wall, China has more than once spilled out over its borders, leaving the Wall all alone and without meaning in the midst of the grey steppe, and that it has shrunk back inside the same number of times.

I remembered one of my aunts who in childhood had had a bracelet put on her arm, a bangle which got forgotten and left in place. As she grew plumper, the bracelet became almost buried in her flesh. It seemed to me that something of the same kind had happened to China. The Wall had alternately squeezed her tight, and slackened off. For some years now it had seemed about right for her size. As for the future, who could say... Each time I saw my aunt,

I recalled the story of her bangle which continued to obsess me, I really don't know why, because in spite of myself I could not stop thinking of what would have happened if the bangle had not been taken off in time, and, taking things to their limit, I could hear it jangling incessantly after her death, hanging all too loosely on the wrist of her skeleton... I lay my head in my hands, embarrassed at having imagined China herself decomposing with a trivial adornment around her wrist...

It was a starless night, but the moonlight gave off such a strong sense of indolence that you could believe that in the morning everyone would abandon all activity—that nomads, birds, and even states would lie flat out, exhausted, as lifeless as corpses laid out beside each other, as we two then were...

We have at last learned the name of the nomad chief: he is called Timur i Leng, which means Timur the Lame. He is said to have waged a fearsome war against the Ottomans, and after having captured their king—called Thunder—he had him paraded him from one end of the vast steppes to the other.

It seems he'll soon be after us. Now it is all becoming clearer—the order for the rebuilding of the Wall, as well as the temporary calm which we all hastened to describe as a 'puzzle' as we do for anything we can't understand in the workings of the state. While he was dealing with the Turks, the one-legged terror did not constitute a threat. But now...

A returning messenger who stopped here last night brought us disturbing news. In the western marches of our Empire, right opposite our Wall and barely a thousand feet from it, the Barbarians had built a kind of tower, made not from stone but from severed heads. The edifice as it was described to us was not tall—about as high as two men—and from a military point of view it was no threat at all to the Wall, but the terror those heads exude is more effective than a hundred fortresses. Despite the meetings with soldiers and masons where it was explained that the pile was, in comparison to our Wall, no more significant than a scarecrow (the crows that nonetheless swarmed around it had actually suggested the comparison), everyone, soldiers included, felt the wind of panic pass through them. 'I've never had so many letters to take to the capital,' the messenger declared as he patted his leather saddlebag. He said most of them had been penned by officers' wives, writing to their aristocratic lady-friends to report intolerable migraines and so forth, which was a way of asking them to please see if they could get their husbands transferred to another posting.

The messenger also said that the pestilential air that the head-heap exhaled was so unbearable that for the first time in its existence the Wall had apparently contracted, and the messenger had prayed to God that the rebuilding work which had been launched at such an opportune moment should be completed as quickly as possible.

The messenger's tale left us all utterly depressed. Without admitting it to ourselves we were aware that we would henceforth cast a quite different eye on the Wall's damaged parts, on its cracks and crumbly patches. Our minds obstinately kept turning towards the pile of severed heads. Once the messenger had left, my deputy pointed out that the wise old saying 'skull on stone breaks nothing but bone'—a phrase whose brushstrokes we mastered at primary school thanks to our teachers' liberal use of the rod—had become obsolete. The way things looked now, heads seemed more likely than anything else to be the weapon of choice against the Wall.

Still no troop movements on the border. A brutal earthquake has shaken everything save the Wall, which has long known how to cope with tremors. The silence that reigned after the last shock subsided seemed deeper than ever... I have the impression that the rebuilding work is being done carelessly and just for show. The day before the quake, the building used as a watchtower, on our right, collapsed again, after being rebuilt once before. It all leads me to think that treason has crept into the Imperial Palace. My deputy has a different view. He has long been convinced that people in the capital are so deeply sunk in pleasure and debauchery that few of them ever think of the existence of nomads and frontiers. Only yesterday he was telling me that he'd heard people say that a new kind of mirror has been invented—mirrors that more than double the size of a man's penis. Ladies take them into their bedchambers to arouse themselves before making love.

Our only comfort is that there doesn't seem to be the slightest movement on the other side of the Wall, except for a few scouts who flash past on horseback now and then, and sometimes we also see small groups of ragged Turkish soldiers. When the Turks first appeared, toward the end of summer, our look-outs were alarmed. Our first thought was that they might be attack units disguised as defeated Turks, but then we got reports from spies who had been infiltrated among them that in fact they were the remnants of the Ottoman army Timur had routed at Chubukabad. They've been wandering up and down the frontier for a long time now. Most of them are old men, and, when evening comes, their thoughts go back to those distant lands with fearsome names where they fought, and also presumably to their Sultan Bayazed, whose memory they trail with them across the steppe like a dead flash of lightning.

More than once they have asked for work on the Wall rebuilding project; after the repeated collapses of the right-hand tower, one of them, who was so persistent that he actually got to see me personally, told me in bad Chinese that he'd once seen in a far distant land a bridge in one of whose piers a man had been walled up. He pointed to his eye as he swore that he had really *seen* it, and even asked for a scrap of cardboard so he could draw the shape of the bridge for me. It was only a small bridge, he said, but to stop it collapsing a sacrifice had had to be made. How then could this huge Wall of China stay standing without an offering of the same kind?

He came back to see me a few days later and told the same story once more, but this time he made a lavishly detailed drawing of the bridge.

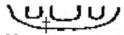

When I asked him why he'd pictured it upside down, he went pale. 'I don't know,' he replied, 'but perhaps it is because that is the way it looks in the water... Anyway, the night before last, that's how I saw it in my dream. Top down.' After he had left we took some time to look at the bizarre sketch he had made. He explained that the symbol † marked the place of the sacrifice. After I stared at it hard for a long while, I thought I could see the bridge beginning to quiver. Or was that because the Turk had told me that he remembered the bridge's reflection in the river better than the bridge itself? If I may say so, it was a way of seeing things from an aquatic point of view—a perspective, the Turk had explained, thought to diverge completely from a human point of view, for instance, or from a so-to-speak *terran* perspective. It was the waters that had demanded the sacrifice of immurement (at least, that's what the legend said)—that is to say, sentencing a man to death.

Late that night, slant beams of moonlight falling on masonry made human shapes appear here and there on the side of the Wall. 'Accursed Turk!' I swore under my breath, believing it was he who had stirred up such morbid images in my mind. It then struck me that the upturned bridge was perhaps the very model of the way tidings good and bad move around our sublunar world. It was very likely that nations did indeed pass messages to each other in that way—signals announcing the coming of their official delegations, with their letters sealed with black wax, a few hundred or a few thousand years in advance.

## Nomad Kutluk

The chiefs have gathered at the *kurultai*, and Khan Timur's *yarlik* has come: 'Never venture over the other side,' it says, 'for that way lies your perdition.' But the more I'm told not to, the more I want to step over and see the cities and the women who are doubled in burnished glass, wearing nothing but a gauze they call *mend-afsh* (silk), women with a pleasure-slit sweeter than honey, but this damned rock-heap won't let me, it obstructs me, it oppresses me, and I would like to strike it down with my dagger, though I know steel has no power over it, for it even withstood the earthquake but two days ago. When the shudder and the masonry wrestled each other, I screamed aloud to the tremor: 'You alone may bring it down!' But it made no difference, the Wall had the better of it, it smothered the quake and I wept as I watched the earthquake's last spasms, like a bull who's had its throat cut, until, alas, I saw it expire, and my God did I feel sad, as sad as that other time in the plain of Bek-Pek-Dala, when I said to Commander Abaga, 'I don't know why, but I feel like screaming,' and he said, 'This steppe is called Bek-Pek-Dala, the steppe of hunger, and if you don't feel your own hunger, you'll feel the hunger of others, so spur your steed, my son.' That's what they all tell me: spur your steed, never let it stop, son of the steppe, but this lump of stone is stopping me, it's in my way, it's rubbing up against my horse, it's calling to its bones, and I myself feel drawn in to its funereal mortar, I don't know how but it's made my face go ashen, it's making me melt and blanch, aaah…

# Inspector Shung

The days drag themselves along as wearily as if they had been broken by old age. We haven't yet managed to recuperate from the shock we had at the end of this week.

Ever since a man in a chariot halted at our tower and said, 'I am from Number 22 Department of Music,' I have felt a foreboding of evil, or something very much like it. When I asked him what the role of his department was and whether he really meant to put on concerts or operatic pieces for the soldiers and workers on the Wall rebuilding project, he laughed out long and loud: 'Our Department hasn't been involved in that sort of thing for ages!' What he then explained to us was so astounding that at one point my deputy interrupted him with a plaintive query: 'Is all that really true, or is this a joke?'

We had of course heard that, over the years, some departments and sections of the celestial hierarchy, while retaining their traditional names, had seen their functions entirely transformed—but to learn that things had gone so far as to make supplying the Emperor with aphrodisiacs the main job of the navy's top brass while the management of the fleet was now in the hands of the Palace's head eunuch, well, nobody could get his mind around that. But that's not the whole story, he said. 'Do you know who's now in charge of the copper mines and the foundries? Or who's the brains behind foreign policy these days? Or the man in charge of public works?'

Our jaws dropped as, with smug satisfaction at his listeners' bewilderment, he answered some of his own questions as if he was throwing old bones to hungry dogs. Lowering his voice, he confided that the institution now responsible for castrating eunuchs and for running the secret service was the National Library. Leaving us no time at all to catch our breath, he went on to reveal that in recent times the clan of the eunuchs at the Imperial Palace had seized an untold amount of power. In his view they would soon be in complete control of government, and then China might no longer be called the Celestial Empire, or the Middle Empire, but could easily come to be known as the Empire of Celestial Castration...

He guffawed for a while, then his face darkened. 'You may well laugh,' he said, 'but you don't realize what horrors that would bring in its wake.' Far from smiling, let alone laughing, our expressions had turned as black as pitch. Despite which, he carried on prefacing all his remarks with, 'You may well laugh, but...' In his mind we were laughing without realizing the calamity that would come of it. Because we did not know that emasculation multiplies a man's thirst for power ten-fold, and so on.

As the evening wore on, and as he drank ever more copiously, especially toward the end, the pleasure of lording it over us and his pride in coming from the capital pushed him on to revealing ever more frightful secrets. He probably said too much, but even so, none of his words was without weight, for you could sense that they gave a faithful representation of reality. When we broached the threat from the North, he snorted with laughter as thunderously as ever before. 'War with the nomads? How can you be so naïve, my poor dear civil servants, as to believe in such nonsense? The Wall rebuilding project? It's got nothing to do with the prospect of battle! On the contrary, it's the first article of the secret pact with the Barbarians. Why are you looking at me with the glassy stare of a boiled cod? Yes, that's right, the repair work was one of the Barbarians' demands.'

'Oh no!' my deputy groaned as he put his head between his hands.

Our visitor went on in a more measured manner. To be sure, China had raised the Wall to protect itself from the nomadic hordes, but so much time had passed since then that things had undergone a profound change.

'Yes,' he said, 'things have changed a heap. It's true China was afraid of the Barbarians for many a long year, and at some future time she may well have reason to fear them again. But there have also been periods when the Barbarians were afraid of China. We're in one such period right now. The Barbarians are afraid of China. And that's why they asked, quite firmly, for the Wall to be rebuilt.'

'But that's crazy!' my deputy said. 'To be fearful of a state and at the same time to ask it to strengthen its defences makes no sense at all!'

'Heavens above!' our visitor exclaimed. 'Why are you so impatient? Let me finish my explanation... You stare at me with your big eyes, you interrupt me like a flock of geese, all because you do not know what's at the bottom of it. The key to the puzzle is called: fear. Or to be more precise, it is the nature of that fear... Now, listen carefully, and get it into your heads: China's fear and the Barbarians' fear, though they are both called *fear* in Chinese, are not the same thing at all. China fears the destructive power of the Barbarians; the Barbarians fear the softening effects of China. Its palaces, its women, its silk. All of that in their eyes spells death, just as the lances and dust of the nomads spell the end for China. That's how this strange Wall, which rises up as an obstacle between them, has sometimes served the interests of one side, and sometimes the other. Right now it's the nomads' turn...'

The thought of insulting him to his face or calling him an impostor, a clown, or a bullshitter, left my mind for good. Like everything he'd said so far, this had to be true. I had a vague memory of Genghis Khan's conquest of China. He overthrew our Emperors and put his own men in their place, then turned on those same men because they had apparently gone soft. Hadn't Yan Jey, one of our ministers, been convicted a few years back for having asserted, one evening after dinner, that the last four generations of the Ming dynasty, if not its entire ascendance as well, was basically Mongol?

So the repairs to the Wall had been requested by the Barbarians. Timur, more foresighted than his predecessors, had reckoned that invading China was not only pointless, but impossible. What China loses by the sword it retakes by silk. So Timur had chosen to have the border closed, instead of attacking. That is what explains the calm which settled over both sides of the Wall as soon as the delegation came over. What the rest of us had ascribed so unthinkingly to an enigma, to frivolousness, even to a hallucination engendered by penis-enlarging mirrors, was actually the straightforward outcome of a bilateral accord.

That night a swarm of thoughts buzzed around in my head. States are always either wiser or more foolish than we think they are. Snatches of conversation with officials who had been posted on the other side came back to my mind, but I now saw them in a different light. The ghost of Genghis Khan has weakened, I used to hear from people who'd carried out espionage in the Northlands. But we heard them without paying much attention, as we reckoned that these were just tales of the Barbarians: they've gone softer, they've got harder, and taking that sort of thing seriously was like trying to interpret the shapes made in the sky by flights of storks. But that was not right at all. Something really was going on out there in the grey steppes, and the more I thought about it, the more important it seemed to be. A great change was taking hold of the world. Nomadism was on its last legs, and Timur, the man whom the Heavens had had the whimsy to make lame, was there to establish a new balance of power. He had brought a whole multitude of peoples to follow a single religion, Islam, and now he was trying to settle them on a territory that could be made into a state. The numerous incursions of these different nations, which had previously seemed incomprehensible, would now probably come to a halt on the surface of the earth, though it was not at all clear whether that was a good thing or a bad one, since you can never be sure whether a barbarian contained is more dangerous than one let loose... I imagined Timur standing like a pikestaff at the very heart of Asia and all around him nomadic peoples barely responding to his exhortations to stop their wild forays...

From the high battlements I could see a whole section of the Wall which the moonlight seemed to split open all the way along. I tried to imagine what Timur could have thought when he had first been shown a sketch of it. He must surely have thought: *I'll knock it down, raze it to the ground, plant grass over it so its line can never be recovered*; then, pondering on how to protect his monastically strict kingdom from the softening wind of permissiveness, he must have realized that Heaven itself could not have presented him with a gift more precious than that Wall.

Next day, before dawn, when our visitor mounted his chariot to be on his way, I was tempted to ask him just what the Number 22 Department of Music was, but for reasons I'm unsure of, I felt embarrassed to do so. Not so much politeness, I guess, as the fear of hearing some new abomination. 'May you break your damn neck!' my deputy cursed as the four-in-hand clattered noisily away between two heaps of rubble. Feeling vanquished, we looked out over a landscape which, despite having sated our eyes for years on end, now looked quite different. We had cursed our guest by wishing his chariot to turn end over end, but in fact it was he who had already taken his revenge by turning our minds upside down.

So the Wall was not what we had thought it was. Apparently frozen in time and unmovable in place while all beneath it shifted with the wind—borders, times, alliances, even eternal China herself—the Wall was actually quite the opposite. It was the Wall which moved. More faithless than a woman, more changeable than the clouds in the sky, it stretched its stony body out over thousands of leagues to hide the fact that it was an empty shell, a wrap round an inner void.

Each day that passed was ever more wearisome, and we came to realize to what degree we had become part and parcel of the Wall. We cursed it as we felt, now that it had betrayed us, how much more suffering it was bringing us. Our visitor's prediction that the Wall would one day serve China again was a meagre consolation, as was that other view which held that the Wall's inner changes were perhaps what constituted its real strength, for without them it would have been nothing more than a lifeless corpse.

When I looked at it all covered with frost in the early mornings, I was overcome with gloomy thoughts. It would certainly survive us all. It would look just the same—greyish and mysterious—even when all humanity had disappeared. It would rust on humanity's cadaver, like the bangle on my aunt who had been rotting six feet under for years.

The death of a nomad scout at the foot of the Wall woke us from our torpor. We had seen him now and again galloping ever closer to the Wall, as if he had been trying to stick to it, until he finally crashed straight into it like a sightless bird.

We did not wait for any instruction but prepared ourselves to provide an account of the event to a commission of inquiry, from our own side or else from the Barbarians'. As we examined the bloodstains streaked along the Wall over fifty feet and more (it seems that even after injuring himself the rider spurred his horse ever on), my mind ran back to that far-off bridge which had been said to demand a sacrifice. Good Lord, I thought, can they have been in contact with each other so quickly?

I also mused about the distance that such a portent can cover, about the migration of forebodings and also, of course, about the mystery surrounding the image of the upturned bridge. It was one among the hundreds of misleading images this world provides us with and which can only ever be seen back to front.

# The Ghost of Nomad Kutluk

Now that I am on this side and no longer need a steed or any kind of bird to get around, since a breath of wind or even, on calm nights, a pale moonbeam will do the job for me—now that I am in the beyond I am no longer astounded by the thick-headedness of the folk down below or by their infuriating narrow-mindedness.

That narrowness must surely lie at the root of their superficial judgement of all things, as is notably the case (to take only one instance of the stupid blunders that I was unfortunate enough to encounter) of the Great Wall of China, to which people down below on earth attribute huge importance, whereas it is in reality only a ridiculous fence, especially when you compare it to a real barrier like the true Wall, the Mother-Wall, the one which makes all others pale into the insignificance of feeble copies, or, to call it, as many do, that bourn from where no traveller returns—the wall that comes between life and death.

So of course I no longer need a horse; similarly, foreign languages, learning and all the other things understood to be part of civilization, are of no use to me now. Souls manage to communicate perfectly well without them.

That horrible fall into the abyss, which came just after I thrashed my feeble body like a rag on the curbstone of China, was enough to make me realize things which it would have taken me thousands of years to understand down there. The knowledge taught by fear is incomparably superior to the product of all civilizations and academies put together, and I think that's the main if not the sole reason why we are forbidden to return, even for a day. It is probably thought that we would need barely a few weeks to become masters of the planet, and that would clearly not be to the taste of the gods.

Strange to say, although we spirits smile wryly as we talk of our mistakes, resentments, clashes and conflicts of yore, most of us up here would still like to go back, even if for only the briefest sojourn. Some can't wait to denounce their murderers, others want to leak state secrets or to elucidate mysteries they took with them to the grave, but for most of us, it's plain nostalgia. Of course, our desire to see our nearest and dearest is also shot through with the wish to tell but the tiniest part of the wonders we have seen from this side.

Every ten or fifteen thousand years the rumour goes around that home visits are going to be allowed. The great mass of ghosts starts to hurry toward the Wall. But then we see it looming before us, a great sinister mass in the darkness of the night. The look-outs are blind, so it is said. Crossings happen in one direction only, from there to here…never from here to there.

Buoyed by the whisper that one day there will be two-way travel through the Wall, we carry on hoping all the same. Some cannot hold back their tears. They claim they've been expected for all eternity by beings who are dear to them, or by temples where they would try to pour balm on wounded minds, or even by whole nations that are dying to see them return. They say they have invitations, which they wave like banners from afar, certificates from people who say they're prepared to give them board and lodging and who will even stand surety for their safe return. They parade academic insignia topped by royal crowns, and other sacred stamps, occasionally of dubious origin. But the gates never open, not for anyone.

Spirits get angry, start to protest, and make a racket that can be heard at the top of the watchtowers. They yell that it's the same old story as on earth, that nothing has changed, that it's just as strict, just as inhuman...

Since it is another case of crossing a boundary, we who have experience of walls and other kinds of barriers cherish the hope that we may be granted special favour. Sometimes we gather among ourselves: some show off the scars from the spears and bullets that went through them, others show the tears made in their skin by barbed wire, or the holes made in their chests by the tips of embassy railings. We imagine those wounds will suffice to soften the hearts of the guardians of the gate. But we soon realize those are just vain hopes and that no one will be granted a *laissez-passer*.

When the others see how we are being treated, they lose all hope. Small, defeated groups straggle away, reckoning that the laws will be relaxed one fine day, and they start to listen out once again for a new rumour to cheer them up.

Last time, in the waiting crowd, someone pointed out a fellow called Jesus Christ... They've been making every imaginable special case for him for all eternity, they even sing hymns in his honour. What's more, his emblem shining from the roofs of cathedrals shows that of us all over here, he is certainly the one most expected back on earth.

As a matter of fact, even he is not optimistic. He comes and goes at the base of the Wall, displaying from afar the marks of the nails with which they crucified him, but the guardians pretend not to see them. Unless, as we have long suspected, the guardians are truly eyeless.

□

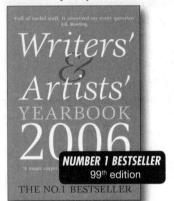
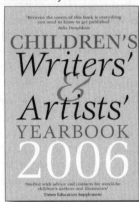

GRANTA

# WHITE SANDS

## Geoff Dyer

My wife and I were driving south on Highway 54 from Alamogordo to El Paso. We'd spent the afternoon at White Sands and my brain was still scorched from the glare. I worried that I might even have done some permanent damage to my eyes. The sand is made of gypsum—whatever that is—and is as bright as new-fallen snow. Brighter, actually. It's quite unbelievable that anything can be so bright. Looking at that sand is like staring at the sun. The underside of my chin was burned from the sun bouncing up off the white sand. It's a good name for the National Park, White Sands, though we thought the place a bit disappointing at first. The sand was a little discoloured, not quite white. Then, as we drove further, the sand started to creep on to the road and it became whiter and soon everything was white, even the road, and then there was no road, just this bright whiteness. We parked the car and walked into it, into the whiteness. It was hard to believe that such a place existed. The sky was pristine blue but the thing that must, that really must be emphasized, is the whiteness of the sand which could not have been any whiter. There was no shade to speak of but we sat and sheltered as best we could, huddled together under a sarong.

I said, 'Life like a dome of many-coloured glass stains the white radiance of eternity.'

'It's like being dead here, isn't it?' said Jessica.

'Yes,' I said. 'There's no life. Hence the white radiance. Unstained.'

We would like to have stayed longer in that unstained wilderness but we had to get to El Paso that night. We walked back to the car and drove out of the park. Ideally one would spend at least a day at the aptly named White Sands but there was nothing we could do about it. Not that that made leaving any easier. It's no good just having a glimpse of a desert, but if it's a choice between a glimpse and nothing at all I would always settle for a glimpse. Frustrating though that is.

Jessica was driving. It was early evening. We were about sixty miles south of Alamogordo and the light was fading. A freight train was running parallel to the road, also heading south.

'Hitch-hiker!' I said, pointing. 'Shall we pick him up?'

'Shall we?' My wife was slowing down. We could see him more clearly now, a black guy, in his late twenties, clean and not looking like a maniac or someone who smelled bad. We slowed to a crawl and took a good look at him. He looked fine. I lowered my window, the passenger window. He had a nice smile.

'Where ya going?' he said.

'El Paso,' I said.

'That'd be great for me.'

'Sure. Get in.'

He opened the door and climbed into the back seat. Our eyes met in the mirror. Jessica said, 'Hi.'

''Preciate it,' he said.

'You're welcome.' Jessica accelerated and soon we were back up to seventy and drawing level once again with the long freight train to our left.

'Where've you come from?' I asked, twisting round in my seat. I could see now that he was perhaps older than I had initially thought. He had deep lines in his face but his eyes were kind and his smile was still nice.

'Albuquerque,' he said. I was slightly surprised. The logical way to have got to El Paso from Albuquerque would have been to go straight down I-25. 'Where you from?' he asked.

'London,' I said. 'England.'

'The Kingdom,' he said.

'Right.' I was facing straight ahead again because I worried that twisting around in my seat would give me a cricked neck, to which I am prone.

'I thought so,' he said. 'I love your accent.'

'What about you?'

'Arkansas originally.'

'That's where my mother's from,' said Jessica. 'El Dorado.'

'I'm from Little Rock,' he said.

'Like Pharoah Sanders,' I said. It was a pointless thing to have said but I have this need to show off, to show that I know things; in this instance to show that I knew about jazz, about black jazz musicians. The guy, evidently, was not a jazz fan. He nodded but said nothing and we prepared to settle into the occasionally interrupted silence that tends to work best in these situations. We had established where we were all from and a pleasant atmosphere filled the car.

Less than a minute later, this pleasant atmosphere was changed absolutely by a sign:

NOTICE

DO NOT PICK UP HITCH-HIKERS

DETENTION FACILITIES IN AREA

I had seen the sign. Jessica had seen the sign. Our hitch-hiker had seen the sign. We had all seen the sign and the sign had changed our relationship totally. What struck me was the plural: not a detention facility but detention facili*ties*. Several of them. The notice—and I took some heart from the fact that the sign described itself as a 'notice' rather than a 'warning'—did not specify *how* many, but there were, evidently, more than one. I did not glance at Jessica. She did not glance at me. There was no need because at some level everyone was glancing at everyone else. As well as not glancing, no one said a word. I have always believed in the notion of the vibe: good vibes, bad vibes. After we saw the sign the vibe in the car—which had been a good vibe— changed completely and became a very bad vibe. This was a physical fact. Somehow the actual molecules in the car underwent a chemical change. The car was not the same place it had been just a minute earlier. And the sky had grown darker—that was another factor.

We soon came to the facilities which had unmistakably been designed with detention in mind. Both places—there were two of them, one on the right and one on the left—were set back from the road, surrounded by high walls of razor wire, and brightly lit by arc lights. There were no windows. In the intensity and single-mindedness of their desire to contain menace they exuded it. At the same time, both places had something of the quality of Ikea outlets. I wished they were Ikea outlets. It would have been so nice if our hitch-hiker had said that he had come to buy a sofa or some kitchen units and that his car had broken down. We could have sympathized with that. As it was, no one said anything. No one said anything but I know what I was thinking: I was thinking that I had never been in a position where I so wished I could wind back the clock just one or two minutes. I would love to have wound back the clock, would love to have said to Jessica 'Shall we pick him up' and heard her reply 'No, let's not' and just sped past, leaving him where he was. But you cannot wind the clock back in this life, not even by two seconds. Everything that has happened stays happened. Everything has consequences. As a consequence we couldn't have not picked him up but I could have asked him to get out. I could have said, 'Look man, I'm sorry, but in the circumstances would you mind getting the fuck out of our car?'. I could have done this but I didn't, for several reasons. First I was worried that if I did suggest he get out he might go berserk, might kill us. Second, I was worried that by asking—by telling him, really—to get out I would be being rude.

So instead of asking him to get out we drove on in tense silence. The car sped along. There seemed no point in slowing down. In any situation there is always something positive to emphasize. In this one it was the fact that there were no traffic hold-ups at all. Jessica was gripping the wheel. No one was speaking. The silence was unendurable but impossible to break. Unsure what to do, I turned on the radio. We were still tuned to a classic-rock station that we had been listening to earlier in the day, before we got to White Sands, and as soon as the radio came on, in the fading light of New Mexico, I recognized the piano tinkle and swish of 'Riders on the Storm'. I am a big fan of the Doors but I did not want to hear this song now. It was just unbelievable. A few moments later we heard Jim Morrison crooning:

There's a killer on the road
His brain is squirming like a toad...

Having turned on the radio with such disastrously appropriate results it seemed impossible, now, to turn it off. The three of us sat there, listening:

If you give this man a ride
Sweet memory will die...

Jessica followed the advice offered by Jim Morrison elsewhere in his oeuvre. She was keeping her eyes on the road and her hands upon the wheel. I kept my eyes on the road and my hands in my lap. Day was still turning to night. The lights of oncoming cars were dazzling and did not augur well. I wondered if it might be possible to send out a Mayday message in Morse code by blinking our beams. The song continued. Ray Manzarek was doing his little jazzy solo on the electric piano or whatever it was. We are in a totally nightmarish situation, I thought to myself. The rain on the record made it seem like it was raining here as well, under the clear skies of New Mexico, south of Alamogordo, heading towards El Paso. When the song finished I turned down the volume while an advertisement was read out for an upcoming sale of furniture. I had been thinking about getting murdered by a hitch-hiker and then Jim Morrison had come on the radio with this song about a sicko hitcher whose brain was squirming like a toad. A little while earlier I had been thinking about Ikea and now there was this advertisement for a furniture sale. Was it possible that the radio was tuned, in some way, to my thoughts? If so would it next play a song about thought itself? Did such a song even exist in the classic rock canon? Before I could pursue this thought the guy in the back seat cleared his throat. In the tense atmosphere of the car the sound was like the blast of a gun going off.

'Listen, man,' he said.

'Yes?' I said. Jessica had said 'Yes?' too, at exactly the same time, and the sound of that double-barrelled query erupted into the car in a volley of desperate good manners.

'Lemme explain.'

An explanation was so precisely what we wanted. In the circumstances the only thing we could have wanted more was an unsolicited offer to get out of our car and turn himself in to the authorities.

I caught his eyes in the mirror. You often see this in films: the eyes of the person in the car framed by the rear-view mirror which is framed, in turn, by the windshield which is framed, in turn, by the cinema screen. Basically the look in those eyes is never benign. It is always heavy with foreboding. I met his eyes. Our eyes met. Because of all these associations it was impossible to read the look in his eyes. Also, I had recently seen an exhibition of photographs by Taryn Simon called *The Innocents*. The pictures were of men and women— usually black—who had been convicted of terrible crimes. Some of them had served twenty years of their unbelievably long sentences (hundreds and hundreds of years in some cases) but then, having won the right to DNA testing, they'd had their convictions overturned. It was not just that there was an element of doubt or that the conviction was unsafe because of some procedural technicality (cops falsifying evidence of a crime which they *knew* the suspect was guilty of but could not quite prove). No, there was simply no way they could have done the terrible things for which they had been convicted. Looking at these faces you try to deduce innocence or guilt, but it is impossible. Innocent people can look guilty and guilty people can look innocent. Anyone can look like anything. Innocent or guilty: from the faces it is impossible to judge. Also, although it is terrible that they were convicted of these terrible crimes, these crimes were committed by *someone*. It is even possible that the reason some of these people had been wrongly convicted was because these crimes—these terrible crimes—had been committed by the person in the back of our car who, speaking slowly, said, 'Guess that sign freaked you out, huh?'

'That is putting it mildly,' I said. 'Also, frankly, that song did not exactly set our minds at ease.'

'Well, let me tell you what happened.'

'That would be great,' I said. I sometimes think that this is all any of us really want from our time on earth: an explanation. Set the record straight. Come clean. Let us know where we stand so that we can make well-informed decisions about how to proceed. *Or do you want me to just beat it out of you?*

'I did some things in my past. I been to jail. I did some time. You hear what I'm saying? I got out more'n a year ago. But now I'm just hitching, trying to get to where I need to be. I tell you brother, I just want to get to El Paso.'

'Well, in the circumstances,' I said. I cleared my throat. It was one of those situations in which no one could speak without first clearing their throat. 'In the circumstances I think it would be better all round if we could just drop you off.'

'Better for you. Not better for me.'

'Well I suppose that's true but, in the circumstances...' As well as constantly clearing my throat I was constantly using the phrase 'in the circumstances'. In the circumstances it was inevitable. 'Well, the truth is,' I went on, 'we were hoping to have a nice relaxing ride and now that doesn't seem at all possible. In the circumstances, in fact, it seems extremely unlikely.'

'See, here's the thing,' he said. 'I am not inclined to get out of the car.' It must be emphasized that he did not say this at all threateningly. He was simply stating his position, but it was impossible to state this particular position without conveying an element of threat. I was worried that he was the kind of person who suffered from mood swings. Violent mood swings. I suffer from them myself. But now my mood was not swinging so much as plunging or, if such a thing is possible, swinging violently in one direction. Jessica was gripping the wheel and keeping her eyes on the road. I was starting in some way to feel that it was predominantly her fault that we had got into this situation. If we had been on our own—I mean if we had somehow been in this same situation (i.e. not on our own) but somehow *on our own*—I would probably have lost my temper and told her as much.

'Lemme explain a few things,' he said. Because I was worried about cricking my neck I didn't twist around in my seat. I kept staring straight ahead into the darkness and the oncoming lights and the red tail-lights of cars in front of us. He had been in a supermarket just buying things, he said. His wife had been having an affair with another guy and this guy's brother worked in the supermarket and one day, when he was meant to be at work but had bunked off because he had flu...

I was looking at the cars coming, the hypnotic blur of lights, the inky sky, wondering what time we might get to El Paso...

And then when he came back to the supermarket... I realized I had drifted off, lost track of the story. In truth it wasn't a very good story, or at least he wasn't a very good storyteller. He kept bringing in all this irrelevant detail. I was very interested in his story but not in the way he told it. A few minutes earlier I was worried that he might be a murderer; now I was worried that he might be a bore but it was possible, of course, that he was a murderer and a bore. I had been feeling for several years now that I was losing the ability to concentrate, to listen to what people said, but I had never before reached such a pitch of inattentiveness at a time when it was important—so obviously in my best interests—to concentrate. It was so important to listen, to follow his story carefully, to pay attention, but I couldn't. I wanted to, I should have, but I couldn't. I just couldn't. It is because there are people like me doing jury service, people who can't follow what other people are saying, that there are so many wrongful convictions, so many miscarriages of justice. Whatever I was meant to be thinking about and concentrating on, I thought to myself, I was always thinking about something else, and that something else was always myself and my problems. As I was thinking this I realized that his voice had fallen silent. He had come to the end of his story. The defence had rested its case.

'We need petrol,' said Jessica.

'She means gas,' I said. A few miles later we pulled into a gas station and stopped. I hate putting gas in a car, especially in America where you have to pay first and it's all quite complicated and potentially oily. On this occasion, though, both Jessica and I wanted to put the gas in so that we would not be left alone in the car with this guy but we could not both get out because then he might have clambered over the seats and driven off without us. Except he could not drive off because we needed the key to unlock the fuel cap. I was not thinking straight because of the hitch-hiker and everything pertaining to the hitch-hiker situation. Both Jessica and I got out of the car. I did the filling up. It was quite easy. I watched the numbers—dollars, gallons and gallons of gas—spinning round the gauge on the gas pump. Although it was not my main concern it was impossible not to be struck by how much cheaper petrol was in America than in England.

Then our new friend got out of the car too. He was wearing black jeans and trainers. The trainers were not black but they were quite old. Jessica got back in the car. I was pumping gas. He looked at me. We were about the same height except he was a bit shorter. Our eyes met. When they had met before it was in the rear-view mirror of the car but now they were really meeting. In the neon of the gas station his eyes had a look that was subject to any number of interpretations. We looked at each other man to man. Black man and white man, English man and American man.

'I need to take a leak,' he said.

'Right,' I said. 'Go right ahead.' I said this in as neutral a tone as possible. I made sure my facial expression gave nothing away and then, worried that this non-expression manifested itself as a rigidity of expression which in fact gave everything away, I relaxed and smiled a bit.

'You ain't gonna up and leave me here are you?' he said.

'Leave you here?' I said. 'No, of course not.'

'You sure about that, brother?'

'I swear,' I said. He nodded and began walking slowly to the restrooms. He was dragging his left leg slightly. He took his time and did not look back. I watched his retreating form. As soon as he disappeared inside I released the trigger of the fuel line, clattered it out of the side of the car and banged it back into the metal holster of the pump. It fell noisily to the ground.

'You need to push the lever back up,' said Jessica. I did that. I pushed the lever back up and settled the awkward nozzle of the fuel hose back into it.

'Quickly!' said Jessica. I twisted the cap back on to the fuel tank but I did it too quickly and it would not go on properly and then, when I had got it on properly, I had problems with the key which I could neither turn nor extricate. There is much truth in the old adage 'more haste, less speed'. Eventually the lock turned and after much wiggling the key came out. I tossed it to Jessica who dropped it.

'Butterfingers!' I said.

'Why didn't you just *hand* it to me?' she said.

'Why can't you catch?' I said. I picked up the key, handed it to her and ran round the front of the car while she turned the key in the ignition. The engine roared into life.

'Go! Go! Go!' I shouted as I climbed into the passenger door. Jessica pulled away calmly and quickly, without squealing the tyres, and I shut the door.

We exited the gas station safely and smoothly and in seconds were out on the road. At first we were elated to have made our getaway like this. We high-fived each other. Ha ha!

'Did you like the way I said "I swear"?' I said.

'Genius!' said Jessica. We went on like this for a bit but we soon ran out of steam because although we still felt a bit elated we were starting to feel a bit ashamed too, and then, bit by bit, the elation ebbed away.

'Your door's not shut,' Jessica said after a while.

'Yes it is,' I said.

'No it's not,' said Jessica. I opened the door a crack and slammed it shut, shutter than it had been shut before.

'Sorry,' I said. 'You were right.'

'Doesn't matter,' said Jessica. Then, 'Was that a really terrible thing we just did?'

'I think it might have been.'

'Do you think it was racist?'

'I think it was just kind of rude. Judgemental. Rash.'

'Think how he's going to feel when he comes out of the toilet. He'll be so let down. He'll feel we treated him so shabbily.'

We drove on. The scene was the same—cars, lights, almost darkness. We were safe but perhaps we had always been safe. Now that we were out of danger it seemed possible that there had never been any danger.

'It's as if he were testing us,' said Jessica.

'I know. It's never a good feeling, failing a test,' I said. 'I still remember how I felt when I was seventeen and failed my driving test.'

'How did you feel?'

'I don't remember exactly,' I said. 'Not great. What about you? You probably passed first time.'

'I did,' she said, but there was no avoiding the real subject of the moment. After a pause Jessica said, 'Should we go back?'

'Perhaps we should.'

'But we won't, right?'

'Absolutely not,' I said and we both laughed. We drove in silence for several minutes. We were no longer elated but the vibe in the car was good again even though we were still ashamed, innocent of nothing and guilty of nothing, relieved at what we had done and full of regret about what we had done.

'You know those urban legends?' said Jessica.

'The vanishing hitch-hiker?'

'Yes. There's probably an axe in the back seat.'

I twisted around to look—a bit awkward with the seat belt. There was nothing on the back seat and nothing on the floor either, except two Coke cans and a bottle of water, all empty, and a torn map of White Sands.

'Nothing,' I said, rubbing my neck. We drove on. It was quite dark now. Night had fallen on New Mexico.

The dashboard lights glowed faintly. The fuel gauge was pointing almost to full.

'Well,' I said. 'We performed one useful service. At least we got him away from that area where it told you not to pick up hitch-hikers. He should be really grateful for that.' I said this but as I imagined him back there, coming out of the restroom and looking round the gas-station forecourt, I knew that gratitude would not be uppermost in his mind. There would have been plenty of other cars coming and going but he must have known, deep down, that the car he wanted to see, the car whose make he would have known—it was a Ford but beyond that I had not taken any notice—and which he hoped would still be there would be long gone. I could imagine how he felt and I was glad that I was not him feeling these things and I was glad, also, that it was just the two of us again, safe and in our car, married, and speeding towards El Paso. □

# THUG

## The True Story of India's Murderous Cult

by Mike Dash – author of *Tulipomania* and *Batavia's Graveyard*

'Dash has an historian's passion for the causes and consequences of
human behaviour, and turns his extensive research into an
idiosyncratic account' *Times Literary Supplement*

GRANTA

# THE SHIP AT ANCHOR
## Frederic Tuten

Mother was old now. After all the years of being her son, I could finally judge her age: old. I wanted to say, 'Just yesterday you were still young, Mom, but today you're old.' But that is not the thing you say to a mother, especially when she's come to visit and is settled by you in a wicker chair on a porch.

The boy was drawing, the sun was sliding into the pocket of the horizon; the ship lay tethered to a roving sea.

'The sea is roving under our eyes,' my mother said.

'The sea is roving, Dad,' the boy repeated. He was fond of replaying certain words when their sounds suggested a shape or an image to him. He often made drawings of sounds, like the word 'sound' itself, which looked like an empty cave with a hanging light bulb, or the word 'pirate', which he once represented—in his more literal, realist period—as a rat-shaped pie with an eye patch and a needle-thin sword.

That was just a visual pun, I explained, a translation of parts of a word to a picture, and thus was much less interesting than his usual, more abstract and evocative images. He agreed, he said, but it was much harder to make images representing the heart of a word. Those images were painful to make, he said, because they did not come from his eyes but from a place deep inside him, from a place he had no words to describe.

From your soul, I wanted to say, but explaining that would have taken him too soon to a world he would one day, and on his own, discover. For now, he was drawing from life the ship at anchor in a flat sea. He put a full red moon above her bow though there was none there in the sky, nothing glowing there at all, not even a hint of a star as the night fell. Soon we would have to put on the porch lights and soon we would have to go into the house.

'This will be for you, Nana,' he said, holding up the unfinished drawing to his grandmother.

'Why don't I take you along with it,' she said. 'Then I can have both of you all the time.'

He laughed. 'Nana, my Nana,' he said.

'Do you want me to get you some tea?' I asked my mother.

'I'll be going home soon,' she answered. 'Stay here with me a while longer and let's devour the time together.'

'Let's devour the whole night,' I said. 'Anyway, what's the point of going home when you're already home?' I liked her, my mother. I loved her as much as I had loved my wife.

The boy looked up from his drawing and said, 'Don't go, Nana.'

'I'll think about that,' she said. 'Come up here and give me a big hug first.'

He rushed to her, throwing his arms about her neck.

'Stay with us, please,' he said.

'Well, since you ask me so nicely, my dear boy,' she said, 'I think maybe I will.'

'Stay forever,' he said.

'Forever's a long time, don't you think?'

'Not long enough, Nana.'

'Forever's an eternity. I'd gladly spend an eternity with you, just as we are, right now,' she said, hugging him to her.

It was soon his bedtime. He made no fuss but asked that his Nana come up and read to him, as she always did when she stayed with us.

Of course she would, she said, since little else in the world made her happier than to read to him, to be with him, to kiss those cheeks so smooth with childhood, and his eyes, she said, to kiss those eyes so sweet with life. She took his hand, letting him lead her, step by step, up the stairs to his blue room papered with stars.

When they left, I brought out my binoculars and took a long look at the ship in the last light. She was a shabby hulk, black paint scaling off the bow, rigging flopping in the breeze, lines laying about uncoiled in slack heaps. Some men appeared now and then, smoking in a shiftless way, looking over the gunwales toward the shore, towards me, a speck on a porch. I waved, but no one answered.

The ship had lay there all day and into dusk and now, at night, lolled about with her running lights in dull glow, like a string of dirty pearls. When I went up to see the boy, the ship was out there, and even after I kissed him goodnight and turned off the light she was still there.

He was reading one of his Tintin books when I came in, and looked up at me at the last possible moment before he felt it impolite not to do so. He had good manners, in any case. You carry your civilization with you; his Nana had taught him that at an age when it could stick. He took to the idea instantly, seeing it as part of a game, which indeed it is. That was what had made him seem older than his years—his manners, and the kindness beneath them, which gave them value.

'I'm sorry,' I said. 'I know you want to go on reading but it's time for sleep.'

'Well,' he said, as if considering the point, 'Why don't you read to me.'

'It would be the same thing,' I said, 'because you would still be up and awake.'

He nodded. He seldom argued unless he thought I or the world was being unfair. 'Unjust' was his ultimate word of disapproval. A friend who had struck him in the back or a teacher who had berated him for another's wrongdoing was unjust, as was the world which caused night to come before its time. Tintin was his hero, because he was a boy who sought justice and fought to set the world right in all places and at all times of day.

'What does that ship want out there, Dad?' he asked.

'Who knows? Nothing much; it's just floating about until something better comes along.' The odd truth was that she didn't drift much the whole day, her position staying fixed as the sea dragged at her anchor and the wind pulled her from stem to stern, roving her about.

'You know,' he said, 'there's a ship just like that in Tintin, where the sailors keep the captain drunk so they can do whatever they want.'

'What did they want, my son?'

'To do mischief, Dad.'

'You must know a lot about that stuff.'

'Not me, Dad. I just do good mischief.'

'The mischief is that you just tricked me into letting you stay awake three more minutes.'

He laughed, having seen the justice in that.

'Goodnight then, Dad.' He waited for me to kiss him. The final one until morning and the protective seal against the bumps in the night.

I turned out the light and left the door open a fist wide so he'd see the reassuring hall light if he woke up in the dark. I stood by the door a few moments until I was certain he was asleep and safe in his dreams. Then I made another visit.

My mother was in her room reading. Ever since I could remember, she read in bed before going to sleep. One of her few certainties, everything else just slips away, she always said. As her husband did— in good health, in good mood. In love with his wife, with his work, with his son, me.

In a second he was gone. Mid-sentence, so to speak. On the phone laughing with an old friend one minute and in the mute other world the next, the phone still in his hand. Comical, actually. As if Death had no interest in hearing the whole conversation. What is so pressing that makes Death so curt, so interruptive of the narrative? Death, clearly, has no sense or desire for the complete story, which means he has no curiosity. Which is why he is so flat, so empty. A silhouette of action.

'Reading again, Mom? After lights out!'

'Oh! Just catching up with the past,' she said. She had earlier gone down to my library and pulled out *The Pilgrim's Progress*.

'A heavy stone before sleep, don't you think, Mom?'

'Not heavy enough,' she said. 'I was looking for *The Magic Mountain*, but you seem to be all out.'

'I'll have it for next time,' I said, 'and in German.'

'Does he miss her very much?' she asked abruptly.

'He doesn't say. But until a little while ago he used to call out for her in his sleep.'

'You know that I generally love you,' she said, turning from her book, 'but I love him more.'

'Maybe you just love him more freshly. In any case, I would feel the same.'

'I'd like to be around a while longer, long enough to see him when he first falls in love. That would be sweet,' she said.

'He's always in love now,' I said. 'Every week a new fling.'

'Not that way,' she said. 'The passionate way, I mean.'

She was once a beautiful woman, my mother; she was a handsome one now, more vain of her figure then when she was young, when she said that only the mind mattered, that while the body grew old and ugly, the mind lasted in its attractiveness. Mothers always tell their sons that, hoping they will not be stupid when they grow up, hoping they will not mistake the beautiful form for the soul in it, although sometimes the two may be joined.

'You mean the sexual way, Mom. Isn't that what you mean?'

'That too, of course. But mostly, I want to be there to help mend his broken heart the first time it gets broken.'

'Anyway,' I said, mouthing the platitude one says to the old: 'You still have a long time ahead of you.' She gave me a sly look: it said, who's kidding whom?

'Let me have ten more years, until he's seventeen. He'll be fully ripe then for love.'

'And what about you, Mom? Are you ripe for another love?'

'Not just now,' she said. 'Right now, I'm just roving. I'd rather meet a new book than a new man.'

'I thought you had read them all,' I said.

'Just the good ones.'

I took her hand and kissed it. 'You'll outlive us all, Mom.'

'I'd rather not,' she said. 'I'd just be left alone with bad books in bad bindings.'

I kissed her hand again, longer this time. And then once again. It was an old hand, like the parchment of a pirate map.

'Sweet dreams,' I said. 'Till morning.' Exactly her words to me at bedtime when I was my son's age. She'd blow me a kiss, and I'd imagine the cloud of her breath coating me with an invisible armour against all the world's harm.

'I may make an early start,' she said. 'I may be gone before you wake.'

I shrugged and turned up my palms as if to say, 'As you wish.' My protests would have been pointless. Not my son's though: what is more persuasive, after all, than a child's earnest plea?

I went out and across the field to my studio. My mother's light was still on even some while after I started trying to work. Where was she now in Bunyan's pilgrimage, I wondered, and what was so compelling about it to keep her awake for so long? The world and its stories, we're famished for them, and maybe, I thought, that is why Death is so jealous of us, since he has no story and is just an agent of terminations.

I was not an exceptional painter. I had gotten used to that idea long ago, before the boy was born, before I met my wife and fell in love with her. It was good for us that I had made that accommodation with myself before we met or I would have been an unhappy husband and a miserable father, gnawing at myself for my limits. What I could do well, I did. I found pleasure in the work so long as I did not yearn for what I was incapable of becoming in my dreams—an artist who painted what had never before been seen and who thus made the world newer and more interesting. The boy might one day do that. He was, I liked to think, already on that path.

I excelled in paintings of seascapes and harbour scenes, boats in port at sunset—lighthouses on cliffs in the whirl of a white storm I also did very successfully. Not very original work, but mine, I liked to think; work which was rewarded not lavishly but sufficiently well to keep a decent life.

For my own pleasure, perhaps for the glow, the vanity of the association, I made copies of narrative paintings long disregarded by the Modernists but still beloved by a few, myself included, obviously. Poussin was then in progress on my easel. Not him, naturally, but his painting in which shepherds are contemplating a plinth inscribed with the words EGO IN ARCADIA SUM. 'Even in Arcadia I am', meaning Death is omnipresent, even in the most beautiful places, where life richly abounds, where bounty reigns. I had still to finish the figure of the shepherdess, a woman ravishingly solid, and simple, like an Ionian temple in a sacred grove of cypresses.

I had been stuck for a while trying to complete her, because each time I painted her face, it was not the face Poussin had rendered but the young face of my dead wife. As if my mind saw one thing but my hand another, and nothing I did made the face look as I intended.

I sometimes thought it a good thing, a sign of something original living within me. But, finally, I could not bring myself to let my little hint of romantic autobiography disfigure Poussin's masterpiece, so I sponged out my wife's face, leaving the shepherdess's torso headless, in white, anonymous space. Audacity in art and in life was never my style. Even at the end, when Death comes and pays his one and only visit, I know that I'll follow him meekly, acquiescent and compliant. 'No trouble,' I'll say. 'Here I come.'

I stayed in this self-defeating mood—the best to keep one from working—for who knows how long, when the boy rushed in barefoot, pale, and frightened.

'Did you have a bad dream?' I asked, lifting him up in my arms.

He did, and when he woke he went first to my room, where I was not, and then to his Nana's room, where she was sleeping in a strange way. When he tried to wake her she would not wake. And so he came to me.

She was still in her bed sleeping, her book open. She was sleeping with blank eyes fixed on words. Was the story that bad, Mom, I wanted to ask, that you would rather have died than continue reading it, calling for Death to spare you from another boring syllable?

Nana was sleeping a sleep of sorts, I told my son. The sleep that carries you to the edge of life and then drops you into another life, one which we could not join while still awake. That is what I told him.

She was now where his mother had gone, where we all one day would go, where our souls would go, his and mine, too. The soul, I said, thinking it now was the best time to tell him, was that strange, unknown, invisible thing he felt inside him when he made drawings of sounds.

He knew that, he said, he had known it for a long time because Nana had taught him that long ago. But all that didn't matter because he wanted his Nana here, with him, and not there with them.

'With whom do you mean?' I asked.

'With the men in the ship,' he said. He had dreamt that she was taken there, and that was what had woken him, his dream of her being carried away to the ship. So he was glad when he saw that she was still there in bed, until he realized, when she would not wake, that it was the other, invisible part of her they had taken away.

'That was a sweet dream,' I said, 'but only a dream.'

'It was not a dream,' he said. She was there on that ship and, he added firmly, we should go there and rescue her.

'Tomorrow,' I said, 'in the morning,' after he had a good night's sleep and thought things over in the daylight, in the light that dispelled dreams and brought them to reason.

'It'll be too late then, Dad,' he said. 'We'll never get her back if we wait.' My boy looked so much older now, when he spoke, older than I was, older and more knowing than the sea when it lies flat and blue in its bed.

'I believe you, my dear boy,' I said. 'Yes, of course, we must go.'

And off we went, down to the dinghy, the boy at the prow and me at the oars, and we rowed out to the ship, glowing cherry red under the full red moon.

And no sooner had we reached the ship's black hull then we were wafted aloft by a magical wind to its disorderly deck, and just as soon, as if on an elevator cloud, we floated below to a drab galley amidships and landed among a sullen, noisy crew and its unshaven, peg-legged Captain—who got right down to business.

'You can't have her,' he said.

'Then Death will,' the boy said.

The crew went silent and looked about apprehensively. I was astonished at his words, almost as much I was by all the events that had led to them. He seemed so certain, my boy, of things unknown and strange, and it was clear that he was strongly in charge and that I was now under his wing.

Then the Captain laughed and, emboldened by him, the others followed suit, but hollowly.

'What do you know about this matter, my little fellow?' he asked nervously.

'Enough to make you be sorry,' my son said.

'Sit down,' the Captain said, 'and let's palaver like gentlemen of the world.'

He waved his arm and suddenly the galley glowed with rich furniture and golden lamps, and there appeared out of the air a huge candle-lit table heaped with golden bowls of fruit and nuggets of chocolates wrapped in gold tissue. The Captain beckoned my son to sit beside him, waving me to the table's other end, where I sat beside a man in silver trousers and a shirt so blue I could see the sky.

'Well, lad, what have you got to say?' the Captain asked, spearing a red pear with a silver poniard.

'Well, sir, I want Nana's soul and I want it back inside her.'

'I have her soul, but I can't undo what Death has done, and neither can you. So that's the final word on that,' he said, slicing his pear to a sliver the weight of a breath.

The crew murmured their approval of their Captain's firmness.

'Hear, hear,' my tablemate called out.

'I understand, Captain,' my boy said. 'Death has his power and you have yours.'

'Quite,' the Captain said.

'But you've stolen my Nana's soul from Death.'

'Let's say we got it on its way to somewhere else. Right, my lads?'

I understood at last that we were on a pirate ship of souls. That these pirates had waylaid my mother's soul from its true journey through the world's seamless mystery.

'What do you do with the souls you've pirated?' I asked.

'We shred them for mulch,' he said, with a big wink of the eye that was not patched.

'We trade them,' another pirate said. 'Small souls for larger, large souls for grand souls, grand souls for noble ones.'

'Whom do you trade with?' my boy asked.

'Why with other pirates, of course,' the blue shirt answered.

'Enough,' the Captain said. 'We're not here for disquisitions.'

'My Nana had a noble soul, I'm sure,' the boy said.

'Of great value, of incredible value, of priceless value. What have you of trading value to match her worth?' the captain asked.

My son whispered into the Captain's ear, whispered something that piqued the pirate chief to cough up a sigh of a thousand fish-eyed bubbles.

'Even if you could do that, why would I care?' the Captain said when the last bubble burst into a little hand of flame.

'Because then you can always see Him.'

'See what?' the Captain shouted.

'See Him,' my boy said.

'Well,' the Captain said, 'this needs some thought.' He called his men to gather around him, speaking to them so softly that I could not catch his words.

One of the pirates exclaimed, 'Trumped by a boy!'

'Still,' the Captain said, turning to my son, 'I don't see the usefulness in having His picture. It's not,' he said in an aside to his crew, 'that He's such a looker.'

'But you may find a use one day,' my son said, ignoring the crew's roar of laughter. 'Maybe you will trade with Him something He wants.'

'That's an idea, Captain,' said the blue shirt, 'maybe we can get Him not to bother us so much, Him always pestering us to give back the souls we've snatched.'

'What would He want to trade, my brave bucko? Nothing pleases Him, nothing interests Him, nothing satisfies Him, except the taking from Life everything that lives.'

'He may want,' my boy said, in a voice firm enough to drive a nail through a beam, 'not to be seen.'

'Show me, boy,' the Captain said, 'then we'll decide who gets what.'

'But you must first promise to give back her soul to where it belongs.'

'Oh! I promise,' the Captain said with a wink to his men.

My boy began drawing on a large white napkin, holding it up to the Captain when he was finished.

'Doesn't look like much to me,' the Captain said, turning the napkin about this way and that.

'It's not a picture of Him,' I said. 'It's a transcription of His name to His image. The boy can do that with most sounds. He can do that with your name, if you want.'

'I have no name,' he said, looking frightened. 'So don't be asking me for one.'

'None of us have names, neither,' said the blue shirt. 'Isn't that right, men?'

'No, no, no,' they said in a chorus. 'None of us have any kind of names.'

'Because when you say His name,' I continued, 'the sound of it vanishes into the air and He vanishes along with it, keeping all His power with him.'

The Captain remained silent for a moment then beckoned his men to gather about him in a circle, where they spoke in crowish barks, very sharp and unsettling. I was fearful and thought of quietly taking my son back the way we came, back to our dinghy and over the dark water, back to our house, where we would be safe.

'Let's go, my boy,' I whispered. 'Let's leave while there's still time.'

'No, Dad,' he said firmly. 'You go, if you want. I need to stay.'

I was so amazed by his audacity that I almost forgot that he was just a boy and that I was his father and had a father's authority. But just as I was about to assert myself, the Captain broke from his men and returned to us, his armed crossed, his face a powdery white smoke.

'We have decided to keep your drawing and to keep your grandmother's soul, to boot. What do you say to that?'

'That Death has many names in many languages, and that now you have His image in only one of them. You can steal my picture but you still won't have the drawings of his other names, drawings that I could trade with you when you needed me to.'

'A valiant answer from such a small boy. But then, even for a brave boy, you are brave,' the Captain said, giving me a look I took to mean that in the area of courage the son surpassed the father.

The blue shirt came up and whispered into the Captain's ear, a long whisper, the length of a woollen string. The Captain nodded slowly and turned to me and my son.

'Let's go above deck,' he said.

Before I could say a word, we were all above deck, under a black heaven, moonless and distraught. I put my arm about my son's waist and held him fast.

'You've won, my boy,' the Captain said. 'Your grandmother's soul is going where it belongs.'

'Let me see it,' my son said.

'You can't see it,' the blue shirt man said. 'It has no visibility.'

'Nor weight, nor colour, nor odour,' the Captain added. 'It has nothing of the qualities you expect in your world.'

'How will I know you've freed her soul then,' my boy asked, 'how will I know you've kept your word?'

'Stand very still,' the Captain ordered. 'And you right beside him,' he said, pointing to me with his sword. 'Notice, that there is no wind, no breeze, no movement of air, that there is only stillness and the flat screen of night.'

'Yes,' I said, 'there's not the faintest stir.'

'Now, hold your breath, the two of you.'

We stayed very still, not breathing, and suddenly felt, for the quickest of seconds, a feathery whisper brush our faces.

'That's that, then,' the Captain said.

'That's what?' I asked, annoyed by his mumbo-jumbo, by what I thought were his theatrical airs.

'Her last breath just flew by you,' he said; 'her last breath, carrying her soul.'

At his final words, we found ourselves, my boy and I, returned to our house. The ship had vanished, leaving, where it had once been, a black line of sea.

I carried my sleepy son to his bed and left his sleeping self to digest the night. I went to my room, thinking I would read and reflect on the night's strange and wonderful events, and then, at early morning, I would start my mother's procession—my wife's same route—from house to funeral parlour, and from there to the grave. I always kept a stack of books on the night table, books I chose randomly and whose pages I read in no order and in small bites. For this reason I read little fiction, enjoying poetry and aphoristic writings, by artists, especially. It was to Ingres I turned that night, thinking to find a sweet passage to ease me from images of death and pirated souls. 'A true line,' it read, 'is closer to god than any church.' It was a noble thought, designed to assure artists of their value, or to make them feel inadequate and forever striving.

I repeated the sentence a few times and then shut my eyes for the few hours before daylight. Somehow, the artist's words made me more melancholy than the fantastic events on the pirate ship, more sad than my mother's death, which already seemed so long ago, before there were mothers. Those words made me wonder why I ever wanted to be an artist, why I ever wanted to live, though I never thought I wanted to die. I tried very hard to quiet myself, to calm my thoughts, but I could not.

I wondered how my son was faring after such a powerful night, so I went down to his room. But he was not in his bed, which was perfectly made, as if the housekeeper had come and trimmed the sheets and flattened out the blankets. I went from room to room, went up to the attic and down to the basement, searching and searching for my boy. I went to my mother's room, but he was not there either, or, oddly enough, was she. I would think about her later; for the moment, however, I was not concerned about my mother, knowing that wherever her body was mattered little, now that her soul was on its adventures. I had not yet started to grieve her death, so busy was I in the events of the night, but I knew that I had an eternity before me to grieve.

I finally went out to my studio, sure that my son had gone there, where he had often come with his mother to visit me at my work, where he felt safe among the stacks of drawings and tubes of paint, safe in the place where, for all my regrets of not being the artist I had dreamed of being, I had been most happy. He liked my happiness, my boy, as had his mother; it made them feel safe, where nothing much else was safe.

Imagine, I started to say, imagine that my mother had so little control over life as to have her husband die on the phone in mid-sentence, and imagine how she had so little to say over things that she herself had died in mid-read, so to speak. So little control over our life and none in death and its aftermath, no voice to say where your soul went, if it went anywhere at all, granted it had not been plucked from your last breath and stowed aboard a pirate ship for trading.

'Don't give it a thought,' my mother answered, once, when as a boy I asked where we went when we died. I did not give it a thought for a long time, having erased the question from my view until my wife died. But soon after, I wondered whether the dead ever missed the living, or whether they entered a new world where nothing of the past lived and where no one who had lived in it any longer mattered. My mother dreamed of an eternity spent in a library, where she could read all the books of the world in all their languages. How many millions of books there would be, Mom, I said, awed by such a vast project. Yes, she said, but one day, in just another day of eternity, she would have read every book ever written, and then where would she be?

The studio—except for the feeling of stale dust and emptiness— was much as I had left it except that the paintings looked tired, sagging on their stretchers. Paintings need to be seen or they languish, wither and die on the vine. My unfinished Poussin was leaning—languishing—against a windowless wall, though I was sure I had left it on the easel when I went out to visit the ship at anchor. I would have loved to have finished that canvas, and this time I hoped I would have the courage to paint my wife's face where the shepherdess's was supposed to be. The courage to leave, for however long it lasted, a trace of my heart.

My son was not in the studio, even though the morning sunlight now flooded the large sad room. What I mean is, that although it was light, he had still not appeared. Whatever that meant, I was worried now, because I missed him so much, and I was frightened of a life where I would always miss him.

'I miss you, too, of course,' I said guiltily to my wife, in case she had read my thoughts from somewhere in the universe. 'And I will miss you, as well,' I said to my mother, not wanting her to feel left unloved. But of course, missing a son is different from missing all others, who return to you in various guises. Unlike the sparrows, sons do not return in the spring.

In the middle of my musings, the door opened and my son came in with a beautiful young woman. He was tall now, with a faint red moustache, and he walked with a seaman's gait, as if to steady himself against the rolling deck of the world. He had his arm about the beautiful woman's waist. She was full of smiles for him and he held her like a man confident he is loved. I was happy for him and wished my mother could see him, a young man in love.

'Dad,' he sighed, in a low sigh of evocation, memory and longing. Then he slowly looked about the studio, even above, at the beams under the high open ceiling, looked about as if searching for me and our old life there. But I was nowhere to be found. □

*For Kenji*

GRANTA

# THE FALCON
## Gilad Evron

TRANSLATED FROM THE HEBREW
BY EVAN FALLENBERG

In general, whenever Mooly, the commander of Gihon, washes his hands, the circular motions whip up colourful bursting soap bubbles, his long, sturdy fingers embrace one another as they rotate and he rinses off the soap with water, lathers up again and rinses, wiping them scrupulously on a dry towel and then once again, towelling between his fingers.

That same thoroughness and attention to cleanliness and perfection are evident in the Gihon commander's uniform. Even after a day of muddy or dust-filled military activity, in dry, parching heat or suffocating humidity, the stains on his uniform always appear like a crusty peel of colour that can be removed with the flick of a finger. His uniforms always retain the marks of ironing, the pleats, the stiffness of starch and the shiny freshness of new cloth, even if they are not new.

The Gihon commander's presence of mind, too, suits clean uniforms and dry hands. He has made a name for himself with the rational moderation of his command, his highly responsible nature, and the exemplary order evident in every aspect of his unit's functioning. His complete devotion to his soldiers and his concern for their every need are, on occasion, overly pedantic, but he is equally insistent about maintaining time schedules and carrying out minor commands as well as major ones, so that the slightest hint of impropriety toward the occupied population by soldiers of the Gihon unit is enough for him to put them on trial and to allow himself a very rare expression of anger.

He once called Gihon a limb of his own body.

Generally speaking, relations with his wife and his two young daughters are good, though in his capacity as officer in a combat unit he does not see them on a daily basis. Every other Friday, when the girls hear his car come to a halt in the parking area of their one-storey house, on the other side of the hedge in their garden, they run out to give him a hug. They take his short-barrelled sub-machine gun from him, brandishing it proudly through the front door of the house, shouting gaily, Father's home! During the summer months, at the hour Mooly customarily waters his small garden and takes pleasure in the growth of seedlings recently planted, it sometimes happens that the neighbour, a young accountant, extends his hand in greeting over the hedge that separates their grassy yards.

His wife generally greets him as he sets down his suitcase in the foyer, under the hat rack affixed there even though neither of them wears hats. They hug and kiss, his wife says his name two or three times in a pleasant, girlish tone—*Mooly, Mooly, Moolili*—and he mumbles variations on her name—*Naomileh, Nomishin, Nomishini*—while the girls cling to the pleats of his trousers. He sits with the girls in the living room and they chat with him and are happy in his presence, undoing his shoelaces and tugging on his boots, together, until they manage to remove them triumphantly and noisily from his large feet. After that they roll his socks off and count his toes, in order—in their words—'to make sure nobody has stolen one', and then they grab the laces, dragging the boots behind them, each girl with her own, into the garden.

When he enters his bedroom and undresses in order to change into civilian clothes, his wife enters too, locking the door behind her. This is the sign that she is prepared for sexual contact. When his sexual organ stands erect, filled with blood, he feels how eager he is to lie with her. This is also the moment he realizes how completely absent his sexual urges were during the previous two weeks. His wife makes do with removing her underpants from beneath her short skirt and they engage in hasty intercourse, knowing from experience that this contact will not last long, breathing heavily and flailing about like fish and trying to swallow their moans, while on the other side of the wall, during the hot months, in the presence of the lawn and the wheel of a bicycle and an army boot, they can hear the neighbour playing like a child with the girls. The voices hum near their ears between the slivers of light that breach the room through the slats of the shutters, and the silhouette of the neighbour holding a hose erect may pass over the wall, or may not, and a lulling melody may be heard from a radio somewhere, music from a sweetened past, or it may not be heard, or may not sweeten. The wife does not expect to reach a state of release from this contact, the first of three they will, in general, conduct over the weekend, unless she surprises herself and gets carried away. In principle she prefers the loss of self-control that full sexual contact provides her with to the occasional masturbation she engages in, in which she remains in control despite the pleasure. In the ensuing silence between the couple, in which they slip in and out of slumber, with the girls' chatter and the tap-tapping of the neighbour's sprinklers in the background, there arises a longing for some moment that perhaps existed or perhaps did not, and that longing pops when thought stumbles upon it and wonders about it—if it does, in fact, stumble upon it.

At sunset they drive to the home of his parents, who live in a small agricultural village. It is a house that has been slightly expanded over the years but which has remained modest; nevertheless, Mooly's mother receives each arriving family member for what she calls 'The Friday Feast' with the ceremoniousness of a grand estate, planting a kiss on one cheek and then the other, declaiming in a tortured French that seems charming to her but which occasionally slips into an incomprehensible tongue-twisting gurgle. *Arrivé!* She invites the family members in. *Quelle famille!* And it is, indeed, a large family: assembled are the brothers and sisters, the married ones and the unmarried ones, the ones with children and those without, friends who will one day become family members, or not, the children, the babies, and those that are no longer babies, a few cousins whose genealogical connection is a mystery to all but who always enjoy this large gathering of the clan, and one lone uncle, for there is always one lone uncle.

They all push into the living room, which is not large but is full of furniture and games and the remains of agricultural machinery that the mother has turned into 'art', and now the room is overflowing, and the babies are put down on the floor to crawl and the adults bend down to cluck their tongues at them and they continue conversations they have not begun or they express opinions on a proposal that has not been clarified, or aired, because the conversation does not develop and is cut short again, because with the pressure of newly arriving guests they are pushed into a different corner, and a platter of refreshments is served to those standing or sitting, or they are sucked out of the house and spewed into the front yard, since the room is too narrow to contain all that compressed human traffic, and cries of exultation at rediscovered acquaintances can be heard, and friendly, energetic slaps on the back, and kisses and caresses, and breathless questions and hazy answers, and cracked plastic drinking cups, and laughter, and mouths, and eyes, and fingers, and shoulders, and hair, and a skullcap, and teeth, and a smile, a smile, a smile, and *Where have you been?* and *What's up?* and *Wow, fantastic!* and memories and zeal, and buried anger, and

joy, and desolation, and *What do you say about the situation?*
Especially they ask the commander of Gihon—Moolish, they call
him—about 'the situation'; even though there are other officers in
the standing army and in the reserves present, they prefer to
interrogate him, as someone whose famed presence of mind conceals
true knowledge, as someone thought of as an authority, and this in
spite of the fact that he is careful always to speak in very general
terms, and in fact almost never satisfies their curiosity, just as he
abstains from discussing any topic that might have political
ramifications. 'I am not a political person,' he says, dissociating
himself every time one of those present attempts to pry from his
mouth some sort of statement of conviction or affirmation. 'A
political person,' he defined it once at one of these meetings, 'is
someone who tries to paint reality in some colour. I choose to look
at reality without colour filters.'

Even when his interrogators take leave of him, their desires
unsatisfied, they are, nonetheless, appeased, for 'their' Moolish's
seriousness pacifies them. With officers like Moolish, they like to say
to one another, we can sleep in peace. But Moolish, in spite of the
crowding and the many faces turned to him in curiosity, is careful to
check, from time to time, that his daughters have found girls their own
age to play with at the fringes of the brouhaha, and if they have not,
then he will verify that they are off in search of cats, their favourite
activity at his parents' house. Cats that move about in silence, in the
shadows, under the leaves of a wide and fleshy palm. *Catch it, catch
it*, they call out to one another, excited, brave, fearful, alone.

The father of the family, too, is spewed out from the crowd in
the room and the foyer. With a bottle of red wine in his hand he
advances toward Mooly, in the yard, as if he has just suddenly
noticed him; even then he is in no hurry. He uncorks the wine bottle
and ostentatiously pours two glasses, one eyebrow raised, as if to
call his son's attention to the fact that these are not plastic cups, but
long-stemmed glass goblets. He invites his son to stroll with him,
taking hold of his elbow as if to hint at serious matters needing
clarification and consideration at a distance from the mob of family
members. They circle the house while taking measured sips from
their wine goblets, until they reach the backyard, which faces a
spacious furrowed field, and they stop, and the father pours once

again from the bottle, and again they drink moderately from their goblets and the father flourishes the bottle as if to show off its quality, and Mooly takes it from him in order to appraise it, and each time it is a different bottle and it is up to the son to tilt his head as if he were a connoisseur. But it is never possible for him to read the label, since the light from the cold neon bulb affixed to the wall of the house is only strong enough to illuminate in silent pallor the furrows made by the plough, or the heads of the watermelons sown each year, which look like children's heads dotting the earth, growing smaller as they stretch from the straw at the edge of the yard to the top of the little hill, behind which stand the tops of several old, disfigured and stubborn cypress trees. From some wedding hall somewhere a vocalist can be heard screeching at some party, and his voice is carried by the wind, so that sometimes it is clear and flowing and sometimes far off and nearly muted, but it is always there, for people marry and reproduce incessantly, and the voice is enough to turn the field and the hill into scenery that conceals the suburbs of the city nearby, and just knowing that the city is lying in wait, right on the other side of the hill, planning its conquest with hordes of people and poisoned sewage, just knowing this depresses and embitters the father so that he tends to drink, and then he feels better. But sometimes he does not feel better, because he remembers that once, when he built his home, the wilderness that surrounded his house extended on and on, and only then, he says, he felt truly free.

Their glasses are filled for the third time and the father jiggles the bottle to prove that it has been emptied, and they stand sipping their third glass of wine slowly, as if to encourage one another to speak. Sometimes they do speak, and on occasion the father even utters a harsh and summarizing statement concerning his life. The son remains silent as if to give the words their due, but then he says, with reluctance, that his father is talking nonsense. After a silence that is meant to express a rethinking and even irony, the father says that perhaps he has, indeed, been talking nonsense. The son is slightly sorry about these pronouncements, but since he has heard them so many times they lose their meaning each time he hears them. With greater vigour he experiences the pleasant sensation of the wine spreading through his limbs. He hugs his father's shoulders and kneads them, loosening him up. When they do not speak—and

during most of their time behind the house drinking they do not—
and when the father is not uttering his statements of nonsense, he
does not hug his father's shoulders.

They may stand like that for quite a long while facing the field,
until the voices that always rise up from the house in search of
Moolish reach their ears. Where's Moolish gone? And where's the
father? They always turn and re-enter the house. Moderately.

On their drive back home, the pleasant sensation in his body
brought about by the wine dissipates a little, and Naomi, his wife,
cautiously expresses a measure of disappointment in the family
gathering. In anticipation of the well-attended get-together she is
roused each time by new expectations and even excitement, but each
time at the end of the evening she feels like some opportunity has
been missed. She assumes the reason is her inability to engage in
meaningful communication in the overcrowding and tumult that
always swamp the tiny house. There are, among the guests, those
who interest her, but nothing can possibly develop in such
overcrowding. What's even more frustrating is that she knows this
is how it will be, and nonetheless develops expectations as the
gathering grows near, and then disappointment creeps in, and with
it anger, mostly toward the 'Arrivé!' of his mother and her gurgled
'Bon appetit!' That pretentious French! That artificiality! Suddenly
she is boiling mad without knowing why, and only belatedly does
she take note of the impression her words are likely to make on her
husband and on her daughters in the back seat of the car. But the
two little girls are asleep and her husband expresses sympathy and
says, moderately, that he understands how she feels.

In spite of everything, the return home is pleasant. Their small
community is quiet and dark, the well-tended green yards stand guard
in the shadows over comely, unostentatious houses, the girls fall asleep
again as soon as they are carried to their beds, the snacks that the
couple tiredly nibble together in the kitchen are crispy as they should
be, the crickets are chirping outside, the sprinklers tap-tap just as
sprinklers should do, the rumble of a faraway car can be heard from
the main road a long way off, and sexual desire spills into their limbs
again and encircles them and thrusts them together, and softens, and
stimulates. This time, without the hastiness of the first sexual contact,
they climb into bed in anticipation of pleasure that will last for a long

while. Their familiarity enables each of them to know what gives the other the most pleasure, so they do not rush to reach what is most powerfully stimulating. Thus, even if Naomi licks, for example, the sexual organ of Moolili-Moolili, or gently suckles his testicles, she does not exaggerate, knowing that he is liable to spurt his semen before he wishes to, while he manages, in spite of fingers whose touch is not particularly graceful or delicate, to expose her clitoris, naked beneath the flap of flesh and the soft, tight curls, though he does not pounce for fear of over-stimulation. And the world shrinks gradually to contain only their bodies, their sexual organs, until it beats inside them alone and, whenever possible, if in the midst of the excitement and the passion and the increasingly tight movement one manages to insert his or her tongue into the other's mouth while the saliva is still flowing, they might even attain release simultaneously. On occasion they do manage it, and then they feel for a while that they are a couple suited to one another, that they are happy and satisfied and that they have fulfilled their idea of a good marriage to its very limits.

The commander of Gihon devotes the following day to his family. The girls ride on his back on the living-room carpet and proudly show off their drawings, helping him in the garden with their tiny plastic trowels to plant flowers in the small, loose-soil beds, but as autumn approaches they make do with weeding dry grasses and putting forth serious suggestions with regards to a suitable animal for the cage behind the house that perhaps once housed a killer dog but that later became a tool shed, though it would be quite fitting for some new animal to reside there, and the three of them wave to Mama behind the wall of decoratively spaced cinder blocks that hides the kitchen appliances and the toil that takes place in their vicinity. 'Mama, can you see me?' Mama is washing Father's clothes, drying them, ironing them, airing Father's suitcase. 'Mama, can you see us?' She prepares lunch, perhaps some guests will show up, maybe a neighbour will pop by. 'Mama, we're here!' And while she works Mama listens to the History Hour programme on the radio and sometimes a wave of anger bubbles up inside her again and her hands ball up into fists until her knuckles turn white, and after that it is all forgotten, since the fresh scent of her hair blows her way with the pleasant wind coming through the decorative spaces in the cinder-block wall. 'Mama! Can you give me a kiss?'

Sometimes married friends show up for lunch, and sometimes not, sometimes with children and sometimes not, with a dog, without a dog, and the day is a bit slow, a bit tiresome, cloudy or not, hot or not, and it is time for the afternoon siesta, and how nice when a little playmate comes over to invite his two little friends to his house, and the next generation walks down the sidewalk in single file, and the red wine blurs the adults' senses and a sort of sadness, whose source no one can identify, settles heavily upon them, though no one takes its presence seriously since it is composed of brittle, crumbly matter, and after a brief nap Mooly wakes up, often feeling fatigued and dully impatient rather than refreshed. I'm a human being too, he is sometimes in the habit of pointing out in the army and at home, even when it is hardly to the point, but the couple try, nevertheless, to behave moderately toward one another, summoning gaiety in order to conceal the distress of their approaching separation, when the commander of Gihon returns to the army.

In the evening he kisses his tender daughters, who dissolve in his arms, and promises to 'bring something back with him', and to 'win the war'. He speaks over the phone with his father and promises him all sorts of things, and with his mother, to whom he promises all sorts of different things, and takes his leave of her with an '*Adieu*', and with his brother he jokes good-humouredly and with forgiveness, since his brother always tries to drag him into a political discussion that has 'moral ramifications', in his brother's words, but Mooly patiently explains his objections to introducing politics into the conversation, and he responds with the same amazement he has harboured for years: how is it that his brother cannot adjust to the thought that some people are simply apolitical? This position drives his brother crazy, since it prevents him from clarifying the underlying *principles*, he shouts, and Mooly calms him down by telling an old joke, at which the brother laughs, even though he remarks that the joke is so old that it has grown a long beard.

In the evening the couple finishes packing the suitcase together, they hang the ironed uniform on a clothes hanger, and they discuss Naomi's studies and her job, which are, according to Mooly's assessment, clearly no less important than his own work. Afterwards they shower and undertake their third and last sexual contact of the weekend. It contains neither the buttock-squeezing pressure of their first encounter nor the prolonged bubble of the second. It contains a measure of anxiety, almost anger, and they do not bother with one another; rather, each one concentrates on his own satisfaction, hostile, almost aggressive, a sort of chaos that surprises and stimulates them more than the safe and usual movements of their first two encounters, which at the same time emphasizes the feeling of loneliness, so that even while they are still held together by their throbbing organs they are no longer together. They have parted.

The next afternoon the Gihon unit entered the Palestinian village of Umm-al-Maya in a convoy of armoured vehicles studded with heavy artillery, and took control. The narrow and twisting streets emptied of villagers in an instant, leaving behind in the dirt the quick imprint of a child running, the shadow of a hurried glance, the sound of shutters clacking shut and pupils dilating with hatred. The front-line command squad spread out around the perimeter of the village against the harsh backdrop of dark, rocky hills facing two other villages in the distance.

That night, rain began to puncture the earth with heavy drops and to spray deflected water from the rocks, cables swung in the wind against leaning poles, the ground flowed with slippery, sucking mud, lightning flashed in the distance and a freezing cold settled on the hills.

After midnight it was decided that the soldiers should not be permitted to remain in their field tents, which were convulsing in the winds. Rotating sentries from the front-line command stood guard while all the other soldiers from the unit infiltrated the stone houses of the village. They awakened the families of villagers from their sleep, conducted searches, posted a guard, ordered the family to bunk with one another in order to make room for them and within a short while the thickened breath of sleeping soldiers filled the confiscated rooms, and the homey sound of snoring no doubt stuck in the ears of the huddling residents, who became strangers in their own homes in spite of the soldiers' apologies.

The commander of Gihon selected for his own residence a lofty stone house at the edge of the village. A stooped old woman stood in the hallway, shrunken, as two officers under his command, their sub-machine guns close to their hips, searched, passed through, hurriedly scanned each room.

Gilad Evron

The commander of Gihon selected 'the master's study', as the old woman called it, spread out his sleeping bag on a wide old leather sofa, removed his boots, placed them on an embroidered rug and fell asleep immediately.

In the morning, when one of his soldiers brought him his coffee and breakfast, the master of the house was presented to him. Not a young man, ungainly and obese, he wore thick glasses, nodded his head in confusion, and smoked, blowing nervous smoke rings from his thick lips and wheezing. The many twisted folds of skin on his face expressed a storm of emotions and fear.

Mooly introduced himself and invited the master to join him for a cup of coffee. The master of the house introduced himself as Chef Sayed. They drank thick, hot coffee together on the desk. The master's facial muscles spoke even when he was silent, observing the officer diligently, curiously, suspiciously, as Mooly scanned the study, taking note of the triangular windows near the ceiling, the stone walls and floor, the standing lamp that curved like the neck of a swan, and the leather sofa upon which he had slept. It seemed that the master was noticing the room and its contents anew through the impression it made on the officer. Afterwards, with his wheeze and clumsy walk, he led Mooly—at Mooly's request—on a tour of the rest of the rooms of the house, chattering anxiously in his rich English, as if eager to prove innocent of all guilt, which had anyway not been cast upon him.

When they stopped in front of the courtyard, Chef Sayed told him about the large house, which had been built by his grandfather, once the village chief, and about his family members, who had dispersed around the globe to study and work and who did not wish to return to live under Israeli occupation. Further, he related how they had held counsel with regards to who in the family could maintain the house, since it was clear that if no one lived in it, the house would be taken over by someone, and that that someone would make it his own, and how they had chosen him, Chef Sayed, who had, in fact, travelled the world and seen quite a bit and even fathered a child somewhere, but who had ultimately reached a dead end. He accepted their entreaties to return home and live in the spacious house in exchange for a modest salary, and in this way was able to put an end to his failed efforts at finding a source of income. The family talent for action had evaded him, Chef Sayed explained, panting and groaning and gasping as they climbed the stairs to the second floor. He was not fit, so the family opined, for practical living; rather, he was content with what they termed 'inaction'.

The second-storey bedrooms were cold and empty, and the echo of the storm raging outside the windows was trapped inside them. While their gaze drifted, against their will, to the wide expanse of hills fading into the wind and rain, Chef Sayed continued with his chattering, obsequious anxiety, trying to establish a rapport with Mooly for the price of his own humiliation, and said that he too sometimes feared he would succeed at nothing. Occasionally, he admitted, he was indeed struck by chronic 'inaction', compiled by periods of depression from which he emerged weak and tormented, but there were other times during which he was able to read and to delve deeply into his reading, and then an odd happiness would overtake him and he would engage in the cooking that he loved so well and would even take pains to make social contact with his neighbours, who were friendly, if a bit primitive. Anyway, what remained during times like these, in these hills, if not expressions of fraternity and friendliness? It was a rhetorical question, which he answered himself. Were the local population not suffering from Israeli occupation they would most likely be happier, he said, even though he had seen places more miserable than his own which were not under occupation. The big question was whether the pursuit of happiness had any meaning. And what was happiness? 'What's your opinion, Micky?' he asked Mooly, the commander of Gihon, whom he had for some reason renamed 'Micky' with a familiarity that contradicted reality, and with an invasion of privacy that was intolerable, and with an unrivalled desire to bestow his words with the power to change the way things are.

The commander of Gihon was silent for a while, then expressed his official apologies on behalf of the Israeli army for invading Chef Sayed's house, and promised to interfere as little as possible, which was just as he had worded his instructions to the soldiers who had spread throughout the village. 'This is more a lookout and a place from which to maintain control than a target itself,' he said, and then rushed to leave the house.

Chef Sayed was startled by the abrupt end to their conversation and Mooly's sudden departure, and even more startled when he realized where he had led himself with all that chattering. He felt defeated and filled with self-loathing, but he calmed himself down gradually, regulated his laboured breathing and blew a snaking curl of clear smoke against the backdrop of heavy skies.

All day long the soldiers moved about Umm-al-Maya on splattered streets, their boots pulling loose from the mud with a sucking noise, or kicking against insolent rocks. They disappeared behind drifting patches of fog and then reappeared suddenly, shrill noises from their transmitters grating on the ear. Establishing a presence! Domination! And at the same time they protected themselves with the bland euphemisms invented by occupying armies to pad and soften reality.

That evening, the commander of Gihon announced that most of the soldiers would bunk at the lofty home of Chef Sayed. That way, he explained with formidable logic, they would be concentrated in one building, thereby reducing friction between the army and the local population.

Head bowed, Chef Sayed listened to the commander's words, wheezing and groaning, then he shut himself up in his study, lay down on the leather sofa and stared blankly into space, inactive. His old housekeeper set out his lunch in the kitchen.

The soldiers piled into the empty rooms on the second floor, their voices rising and falling, now exulting with friends on their cellular phones, now laughing, now engaged in a quiet tête-à-tête, now fading in the face of the bold hues of rock music bursting forth from a portable radio, or applause from a small television. At times they tried to hush one another like small children who do not wish to disturb their parents' rest, but they were unable to control themselves for very long, and after a while the giggling would commence and grow until it turned into a raging force that hurtled itself down the cold staircase, and then ebbed like a wave, and the stairs settled back down until the soldiers returned, creating a din with the pounding of their boots, in a hurry to use the bathroom on the first floor since the facilities on the second floor were not functioning properly, and the sound of the water flowing in the pipe like hoarse thunder, and mud splattering everywhere. Chef Sayed left his study and ordered the old woman to sweep up after them, so she swept up after them, then swept up after them again until she complained to Chef Sayed that she was exhausted and he went to stand at the bottom of the staircase. When the soldiers spied him standing there in all his sovereign power, with his huge, shapeless face and heavy breathing, they trod softly and stopped shouting, stealing glances at him like children looking to test their proctor, and they climbed the stairs gingerly, then flapped their arms like alighting birds and sent mocking, taunting grimaces in the direction of his terribly strange face and swallowed their sniggers, but when they reached the top of the stairs they broke into a wild roar of laughter, albeit harmless.

Chef Sayed remained stolid, standing with his back to the courtyard on the other side of the glass doors, where droplets were falling from the leaves of the olive trees on to the heavy, rain-sodden earth, and the stone wall glistened from the drops that fell without cease. He gathered strength and continued to stand there until the commander of Gihon entered, removing his wet overcoat next to the front door, while two of his officers took from him the maps and the short-barrelled sub-machine gun, and Chef Sayed nodded a dejected greeting, like someone who assumes that the arrival of the master will enable the establishment of boundaries that were heretofore ill-defined, and Chef Sayed requested his attention to the matter. However, Chef Sayed's shapeless face, his thick lips, his constantly shifting eyes, awakened such repulsion in him that the commander of Gihon did not address his expectations; instead, he nodded briefly, preferring to pursue his own matters, when just precisely at that moment, somewhere on the second floor, a draught blew through. Tiny bells jingled, doors slammed and then a storm of army boots came raining down, shouts could be heard from the staircase and the bodies of men writhing and struggling surged forward on the trail of some dark, unclear movement fluttering above the stairs, and the panting gang of soldiers came to a halt in front of this wonder. Wow! Wow! A falcon! Wow! A falcon! No, a hawk. A vulture! A hawk! Look, it's a falcon. A hawk. A real falcon. A hawk. A falcon. Wow. And the bird of prey, stirred up from somewhere, drummed its giant talons on the glass doors leading to the courtyard at a proud, slow pace, its head held high, glancing madly in every direction, its hooked beak ensconced in a leather cone, from which dangled a strip of leather adorned with a string of tiny bells that hung in overlapping excess like the straps of a straitjacket.

Chef Sayed wheezed and swung his arm toward the soldiers in warning not to come any closer. They obeyed him as one, since this wave of his hand transformed him into an expert. Frozen in place, whispering, trembling, they followed the giant bird's movements and those of his master, the sorcerer. Chef Sayed removed a long leather glove from the closet and pulled it over his hand, stretching it until it reached his elbow. He was fully alert, well aware of his new, enhanced status. He took his time, tightening the strap on the glove and closing the buckle, then he made a high clucking sound that it was hard to believe he was capable of making, and the falcon flew to his outstretched glove to the pleasant ringing of bells. Chef Sayed presented the bird to the bulging eyes and the elated, inflamed whispers of all those present, and, as an actor appealing to his audience from the stage, he requested that the soldiers sweep up after themselves and cease making a mess. He did not notice the resentment of his audience at such a loathsome juxtaposition of the sanctity of the falcon with the profanity of muck. He paused a moment to assess the impression his words had made, then opened the glass door and went out to the courtyard, the falcon erect on his forearm.

The rain had stopped, but the branches of the olive tree and the tiny leaves of a stubborn climbing plant shook in the strong winds, scattering shiny droplets in the light. A breath of fresh, cool, wet, night air blew into the house through the open door. Chef Sayed leashed the bird to a tree next to the stone wall and removed the leather cone, allowing the falcon to present the powerful hook of its beak. He entered the house, loosened the buckle on his glove and dragged himself sluggishly toward the commander of Gihon, who stood watching the bird in the shadow of the wall along with the other soldiers. This had been his family's hunting bird for years, he told them, but now it did almost no hunting any more. Hunting is the sole privilege of the master, and he was not master. Once again Chef Sayed ruined the fairytale atmosphere that had descended on the courtyard, by recalling that it was insufferable in his eyes that the soldiers should be defiling his house as they had done that very day, and with all due respect he requested that they be ordered to clean up after themselves.

Mooly was quiet at first, then ordered the soldiers to return to their rooms upstairs. He was obliged to repeat himself and to reprimand them until they climbed the stairs, their eyes still fixed on the bird, riveted by its powerful essence. It did not spread its wings and did not show off its killer talons by tearing to shreds some scurrying victim, but the soldiers, by some primal instinct, sensed the tension between predator and prey, between the creature scampering in fear and the shadow hovering and growing above it.

For a long while Mooly continued to gaze wearily at the courtyard and at the bird with the timeless eyes, perhaps vaguely recalling similar hunting birds borne on gloves in deserts on the far side of the Syrian rift, wandering, perhaps, all the way to India, crossing lands on the backs of elephants, possibly sinking into the intoxicating colours of arabesques on Persian miniatures, and he dredged up from his childhood the memory of the sweet taste of sticky fingers leafing through the pages of a scented, festive tome, the murmur of an infant searching, searching, for what is he searching? *Mooly, Mooly, Moolish.*

Chef Sayed stubbornly repeated his request, for the third time, to keep the house clean. 'Yes, yes, yes!' the commander of Gihon responded impatiently, wishing to take his leave. But Chef Sayed once again got carried away in frightened prattle, the result of his desire to apologize, to please, to explain, to build a relationship, to annul the threat. He admitted to 'Micky' that he found it difficult to deal with this invasion of his privacy. His impotence in the face of violence depressed him immeasurably. Perhaps that was why he had become overly sensitive in this matter of cleanliness. It was his weakness. No, he was not trying to intimate that they were behaving violently, no, certainly not at all, and it was not so terrible if they kicked up a bit of dirt. Not so terrible. It was only human, so why not? And Mooly, for his part, was compelled by his repulsion to proclaim that the soldiers would clean up after themselves. He would take care of it. And after further consideration he expressed understanding for Chef Sayed's feelings. He could, he said, even relate to his anger. Chef Sayed denied being angry.

'I wish,' Mooly said, 'that we may meet in different, better times.' And he climbed the stairs.

The next day was even colder, and by late afternoon the skies were washed clean of all clouds. Later, tiny stars punctured the upper stratosphere, and later still the dull blast of cannons could be heard from behind the hills sunk in darkness. Transmitters buzzed in the armoured vehicles of the front-line command squad above the village, and soldiers ran in and out of Chef Sayed's house, causing a cold wind to blow through it and leaving a wake of thick, dark chips of mud that looked like dog droppings, and excited shouts on the stairs. Afterwards, they settled down and brought up rations cooked on a small, splattered gas stove in the kitchen-tent, through which the wind billowed, and the meal was accompanied by laughter on the second floor. The sewage pipes overflowed and Chef Sayed, who stood gagging at the doorway to his study, blocked the path of the commander of Gihon when he returned, filthy, the cold clinging to his uniform. In a wheezing fury Sayed demanded that the entrance to his home and the muddied rooms be cleaned. He did not wish to climb the stairs to the second floor. His heart would not allow him, he said, but the old woman could not chase after the soldiers. It's *their* dirt! *They* should clean it up! He should command them to! He had promised!

The order was given. A pair of soldiers swept the wide staircase energetically but not very meticulously, then came back downstairs to continue with the foyer, and then the living room, which was open all the way to the glass courtyard doors where, in the dim, cold air, between the stone wall and the frozen leaves, they could make out the haughty movements and demented gaze of the bird of prey. The instinct for male rivalry and risk-taking bubbled up in the pair of soldiers armed with feather brooms.

What is there about the indifferent falcon with the eye of a predator that so dares and provokes?

They could not stand the temptation and so they stole into the courtyard bearing hot dogs as bait in order to pluck feathers from its aggressive virile magnificence, but the bird inflated its breast suddenly and, with a flash of its wings, transformed itself from hunted to hunter, slipping away from the soldiers and using its eager talons to assail the faces of its attackers. Its beak burst forth like lightning, ready for blood, and the soldiers fought for their honour and their flesh with the blows of startled brooms, the huge clash taking place in the courtyard with a masculine, soldierly, alert and cheering audience on the other side of the glass doors.

The commander of Gihon was on the second floor. The master of the house was splayed across the sofa when the gentle tinkling of the bells reached his ears from above the muffled voices. He rushed out of his room and sighed at what he saw, then shouted noiselessly because his lips were too thick and his body too encumbered; re-entering his study, he stood next to the swan-like neck of the lamp facing the leather sofa, opened the desk drawer, and removed a pistol. He peered through the lenses of his glasses, struggling to open the safety catch, but his fingers were too fat. He moved toward the courtyard, still fumbling for the safety catch but unable to locate it. I'm going to shoot, he wanted to shout, but they noticed him, marked him. A pistol! A pistol! They raced at him, turning the new hunter into the hunted, hands grabbing him from the sides and the back and the front and fingers poking him in the face so that his eyes floated out of focus without the thick lenses and skittered about close to the cold floor on which he was lying, and the hands held him tight, and his breathing was tortured, heavy, and his breath came back to his cheek cool from the stone floor, and the hands held his scrambled face closer and closer to the floor, down, down, down! And the fingers scrutinized his body. Was there a grenade? A grenade? Another pistol? Is he clean? Is he clean?

He was very cold.

Chef Sayed lay on the leather sofa and rubbed its metal buttons with his fingers. A suspect in his own home. A stranger to his sofa. The commander of Gihon sat facing him on the chair in front of the desk and, like a master watchmaker, disassembled the pistol and mentioned matter-of-factly that he assumed Chef Sayed was not a member of one of the organizations at war with Israel, but that possessing a weapon in this area was illegal and a thorough search of the house was necessary. That would explain the sounds he was hearing from his nearby bedroom and dressing room. The search was being conducted with the utmost care so that nothing would be damaged. He was sorry about the incident involving the falcon, and was certain Mr Sayed had heard with his own ears how he had reprimanded the soldiers. He was groping for friendly sounding words to soften the hostile tone of Chef Sayed's heavy, cleft breathing. Weary lungs struggled to push air into the body so that the limbs would not collapse under the weight of the weak and swollen flesh, which aroused disgust. Has he ever considered selling the bird? Mooly asked.

Chef Sayed pulled himself up to a sitting position with great difficulty. The falcon did not belong to him, but to his family, he explained, his breathing asthmatic: it was a deposit in his charge. Long ago they had hunted with the falcon in the hills, just as their forefathers had done in ancient times, but the right to hunt had been forbidden to them ever since 'the times had been torn asunder', as he put it, and the falcon—symbol of lord and master—had 'put on a pair of slippers' and perhaps degenerated because of the meat that was placed before him, and it was possible that he had even lost his killer instinct; but for as long as he remained in the hands of the master of the house he preserved the illusion that its master was the master of his own destiny. Today, however, Chef Sayed said, panting and grunting, both were proven false: the illusion had turned itself inside out, and the falcon, it was now apparent, had restored to itself its killer instinct. Yes, facing two soldiers defending their eye sockets his pride had returned!

Mooly's fingers sailed the sawed-off bullets back and forth across the desktop.

'What is the value of such a falcon?' he asked.

The soldiers who finished their search appeared in the study with a small booty that did not include a weapon, but did include several unmarked video cassettes that aroused suspicion. When Chef Sayed caught sight of these he was seized with horror. He struggled to pull himself to his feet but failed, his face flushed then paled, his large hand reached out toward the soldiers, he attempted to speak but did not succeed and he punched his fist into the leather sofa. The soldiers drew back, their commander's brow knitted in concentration. With a nod of his head he indicated to his soldiers that they should leave, and he turned his attention to Chef Sayed, who was struggling with his voice and trying to rise to his feet. 'Give them back,' his thick lips were moaning, and his face twisted into a whole range of expressions. A repulsive despair was ravaging his face, and Mooly held his arm, attempting to assist him, since the overgrown man appeared as someone who had lost control of his face, and it seemed that if this nervous spasm did not cease the whole persona would crack into pieces.

Chef Sayed eventually settled down, sitting on the sofa like a condemned man and muttering, 'Give them back.' His face fell slack and he began swaying from side to side like a man in prayer, the leather sofa beneath him creaking loudly as he swung like the clapper of a bell, waiting for the blow that would strike him, which indeed it did.

At first it was a few gurgles of mocking laughter from the soldiers on the second floor while they were still inserting the cassette into the slit of the machine, then teasing cries of appreciation, then imitations of women's moans of desire filled the stairwell, a noisy craving lapped at the glass doors of the courtyard, orgasms screamed their way to the study, and Chef Sayed stammered incoherently as if he were choking. In the kitchen, the old woman fell deaf and continued chopping the flesh from plums preserved in their own sweet juices.

'What are you doing? What are you doing?' Chef Sayed muttered, beads of sweat adorning his skin. 'Why don't you tear me to pieces, strip me, vomit me out into the hills? How can you? And you, Commander,' he sobbed to the commander of Gihon, 'you have disemboweled me, eviscerated me, cut me into pieces. Why don't you just hang me up by my testicles, what else is left? What of this body, this stinking sack, this infested blob, is left to me? Even my needs are not mine, my humiliation is no longer mine, my juices, mine, are not mine, all that is mine is not mine: scissors, bowels, boxes, lamp, lamp, extinguish it, extinguish it. The light is too strong. Extinguish it, Micky, extinguish it.'

And 'Micky' extinguished it, the swan-necked lamp, and the sofa sank into the gloom. Bedroom light slithered in, panting, from the bedroom, recorded American orgasms and soldiers' cries of encouragement grunted on the stairway and groans from the leather sofa attested to the heavy body in torment upon it.

Tiny bells then rang from the courtyard, where the falcon's body was banging at the glass door, and the commander of Gihon rushed to see if something contrary to his orders was taking place there. But he found himself alone, looking out at the chilly courtyard, at the large falcon that had just hunted down a mouse next to the glass doors and whose great talons were ripping into the writhing body while its beak stripped the skin and tore out strips of flesh with great force, and swallowed with great force, and looked at him with great force, his gaze completely crazed and completely indifferent.

When he had satisfied his hunger, the falcon spread its glorious wings and floated heavily to his niche in the wall, his string of bells announcing his movements.

Mooly did not remain indifferent. He let his heart leap and soar in the wake of such intense, focused power. He neglected caution, neglected his command, and wandered to the childhood he had nearly forgotten, to impressive backyard victories at his parents' sun-struck house, among thorns and dry, crackling plants, among sweaty, fighting children elated with dreams of grandeur. *Moolili.*

When he returned to the master's study, which was sunk in gloom, he reported to the dark, breathing sofa that the falcon had caught a mouse. Now he was sated. The bird of prey had, it would seem, resumed hunting. This time it was he who wished to draw out their conversation, due to embarrassment, and a desire to make amends, and the burden of silence. In the silence, Chef Sayed's wheezing breaths could be heard like the rasp of a barn owl, breaths that held Mooly's own breathing in their grasp and foreshortened them to match his own so that it was possible, Mooly reflected, for the master of the house to strangle him with his breathing. This was how a thought could affect the body. He plugged his ears. And in this twilight he suddenly blurted that he was willing to pay two months' salary for the bird. Then he said he would pay three. Three months'. He did not weigh his words. He did not consider the circumstances, or his emotions. There was simply feeling and desire, and they were expressed before they could be filtered. And from the moment these words were uttered they billowed through his body and his soul, and Mooly felt a great sense of relief, felt heat in his body, and it was pleasant to him, and his breathing returned to normal. He said, almost with affinity for the man, that sometimes we have to endure difficult tests in order to move forward.

After an hour or so there was a sound of hoarse coughing followed by words that burst forth from the heavy black stain on the sofa that was Chef Sayed. 'Tomorrow we shall discuss it,' he said. 'Tomorrow evening we shall sit down together like gentlemen and we shall discuss it.'

The next morning Chef Sayed set out, wrapped in a woollen overcoat against the strong winds, on the dirt roads soaked with rain, treading clumsily to the greengrocer, whose iron door stood only half open due to the wind and the scarcity of goods, and then to the spice seller, who complained about all the precipitation they were experiencing and wondered how long the soldiers would remain in the village, and to the cheese seller, who opened sealed papers and sliced dripping white slabs that gave off the scent of semen, and weighed and wrapped them and was glad for the money and cursed the soldiers with animosity.

Panting and grunting and wheezing, Chef Sayed continued on his way, exhaling vapour in the cold air.

At home, in the kitchen, he set down his purchases on the butcher-block table and added to them baking powder and flour and sugar, and almonds he removed from a bag, and raisins and figs, and even the plum confection, sticky and sweet, that the old woman had prepared the night before. No sound came from the second floor. The echo of the wind blowing outside the stone walls deafened the sound of the dense breathing of the two soldiers who had finished night-duty and were now sleeping in open-mouthed exhaustion, wrapped in sleeping bags in one of the bedrooms.

Chef Sayed donned his battered leather apron atop his huge belly and expertly sharpened the carving knife on it, slapping the blade first on one side and then the other as if he were smacking a baby's bottom. Then he pulled the long leather glove over his hand and went out to the courtyard, where a whirlwind was ruffling the pale leaves of the olive tree and the tips of the falcon's feathers, who was perched in his niche. Chef Sayed clucked shrilly to it and the bird flew to his arm. Carefully, Chef Sayed slipped the leather cone over its head, obstructing its beak, wrapped the string of bells around its sturdy feet, grasped it by the neck and with thick fingers slammed its head on to a large stone, and with a heavy shoe and a rasping breath, mashed its head into an unidentifiable lump. With the stiff, sharp knife he cut off the head and tossed it into the courtyard. The warm body continued to twitch as he trimmed the long feathers with a short pair of shears. The blood continued to spill out on the stone while he sank the knife into the bird's backside and ripped through it up to the throat, stuck in his thick fingers and yanked out the rubbery, acrid, oozing parts and flung them on to the low roof of the house, where it came down to the wall. Presently, ravens battling the wind landed on the tiled roof, pecked at the pool of flesh and at one another, and squawked with horror in their beaks.

The old woman came out to the courtyard, seated herself on a low stool and began plucking the bird's feathers: the grey ones, the black ones, the white ones, the hard, bristly ones, and the plumed ones. Chef Sayed collected the long feathers into a bag, staring blankly at the plumes as they filled the air and floated and fluttered in every direction. Those that did not stick to the stone, or to a leaf or to a piece of bark rose above the wall and joined the clouds. The old woman went back into the house, the stripped body of the bird dangling at her thigh.

That evening, the dining room table stood set with precision, Western-style, adorned with thin translucent glasses and tiny explosions of light gleaming from the tips of the fork prongs.

Mooly and Chef Sayed moved their napkins to their lips and expressed their delight in the perfectly seasoned meat filled with treasures difficult to imagine in a place like this and during such troubled times: plums, raisins, the choicest rice, almonds, tiny onions, garlic and a variety of thick sauces enriched with sage and saffron and ground pepper and even a hint of cinnamon, which complemented the complexity of the tastes. Only the meat was perhaps a bit tough, yes, a little rubbery, but the stuffing and the sauces disguised its disadvantages and its identity. One might suppose that the feeling of satiety, of refinement, of good taste, would have facilitated contact between them, but Mooly discerned that his dining partner's heart was not in it. He was absent-minded, and came to life a bit only when their conversation turned to the falcon. A pleasant mood settled on Mooly and he began telling about the spacious cage in his backyard that had once housed a horse or a dog but which would be quite suitable for a large falcon, and how especially it would please his daughters. After all, it was impossible not to be amazed at such a wondrous creature, and his daughters would be happy that it was theirs and theirs alone, and their little playmates would come to look at the bird, and he could imagine the joy and, yes—truth be told—the envy of his neighbours. His is a small and pleasant community with well-tended yards and nice people, and it is very quiet, so quiet that his daughters can walk on the sidewalks or in the road without caution, and when he is on a furlough they take his boots for a walk, dragging them along by their shoelaces... He will learn to hunt with the falcon, and he will buy himself the glove, and the leather cap, and the string of tiny bells, and he will learn to cluck his tongue. Because surrounding his community there are still open spaces, and this is a great tradition, aristocratic, once the pastime of kings and barons, while today it has nearly been forgotten, but he will learn it, yes. He will learn to hunt with the falcon. 'But where is it?' he asked. 'The bird. The falcon.'

'You have just eaten it, Mr Micky,' Chef Sayed responded, pointing with his fork at the remains of the meat swimming in its rich sauces. He was wheezing, and his face was more shapeless than ever, more expressionless than ever.

Mooly sat for a moment like a person who does not understand what is being said to him, then he stood up suddenly, knocking his chair to the ground.

'Sit, sit back down and eat!' Chef Sayed shouted, spearing his words with his fork. 'Sit!'

Mooly turned in haste to the courtyard, opened the glass doors to the night wind and with a churning stomach stepped out and vomited the digested remains of the falcon on to its undigested head, and on to the empty eye sockets that had been plucked clean by the ravens' beaks.

Chef Sayed's shouts were punctuated by his coughing. 'Sit, sit and eat! Sit!' He could not cease this convulsive coughing, which was no less powerful than Mooly's nauseous heaving. When Mooly returned to the table, wiping his face, Chef Sayed was still coughing and choking and shouting, and his shapeless form aroused greater repulsion than ever. The commander of Gihon removed his short-barrelled sub-machine gun from the back of his chair, opened the safety catch and shot Chef Sayed in the head. *Mooly. Moolili.*  □

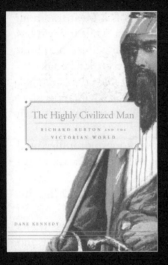

# THE HIGHLY CIVILIZED MAN
Richard Burton and the Victorian World

## DANE KENNEDY

"Fresh, lively, and entertaining, Dane Kennedy's new assessment of Richard Burton punctures the tired stereotypes that have long dogged Burton scholarship. Kennedy reads Burton within a series of key Victorian debates around science, sex, religion, race and empire, yet still holds onto his subject's remarkable individuality. Eminently readable, satisfyingly erudite, and always fair in its judgments, this is the biography Burton deserves."
—Philippa Levine,
University of Southern California
New in cloth

## STUTTER

### MARC SHELL

One person can't help stuttering. The other can't help laughing. And in the way one bodily betrayal of better intentions mirrors the other, we find ourselves in the gray area where mind and body connect—and, at the damnedest moments—disconnect. In a book that explores the phenomenon of stuttering from its practical and physical aspects to its historical profile to its existential implications, Marc Shell plumbs the depths of this murky region between will and flesh, intention and expression, idea and word.
New in cloth

GRANTA

# THE WEATHER WHERE WE ARE

Eight reflections on climate change
and one on the tsunami
from writers around the world

# Margaret Atwood
## The Arctic

In the South—by this I mean any part of the earth with trees that grow up instead of sideways—it's hard to see the climate changing. A severe windstorm here, a warm winter or a drought or a flood there, but haven't there been severe windstorms and warm winters and droughts and floods before? Plants grow back, they regenerate after die-off, they cover over the scars. Species creep northward, but at least there are species. Things can't be that bad, you say, as you water your garden: Look how well the dandelions are doing!

In the Arctic it's different. Everything is so visible. Everything—except the rocks—is so fragile. There are trees, but they don't convert the limited sun-energy available to them into wood. They spider along the ground, two hundred years old and only a foot wide. Kill one and it won't be back soon. It's the same with the ice.

Arctic ice is life-giving. Small organisms grow on the undersides of floating ice pans and icebergs, fish eat the organisms, whales and seals eat the fish, polar bears eat the seals. Ice gets into the sea in two ways: it falls in from calving glaciers, or it forms during the winter. Both kinds are spectacular, and both are essential. But the Arctic ice is dying. You can see it happening. There's no cover-up.

My partner and I have gone up there now over a four-year span—'up there' being the eastern Arctic, on the Greenland side and also the Canadian side, at lower altitudes, middle altitudes, and upper-middle altitudes. We go because we love it, and because we love it we worry about it. Everywhere it's the same. The Greenland ice cap is still calving into the North Atlantic, the icebergs still travel north to the top of Baffin Bay, then turn south and make their way past Newfoundland. But in the summer of 2004 there were almost no floating ice pans. Other glaciers are in retreat: we could see the rock valleys they used to fill, we could see the line they'd reached even a few years before. The shrinkage has been rapid.

Inuit told us stories about how hard it's become for polar bears and hunters to get out on to the ice, the only reliable place to catch seals. The ice was forming later and later every fall, melting earlier and earlier every spring. When you can't depend on the ice, what can you depend on? It would be as if—down south—the highways were to melt. And then what?

The canary in the mine used to be our warning signal: it keeled over and men knew they were in danger. Now it's the polar bears on the shore, dying of starvation.

The Arctic is an unbelievable region of the earth: strikingly beautiful if you like gigantic skies, enormous landforms, tiny flowers, amazing colours, strange light effects. It's also a region that allows scant margins of error. Fall into the ocean and wait a few minutes, and you're dead. Make a mistake with a walrus or a bear, same result. Make the wrong wardrobe choice, same result again. Melt the Arctic ice, and what follows? No second chances for quite some time.

You could write a science fiction novel about it, except that it wouldn't be science fiction. You could call it *Icemelt*. Suddenly there are no more small organisms, thus no fish up there, thus no seals. That wouldn't affect the average urban condo dweller much. The rising water levels from—say—the melting of the Greenland and Antarctic ice caps would get attention—no more Long Island or Florida, no more Bangladesh, and quite a few islands would disappear—but people could just migrate, couldn't they? Still no huge cause for alarm unless you own a lot of shore-front real estate.

But wait: there's ice under the earth, as well as on top of the sea. It's the permafrost, under the tundra. There's a lot of it, and a lot of tundra as well. Once the permafrost starts to melt, the peat on the tundra—thousands of years of stockpiled organic matter—will start to break down, releasing huge quantities of methane gas. Up goes the air temperature, down goes the oxygen ratio. How long will it take before we all choke and boil to death?

It's hard to write fiction around such scenarios. Fiction is always about people, and to some extent the form determines the outcome of the plot. We always imagine—perhaps we're hard-wired to imagine—a survivor of any possible catastrophe, someone who lives to tell the tale, and also someone to whom the tale can be told. What kind of story would it be with the entire human race gasping to death like beached fish?

What kind of story, indeed? And who wants to hear it?

# John Borneman
## Sri Lanka
December 28, 2004

The morning after Christmas in Unawatune, a village on the southwestern tip of Sri Lanka. We got up around 7.20, went swimming at the beach across from our hotel, returned to our room, showered, and by eight we were one of two couples enjoying breakfast in our hotel's dining room, a small, solid concrete structure with three open sides and a corrugated tin roof on the beach side of the narrow road that runs through the village. Our hotel, the Neptune, was on the other side of the road. By nine we had finished our meal and our final pot of tea and were preparing to leave and go snorkelling, when Parvis, my partner, said, 'The beach has disappeared.' The water was nearly at the level of the dining room, which stood about eight feet above the beach and twenty feet from the water. We stood up and went to the edge to look. The water was lapping at the chairs put out for sunbathing. They began to float and risked being swept into the sea. I said, 'The chairs are disappearing. That's too bad.'

A waiter in the restaurant tried to help a young girl wearing a fashionable black bathing-suit climb over the wall from the beach, as the water seemed to be engulfing her. But she let go of his hand and tried to climb the stairs instead. She was halfway up when the rising water swept the stairs away, too, and the man helped her up out of the water. She laughed and ran out of the restaurant. Everyone else laughed along with her. A wave splashed over the wall and got us a bit wet. By then all the tables in the restaurant were full of tourists, and everyone laughed, again, amused at this unexpected wave. Within seconds, however, the water had risen above the three-foot restaurant wall; dishes, teapots, silverware fell off the tables, which began to float and overturn. The water was dark, not the clear blue in which we earlier swam. It poured over the top of the wall and small waves lapped at everything inside the room. The Sri Lankan waiters stood as dumbfounded as their customers. In an orderly fashion, without a word being exchanged, everyone rose to leave. No rush here in paradise, which is where I told my friends I was going: a sunny spot in a lazy, friendly beach town on the south Sri Lankan coast.

It is all happening too fast to recognize what is happening. I am helpless as I realize that the waves are going to cover us; the water is becoming a rising wall, not a wave, and simply overtaking us. We, like the others, are not able to escape. I ask myself, is this a tidal wave? Parvis is in front of me and seems to be waiting for others to clear out, not in any particular hurry, unfailingly polite as always. I rush towards the exit and say, 'Let's get out, Parvis, don't wait.' But he is thinking, he tells me later, don't panic, take your turn. Seconds later, I am one of the first to begin down the steps to the street, towards the hotel, but an aggressive push by the gushing water on my legs and lower back sweeps me off my feet, and I take a ride down the steps on my ass as if on a water slide. With my left hand I am holding high our guidebook, *Lonely Planet Sri Lanka*, with all the addresses of places we are going to visit. This is only our fourth day out of seventeen planned in Sri Lanka, and, I think, there goes our itinerary. The water grabs the book from my hand. I sense a middle-aged woman, also sliding on her ass, close behind me. I land on my feet about two yards away, but tables and chairs follow me, threatening to knock me down, so I walk, crawl, stumble quickly towards the wall in front of me, which is part of our hotel. To the left side of the entrance I see two windows above the water, which is rising about a foot every ten seconds. A Sri Lankan girl wraps her arms around my neck. She is light, and I drag her, or she floats behind me, toward the window sill, and a Sri Lankan boy hooks his arm in mine as I begin to climb the wall. Or are we simply floating up the wall?

The window sill provides no purchase, no place to grab on to. I am afraid of falling back into the water, which is not only coming straight at me now but has also formed a river through the village street, a swift river that begins to roar and threatens to carry me to my left towards the other end of the village. I suddenly find my hands are able to grasp on to the wooden lattice work between the upper window panes and I grip it, as do the girl and boy next to me, who are screaming hysterically, their dark, round eyes betraying a deathly fear, and a plea for my help. I am silent, though; Parvis later describes me as 'bewildered'. I think, just hold on.

The water had broken the windowpanes, enabling us to resist its pull. But it is still rising, and within less than a minute we are submerged. I hold my breath. The water goes down, and then re-submerges us. This pattern repeats. The boy and girl scream loudly every time the water subsides. After our second submersion, the boy suggests we go through the open window into the building, but I notice the low ceiling and think, better to ride the water outside, we might get trapped under the roof. So we climb as high as we can up the wall. Nothing goes through my mind but to hold on, to focus on the immediate task, to stay calm, to relax—no prayer, no thoughts of others, or of what to do next.

I do, however, take note of the absurdity of the moment, as the water waxes and wanes, comes up, goes down. I keep thinking, it won't stay up forever, it has to retreat, and we will keep rising to the top. But its intensity increases, threatening to pull us into the river and downstream, and it gets louder, competing in my ear with the screams of the boy and girl. My glasses get caught in the girl's long hair, close to a ribbon that holds her hair in place but is coming loose, and as she turns now and then and struggles to climb the wall, to stay above the water, my glasses nearly come off. I think, if I lose them, I can't see! 'My glasses are caught in your hair,' I tell her, but she is in no state to understand. Perhaps she doesn't speak English. Eventually I tear them free from her hair. We endure this for what seems an eternity but is more likely less than ten minutes.

Just as quickly as the water arrived, it begins to go back, steadily. It reveals the boy's leg, and he sees a huge gash above his thigh. He whimpers, then stops; his mouth remains open for a long time, silently screaming. The girl looks at his wound, and then looks at me uncomprehendingly. When the water recedes below the window sill, I jump down. The water now stands slightly above my waist. The boy and girl make garbled noises, grunts, whines, pleading that I should take them with me. I say, just stay calm, and motion, wait, wait, the water is going down, I'll get help. I wade back towards the restaurant, which has collapsed, and I find a concrete slab under the water to stand on, and I survey the scene. Could I make it to our room on the second floor? I notice electric wires in the water. I think, electrocution! The street is empty. Everything is quiet. Risk it, I say to myself. As I move, a young Sri Lankan man emerges from the hotel; he approaches and extends his hand. I say, 'No, I am okay, get the two people on the window sill.'

Then I hear Parvis calling in a panic-stricken voice, 'John, John, John.' I turn the corner and he holds out his arms and rushes towards me. We embrace. 'I thought I lost you,' he says, 'I have been calling for minutes, didn't you hear?' 'No,' I say. We wade through the water on the fully devastated ground floor. The street is still a river, now shallow instead of ten feet deep, littered with furniture, instruments, the head of a Buddha statue, odd pieces of things. We go upstairs to our room. It is untouched. The bathing suit I had put out on the balcony is now dry. The sun continued shining through this whole thing, whatever it was. Why, I think, do I expect the sun to coordinate its activity with the ocean?

We look out on the balcony, where another couple are standing. Parvis tells them they can stay as long as they like. We think out loud: Should we leave or stay? I sit on the bed to take stock of what happened to me, to us. Parvis gets out his camera. 'There's always a second wave,' he says, and he begins to yell to people as they appear in the street/river below us, 'Get out. Get out. A second wave. Leave.' They don't seem to respond, they look dazed. 'You wouldn't believe this,' he says to me, as he takes pictures, 'Look at this, come and look at this.' I join him. 'Look at the water,' he says. It had receded to about a kilometre away from the former beachfront. Furniture, house parts, trees, tuk-tuks, cars, clothes, everything human filled the exposed ocean bed.

We discuss what to take with us. Parvis says one computer. I say, 'Oh no, both.' We gather our documents, passports, money, leave all our clothes, and go downstairs, planning to go inland. The people on the street appear to be mindlessly wading through the water, though then I realize they are looking for the missing.

Parvis goes back upstairs for some reason and finds the young boy who had shared the window sill with me. He is resting on a bed. Some tourists had bandaged the opening in his thigh. I wait for Parvis, get anxious and impatient—the second wave! I yell for him, he answers the first time, yes, then gets angry at me, and refuses to answer. I go upstairs and find him: he has offered to help carry the young boy, who is in shock and cannot walk, and holding on tightly to a blanket and a pillow. Parvis has given his computer to someone else. I retrieve it. As they carry the boy downstairs, the water tugs at the end of his blanket. He drops it, and then his pillow, saying nothing. Local people are urging everyone to leave; there is higher ground behind the hotel. We begin climbing the mountain, including some large, slippery rocks. We take off our shoes or sandals to scale them.

Halfway up the mountain, women are wailing under an open-sided hut. Men are gathered around a woman lying on her back under a blanket. I realize she is dead. There must be more, I think. Further up, a Japanese nurse is treating people's wounds with nothing but a bit of cotton and alcohol. I have scraped knees, several deep cuts on the left foot, with glass embedded in my soles, and a few other scratches. Parvis seems to have nothing, though later he discovers a cut on a toe that becomes infected.

Further up the hill, everyone had a different and unique story they wanted to tell. I sat at the nursing station and listened. I would have liked to take pictures, but it seemed obscene to photograph people in that state. Some were seriously wounded, others, like me, merely cut and bruised. A young man borrowed a notepad and a pen from me to make a list of the missing: a Czech girl, a Polish boy, Japanese, Australian, Brit—and that was the start of his efforts. He said that nine tourists and twelve Sri Lankans from our village had been confirmed dead. The dark-haired girl in the black bathing-suit showed up, totally in control. She was from Singapore and in Sri Lanka with her boyfriend, who had sustained a few deep cuts and scratches across his chest. 'You're the one who climbed out of the water in our restaurant,' I said. 'Yes,' she laughed. As she was being pulled out of the water, the concrete wall of the restaurant was scratching her legs, so she let go, to use the stairs, which then got swept away. 'I was laughing as it collapsed,' she said, 'because I thought, damn, there went my cigarettes!'

We European and Australian and Asian tourists gathered in the villages on the top of the hill, and local people served us tea. The second wave came, and the third, but Unawatune had been evacuated. Some watched the second wave from the hillside. We had water, and a couple of boxes of cookies, but we had no other food. Local phone lines were not working. I ran into a couple of Australians and Brits with cellphones, but their networks only allowed them to call home, which they did, and were told by people at home watching CNN, that a 'tsunami'—I'd never heard the word before—had hit, that thousands of people were dead. A few villagers came by and offered individuals beds or floors in their huts to sleep on, but most of us planned to sleep out in the open. Only mosquitoes to fear.

Just before dark, the men from the village returned from their search for the missing. One of them, a middle-aged man, came up to me. He had found the body of his closest friend, who, he said, greeted him endearingly every morning on his way to work. He would miss that. He offered Parvis and me his bed for the night. Anything to avoid the hard ground, I thought. He repeated his offer—I am an honest man, he asserted, a carpenter, and my house is on the way to the bus route.

Parvis felt bad about leaving. He wanted to share the fate of the others. I thought: no food, no communication, no sign of rescue; we're only a burden; let's make our way inland. We spent the night at the carpenter's house. It was late, and there were only candles, no electricity, so we declined his offer of food and only drank tea with him. He gave us his explanation for the tsunami: the culture of the beach, the drugs, the tourists, the sex—the wave was revenge for these pleasures. The last time something like this had happened was 2,000 years ago, he said, as recorded in some mythical texts. I did not sleep a wink that night (though Parvis did fine), it was either a mosquito that got under our net, or the hardness of the bed.

The next morning, we climbed down a steep mountain passage with our luggage and walked along the beach road to Galle amid massive destruction: debris everywhere, upturned buses, uprooted railroad tracks. Eventually we got a bus to Colombo.

When I switched on my computer, nearly a hundred emails awaited me. My friends and students in Syria, where I was teaching in Aleppo as a Fulbright professor, made anxious enquiries. 'I am really concerned about you and happy new year *alsalam alikom* bye,' wrote Abedasalam, a young waiter who had just been fired from his job at a restaurant I often went to. 'I and rami ask god to you the full health and coming back quickly,' wrote Husam, a clerk who worked down the street from my apartment in the al-Medina souk. When I replied 'bruised but alive' to them and other Syrian and American friends, many wrote back to express relief and joy that their prayers had been answered.

I am not a believer, and the experience of the tsunami only confirmed my agnosticism. It was an arbitrary, capricious event—nature calling. It had nothing to do with my being human, and in that respect was infinitely humbling. To my Syrian friends I wrote, 'But God sent this tsunami, he tried to kill me.'

# Urvashi Butalia
## India

For several years before he died my father greeted the arrival of winter with a mixture of joy and apprehension. Joy because winter meant clear, sunny days, hours of soaking up the warmth, sitting out in the afternoons eating spiced tomatoes, radishes and oranges, drinking *kanji*, the dark fermented juice of black carrots laced with rye that is the Punjabis' staple winter drink. Apprehension because, as he put it each year, 'I don't know if we'll survive another year.' The 'we' included my mother. They were both getting old. The Delhi winter, sunny and sharp, was also bitterly cold, with great differences between day and night temperatures, and no heating inside homes. My father felt the cold acutely. During one bad winter he asked, with some embarrassment, if he could borrow some brightly coloured woollen leg warmers I'd bought in England. He wore them hidden under his trousers, and was grateful for their warmth.

I'm not sure when the weather began to change, but suddenly we realized that winter did not feel so cold, and did not last so long. November was when the cold season began, when we would pull out our shawls and quilts, dust off the mothballs, put them in the sun to air and dry, and then curl up under them, cosy, gorging ourselves on roasted peanuts. The cold would last all through December and January, cold descending as soon as evening fell. Sometimes the night temperatures would be down to three or four degrees. We waited all year for these crisp few months: for the cold, the blue skies, and the delicious caress of the winter sun.

Then we began to get fog. At first, we were delighted. The English weather—rain, mist, fog, greyness—has always held a fascination for us, even when we knew it only from books and films. When you live with forty-five degrees of heat for several months of the year, rain and grey skies are what you long for. A few days of fog and grey skies, people thought, would go down just fine. The trouble was, they weren't a few. The fog went on and on. Lorries got stuck, flights couldn't land, trains couldn't run: milk, fruit and vegetables became scarce and business trips and holidays had to be cancelled. We were told several factors were to blame: global warming, increasing pollution, and the ever growing population of Delhi, which demanded houses rather than fields.

Summer also began to feel different. It became hotter and hotter. In 2004, the heat killed 1,400 people in India. They just collapsed and died. This year we don't yet have proper figures, though the anecdotes are there. In the eastern state of Orissa there's a place called Talcher where thousands of trees have been cut down to make room for the factories of big multinational companies. In Talcher lived a forty-three-year-old woman, Sailabala Kanji, who stepped out of her home at three in the afternoon when the sun was already high in the sky. The temperature was fifty-five degrees. Five minutes and 500 metres later she was dead. I read her story just as I'd finished reading another—about a train in a nearby state, Madhya Pradesh, that had been caught in a flash flood. Two hundred people were stuck in the train with water up to their chests, one cellphone working, and no help for hours. The papers said it was global warming…

It wasn't always like this. Summer nights were cool when we were children. Everyone slept outside, in the open. Air conditioners were unheard of. Come evening and you'd begin to roll up your bedclothes, take them up to the roof, spread them out. At bedtime, buckets of water would be carried up, everything would be sprinkled with water. And then, stars in the sky, and the cool perfume of jasmine in the air, we'd sit down to long nights of storytelling. If it rained, everyone would jump up, roll up the bedclothes, head into the house, and just wait for it to clear, before heading out again. Now you shut yourself up in your room, put the air conditioner on, and cover yourself with a blanket. And if you're poor, you go out to work, head uncovered, body exposed, and you die.

Of course, the weather has always been cruel in India, but it was at least more predictable. You knew the summer would be hot, and the winter cold. March, and the harvest festival of Holi, brought a hint of summer, and by April the heat had begun to kick in, rising until the monsoon broke in June or July. November, and the festival of Diwali brought a hint of winter and by December the warm clothes were out. Now you're guessing much of the time: will the winter be cold, the summer hot? Will the heat come early, the cold late? Nobody, not even the Met department, seems to be able to say for sure.

Perhaps we can adjust to this new uncertainty—people are adapatable and so, up to a point, are the crops they grow. But if the monsoon were to become equally capricious—and its arrival and duration have never been completely dependable—then India would face a very different future. The monsoon is the most essential and cherished of our seasons. The harvest relies on a good monsoon, and therefore the economy relies on a good monsoon. It directly affects our well-being; it can influence the outcome of elections; it's the only season that merits a whole raga to itself in Hindustani music. The story goes that in the court of the Mughal king Akbar, courtiers jealous of the poet Tansen persuaded the ruler to ask the poet to sing the raga Deepak, the music that is dedicated to fire, to a flame. They knew that once he began, he would become so absorbed in his music, that not only would everything else burn with the fire, but he too would die.

But Tansen was cleverer. He agreed to sing, he had little choice. But he spoke to his young daughter, and warned her of what would happen, telling her that as he began to sing, she should take up the raga Malhar, the raga that welcomes the monsoon rains. He sang, and she sang. His music ignited a fire, everything began to burn, her music brought the rain, everything was blessed. A song that everyone across India will recognize is a song that asks for rain

*Allah megh de pani de re chhaya de*
*Re Allah megh de...*

Allah, give us clouds, give us rain, give us shade
Allah, give us clouds...

# James Hamilton-Paterson
## Italy

Having been brought up in Britain I draw on a cultural heritage that includes a national obsession with the weather. Since changeable weather is entirely natural for an island in the East Atlantic, I assume this obsession is simply a fossil from the days when Britain was a maritime nation dependent on the sea for food, trade and defence. Looking back though the weather in my childhood now appears remarkably stable (generally rainy), and I only remember extremes such as the odd torrid summer and, in particular, the notorious winter of 1946–7. Then, the ferocious and lasting cold was made worse by the post-war scarcity of fuel. In our semi-detached house in Eltham my sister and I went to bed in socks and mittens with wartime hot-water bottles made of glazed stoneware.

Twenty-four years ago I moved to Italy where on the whole the weather was not merely better but, being continental, more predictable. True I was living up a mountain in southern Tuscany, in an area that turned out to have a microclimate of its own. But in general, the four seasons were still as clearly marked as in Vivaldi's day. In autumn the grapes and olives were picked, mushrooms rose and leaves fell, mists swirled, the first frosts gripped on clear nights and the air was scented with the roasting of new chestnuts. Winters were usually short and sharp, the tramontana blew icy blasts down from the Russian steppes and there would be a few days' worth of snow (my house was at 700 metres). And then, suddenly one morning, spring would be declared and over the next month the surrounding forests methodically pitched their new, green awnings in preparation for the long hot summer.

Over the years, things changed. As always there were dry years and wet years. But little by little autumn and spring began to lose definition, blurring and shortening until, when I came to leave the mountain two years ago, winter was eliding almost seamlessly into summer, and vice versa. I moved to where I am now, in northern Tuscany not far from the sea. The climate here is noticeably damper: the gutters and drainpipes in this area are made of copper to resist the salt in the wind. Yet the complaints of the locals are the same: spring and autumn—especially autumn—have faded, except in memory. Until the 1960s Italy was still to a great extent an agricultural economy and millions of Italians were small farmers and labourers: peasants, in short. There are still plenty of people of my age or older who instinctively think in terms of crops and the soil, who read the sky and decide to bring pruning forward by a week or postpone the olive harvest until things look more settled. The moon's phases move in their subconscious minds like deadlines do in mine. They still know dozens of the rhymes and saws that once transmitted practical wisdom all over illiterate Europe. These sayings concern when to plant what, and what to wear when: adages that in Britain have largely fallen from memory, leaving only scattered remnants of red skies at night or clouts not being cast. Here in northern Tuscany the old boys and girls buy a yearly almanac, an 'agricultural guide' named after its original nineteenth-century author, Sesto Cajo Baccelli ('elder brother of Settimo, nephew of the famous astronomer and cabbalist Rutilio Benincasa, known as the Soothsayer of Brozzi'). Like *Old Moore's Almanac* in Britain, Sesto Cajo Baccelli's little booklet is updated each year. The months are laid out with information on the agrarian tasks that fall due, together with the phases of the moon (still deemed critical for planting and grafting) and weather guides. As I write this on November 5, I read that old Sesto foresees mists for today. It so happens that after three weeks' rain (also foretold), today is bright but misty.

So here we have a contradiction. Wise old Sesto Baccelli is still read for his immemorial version of the weather. Wise old Ivo my neighbours' gardener and his wise old wife Diva, on the other hand, are insistent that the climate here has been changing for years. 'November the fifth,' she says to me with a reminiscent smile. 'Lovely and sharp at night, it used to be, everybody roasting chestnuts, and a good frost to make the turnip leaves taste better. Not hot like today, with this African sirocco and the grass still needing mowing every few days.' To hear her talk, even the weather has conspired to make the good old days seem still more remote.

What is beyond question, in urbanizing Italy as in the UK, is that even people who have never so much as grown a tray of mustard and cress on a strip of wet flannel in primary school are hooked on the weather. In both countries this is down to television, with its elaborate studio sets, its presenters with fixed grins prancing and pointing at weather maps as computerized cloud-banks mass to menace us all with meteorological hogwash. It's not about information; like the news, it's more a comforting diurnal ritual whose torrents of words and pictures convey mild, empty dramas even less suggestive than the constantly intervening ads. On my visits to England I'm always newly astounded by the sheer length and blather of the TV weather spots. I suppose this befits the nation that invented forecasting. It was Francis Galton, Darwin's cousin and co-founder of the Meteorological Office, who invented the weather map. The idea of regular weather forecasts was the brainchild of Robert FitzRoy. He captained the *Beagle* on her momentous voyage around the world with Darwin, later headed the new Met Office and briefly ran the world's first newspaper weather forecasts in *The Times* until he was sacked for their inaccuracy in 1864 ('Admiral FitzRoy has still to convince the public...'). I wonder that anybody can be bothered to take in these maps with their blinking and flashing overlays and dissolves, and their swirling showers of arrows 'somewhere becoming rain' (did TV weather maps suggest to Larkin the mysteriously beautiful image at the end of 'The Whitsun Weddings'?). We will have to put up with whatever the weather does tomorrow, so to what end all this electronically-aided guesswork as to exactly where between Andover and Southampton the patches of drizzle will die out?

To none, in itself. But these days everyone has watched the other programmes, the ones about climate change. We all know about the mortally-wounded ozone layer, the greenhouse effect, about carbon dioxide and retreating glaciers. We are shocked by the thought of no more skiing, no more polar bears, an Aberdeenshire Riesling, the Sahara edging towards Beachy Head, angelfish in the Solent. We have taken in the TV dramas of hurricanes, perfect storms, tornado-chasers and flood-watchers. We are all gripped with a mild meteo-enviro panic, constantly aware of the weather not as something marginal that has to be lived with but as symptomatic of a planet out of kilter. Every slightly unusual weather pattern is mined for its dire significance and seen as being highly suggestive—if not actual confirmation—of permanent change.

We have all been infected by this. Wise old Ivo and Diva still hedge their bets, Sesto Baccelli in one hand and long memories to draw on of other strange patches of irregular weather. Yesterday evening Diva remarked to me: 'Who knows, Giacomo? Who knows what the weather has done over millions of years, and who knows what it's doing in other galaxies? Whatever is sent we have to endure it, and whatever happens is for the best.' She believes absolutely in those everlasting and merciful hands cupped beneath the human race.

What an interesting reversal it is that we, who until so recently were intimately dependent on the local weather for our food and for our very lives, now buy everything from shops and supermarkets which source their produce from around the globe. Moreover, we're insulated from weather as never before by well-built houses, by central heating and air conditioning. And yet we're still anxious about it. In fact our anxiety has extended well beyond this year's maize or wheat crop until it has become open-ended and melds easily into a general foreboding about the future. Ivo remarked that he's heard the Arctic ice cap may be extinct in 2050. 'But so will you and I be,' I said. We looked at each other and laughed in relief.

# Maarten 't Hart
## The Netherlands

When I went to the University of Leiden in 1962 to study biology, I was required to take a minor in geology. In one of the very first lectures we future biologists were told that a new ice age was at hand. Soon the inter-glacial era in which we lived so snug and warm would come to an end; before the end of the century winters would become harsher. Get your skates out of the grease and have them sharpened, was the message.

How different the message is today, more than forty years later. Due to climate change, the parts of Holland that lie below sea level will soon be in danger. If the polar ice caps melt, much of Holland will be under water. Just a few weeks ago one of the leading Dutch newspapers carried a description of the 'worst-case scenario'. Had the time come for businesses to move east? the article asked.

I live only seven kilometres from the sea in a town which lies on reclaimed land that is six metres below sea level, so I run a fairly big risk. Perhaps the time has come for me to buy a houseboat stocked with emergency rations and moor it in the broad ditch which surrounds my house and garden?

It makes sense to keep an eye out for signs of climate change but it's not a simple thing to do. Are thrushes starting to sing earlier in the year than usual? It doesn't seem as if they are. However birds react to light, not temperature, so they are no use for tracking changes in the weather. Can spring flowers tell us whether climate change is taking place? Does the European hazelnut (*Corylus avellana*), one of the first trees to come into blossom, flower earlier now than in the past? It's hard to say, because the plants behave differently from year to year. Even if your hazelnut is already in bloom at Christmas you still can't say: this time it is remarkably early. Next year it might not bloom until the middle of January.

It's true that a spring flower like the common periwinkle (*Vinca minor*) has been flowering noticeably earlier than it used to. Sometimes you even see its beautiful blue flowers by Christmas. But perhaps this is due to its aggressive growth; once it has spread everywhere in the garden, there are more plants and therefore an increased chance of a few flowers appearing early.

Here, in Holland, there is only one plant from which one can make reasonable deductions about climate change: the broad bean. The broad bean likes the cold and you have to plant it early. But not too early, because then it will rot in the damp, chilly soil. Years ago I used to plant it in the clay soil in my garden around the middle of March and harvest it in the middle of May. If I planted it a bit later to make sure it wouldn't be defeated by cold and damp weather, it would grow well but then there was a risk that black bean-aphids would destroy it at the beginning of June. The black bean-aphid is a cruel organism. It appears suddenly in the tops of the beanstalks. Only ten or so on the first day, but an aphid becomes a grandmother overnight, so there are another hundred aphids the next day and ten thousand the day after that. Soon, large, jet-black, squirming aphids completely cover the plants and transform them into cheerless phantoms.

Planting the broad beans early prevents the aphids from striking. The beans are mature before the aphids show themselves. And if an aphid does appear, I can eliminate it by ruthlessly pinching the tops of the plants.

What have I learned over the past seven years? That planting my broad beans in mid-March is too late. Black bean-aphids will reliably appear at the end of May when the beans are still growing. What has also become apparent to me is that broad beans can be planted earlier, at the end of February—something that was impossible in the past. And even then I have to watch out for aphids because, since the weather in May is warmer and drier than it was, say, fifteen years ago, they show themselves much earlier and in greater numbers.

Due to my experience with broad beans, I believe it is possible to speak of a subtle and irreversible change in the climate. By the end of February the soil has warmed up to the point that broad beans can be planted, and by the end of May it has been so much warmer in the intervening period than in the past that black bean-aphids are appearing earlier than before. Yet we must keep an open mind. The aphids may have mutated to the point that they begin to reproduce earlier. Perhaps we are planting better quality broad beans which can stand the cold and damp better than the kind we used to plant? Nevertheless I cling to the view that climate change is responsible for this revised strategy for the successful raising of broad beans. I'm going to buy a houseboat.

*Translated from the Dutch by Michiel Horn*

# Thomas Keneally
*Australia*

The poet Les Murray once said Australia has two seasons, and they are drought and flood. Certainly, the conventional seasons sweep across a country lush and sub-tropical on the south-eastern and east coast, and semi-arid for much of the rest. But the great and dominating oscillation of weather, the one which influences national wealth and the national spirit, is years long—the El Niño Oscillation. El Niño was named by South American fishermen who noticed warm waters from the Western Pacific turning up off the South American coast and diminishing their fish stocks. Since this happened about Christmas, they gave the phenomenon its name: the Christ Child.

The effect of this water exchange across the Pacific brings drought and fire to Australia, as is the case as I write. This year our city woke to one achingly brilliant blue-sky, blue-sea day after another. By early

June—autumn here—the dazzling skies, denying water, began to take on a sinister aspect. The result has been water restrictions in the big cities—one is not permitted to hose a window or a car or a pavement—and pastures reduced to rubble in the countryside. I recently drove from Sydney to South Australia and have not in a lifetime seen a browner earth except, of course, where environmentally controversial water irrigation schemes exist. This drought is the worst in European-settler memory. Farmers whose ancestors lived plushly in the grand old days, when Britain's population and industries consumed the majority of our produce, are now desperately seeking new ways of making a living, or selling their forebears' farms.

This winter, for the first time in five years, rain arrived in many areas deep inland—in Hay in the Riverina area where an aunt and uncle of mine live, for example. It has not yet been followed up. El Niño is bad news from Peru to Indonesia, and it has been governing this continent for a long time, modifying the Australian seasons before and after the entry of the Europeans.

Global warming complicates this ancient scenario in ways I am not expert enough to comment on, except impressionistically. As anyone will know who has sat through a Test Match at the Sydney Cricket Ground and watched the pyrotechnic evening thunderstorms rolling up from the south, Australia is a place of melodramatic thunderstorms succeeded by strong winds. We are told that temperature rise will make these coastal summer storms more dramatic and destructive than ever. Some phenomenal storms have recently struck Sydney and Brisbane, with cricket-ball sized hail shattering roofs and destroying the paintwork of cars. My daughter was riding in a Sydney cab when a ball of hail smashed the windscreen. Everyone nods and says, Yeah, climate change.

Interestingly, global warning here does not seem to mean fierce summers. Everyone I talk to has a memory of more consistently scorching summers than we get now. Reading the journal of a charming officer of the First Fleet recently, I came across this, written in the early 1790s about Sydney: 'I have been in the West Indies—I have lived there. I know it is a rare instance for the mercury in the thermometer to mount there above 90 degrees; and here I scarcely spend a week in summer without seeing it rise to 100 degrees; sometimes to 105; nay, beyond even that boiling altitude.'

It seems to us now that the temperatures are evening out, drawing a little closer together. There won't be as much snow on the Australian Alps, winters will be warmer, and summers warm but less day-to-day stifling. Valid or not, there is a universal sense that not only is El Niño giving us a rough shake, but that our lives under the sun are not the same.

# James Lasdun
## United States

It is February and the weather forecaster on the early news announces that the National Weather Service has issued a Winter Storm Watch for the Catskill region, with six to twelve inches of snow predicted to fall tomorrow afternoon and through to the following morning.

I've lived in the United States for almost seventeen years, but I still find these official announcements of impending onslaughts from the elements oddly stirring. They remind me of one of the reasons for continuing to live here: the heroic nature of Nature; the large tracts of not-yet-spoiled wilderness, the vividness of the seasons, the exhilarating extremes of weather.

On the midday bulletin, the weatherman ups the estimated snowfall to between nine and fifteen inches, with the possibility of eighteen or more in the higher elevations, where my family and I live. We love a winter storm: school closes and the children go sledding with their friends instead. The power invariably goes out (sometimes the phone too), leaving us to the mercies of our wood stove, and giving us a chance to indulge our fantasies of living like the pioneer settlers from the *Little House on the Prairie* books. But we're careful not to let ourselves get carried away: over the past five or six years we've noticed a tendency for the weather service to overestimate these winter storms, sometimes to the point of predicting large blizzards that simply don't materialize at all.

We've also noticed (as has everyone else who lives here) that the winters themselves have become less dependable. My image of the Northeastern winter was formed in Vermont, where I lived on and off when I first moved to the States. There, the seasons were each sharply delineated. There were even distinct phases within each season: 'mud season', when the ground thawed at the beginning of spring and the dirt roads turned to an unnavigable cold grey slurry; late fall, when the golds and raspberry reds of October gave way to dustier ochres and russets. Mid-winter was always the most spectacular moment; the white clapboard villages glinting in their snow-crusts and diamond-clear icicles, the streams and ponds frozen, the whole landscape buried under three or more feet of sparkling snow. In early March the farmers hung metal buckets under the taps in their sugar maples, and the smell of sap being boiled down for syrup drifted in sweet currents through the cold air. (Methods have changed since then: instead of using buckets and woodshed kettles, the farmers now use reverse-osmosis pumps and electric evaporators, running yellow plastic tubing from tree to tree, so that the woods, as you drive by, look like a series of crime scenes.)

We're not so far north here in the Catskills, but our first winters here, ten, twelve years ago, were on the same dramatic scale. But in recent years, as if stricken by some sort of performance anxiety, this pugnacious season has started faltering. The snow fails, or it comes in as predicted only to be followed by balmy sunshine that melts all but a few north-facing blobs and rags of it in a day. Or the opposite happens: an out-of-control spasm of frigidity so extreme and sudden the stones crack on the town sidewalks and the birds get flash-frozen on the trees.

We blame this erratic behaviour on global warming. Of the two apocalyptic scenarios currently gripping the American psyche, this is the one we choose to subscribe to. Its scientific terms reassure us, although our readiness to invoke it owes as much to blind faith as do the Rapture fantasies of the Christian fundamentalists. Our apocalypse may be more reputably accredited than theirs, but my guess is that the susceptibility to either vision has the same psychological basis: guilt. Precisely because there is still intact wilderness in this country, still visibly in the process of being annihilated, you cannot live here without an overwhelming sense of the destructive character of your own species. You can explain it in terms of divine purpose or human folly, but you can't pretend not to be a part of it: you drive, you fly, you live in a heated building; one way or another you are implicated. We expect to pay a price. Depending on one's temperament, this will articulate itself either in terms of the Book of Revelation or the science pages of the *New York Times*.

Up in the Catskills, we practise a kind of secular flagellantism. We recycle religiously. We've installed low-energy appliances, low-capacity toilet cisterns. We eat mostly organic vegetarian food, wash with biodegradable soaps and detergents. But meanwhile the two cars that make our lives here possible sit mockingly in the driveway, rendering our virtuous endeavours about as meaningless as the rituals of our religious counterparts. Even with our modest (by American standards) lifestyle, no fewer than five planet earths would be required to sustain the world's current population if everyone lived as we do.

By next morning the Winter Storm Watch has been upgraded to a Winter Storm Warning: two to three feet of snow now expected in higher elevations, blizzard conditions, travel advisories, airports closed; the works. Our scepticism gives way to nervous excitement. There are urgent chores to be done: bringing in firewood, filling pans and buckets with water (the well pump won't work if the power goes), running into town to stock up on food and candles... The snow starts falling at around three in the afternoon. Big, puffy flakes that wander through the air like white bumble bees. It's cold enough that they settle right away, and soon everything—trees, house, cars, barn, woodpile—becomes a ghostly, blurry version of itself. By evening the flakes fall harder and faster; an encouragingly businesslike assault. There are already several inches on the ground, and we go to bed with high hopes, raised even higher by the sound of the snow plough thundering up the road at two in the morning. For the first time this winter I allow myself to contemplate the possibility of at least a day or two of my favourite outdoor activity: cross-country skiing.

I'm not the athletic type, but this has been one of the great discoveries of my adult life. There is nothing like gliding through a forest deep in fresh, velvety snow. The evergreens are a deeper green, the white birches glow like alabaster columns, the only sound is the hiss of your own skis—and for once the catch-all American term of approval, 'awesome', seems fully appropriate.

We took it up when we lived in Vermont and during our first winters here in the Catskills we could count on skiing throughout most of the season. But the patchiness of the past several winters has made it an increasingly rare prospect (you need a good twelve inches of cold, dry snow to go comfortably over the rocks and fallen trees in the woods). Last year we never even brought the skis down from the barn.

Perhaps there is no real connection between this and global warming—we're told not to draw conclusions from local short-term fluctuations. On the other hand there are more troubling things going on than a few years of lousy skiing. Maples, the mainstay of the Northern woods, depend on long hard winters to kill off the thrips and other pests that attack them, and in the absence of this invigorating yearly freeze the population is already showing enough signs of severe stress for botanists to be predicting major die-offs. Syrup yields are declining steadily, and south of Canada the industry is generally considered to be on its way out. Meanwhile prolonged droughts in other parts of the state are creating development pressures up here which are hard to resist. The larger land parcels around the Catskill preserve are being broken up, with new houses, lawns and roads spreading deeper into the woods and higher up the mountainsides every year. You can hardly go out these days without running into a new pool-house or chain-link fence.

Something has been troubling my last hour of sleep. I wake to a gentle pattering sound and realize, with a familiar sinking feeling, what it is. An image of singular blight lies outside the window. There must be a good eighteen inches of accumulation; prime skiing quality, no doubt, before the snow turned to rain. The enormous quantity of this mush, combined with its utter uselessness to either the woods or us, gives it a peculiarly depressing quality—like so much waste.

This is a privileged moment to be alive on this planet: simultaneously in sight of its past riches and their future ruination. I see myself aged ninety, a decrepit survivor hanging on after the great climate breakdown of the mid-twenty-first century, after the drowning of Manhattan, after the prairies have turned to desert, after famine and civil war have broken up the Empire and the Korean army has occupied D.C. and the Syrian fleet come steaming up the Hudson; going out to the cactus patch where our wild blueberries used to grow, foraging for a prickly pear or two to sell our new masters, then trying to explain to my incredulous grandchildren what snow was and exactly what it was we used to do with these long, narrow slats of fibreglass gathering dust together in the old barn, with their smooth tops and scaled undersides and pointed, upcurving ends...

# Javier Reverte
*Spain*

Fifty years ago, people had to make every effort to overcome the cold, and for a good part of the year too. I don't remember the heat having much effect on our lives, nor did I consider it a nuisance we had to struggle against. The heat would draw in and we'd say: 'Here comes the warm weather.' During the rest of the year the weather seemed like a vile trick devised by a malign god. In my home city of Madrid we feared the cold. Even now I shiver when I remember my childhood. By contrast, the heat does not occupy a dominant place in my memory.

In my childhood, just after the end of the Spanish Civil War, many of the houses in my district still displayed the signs of bomb damage; in the open spaces and on wasteland you could still find casements, pillboxes, bunkers, machine-gun nests, trenches and thousands of shell and bullet cases. I lived to the west of the city in a district near to the City University. A ferocious battle that lasted for several weeks had been fought here when Franco tried to march in to Madrid in the winter of 1936. Long after the war was over, Madrid was a city besieged by hunger and the standards of hygiene were lamentable. Only streets in the city centre were coated with asphalt; the rest were made of packed earth which turned into mud in winter, and dust in summer. There was no central heating in our homes and we cooked on coal fires. We were simply not equipped to deal with the cold. In my memory, I retain the image of immense snowy peaks that I have never seen again. And, above all, what seems to me to have been lost forever is a sense of the changing seasons.

I have a particularly vivid memory of a snowfall in the winter of 1954 or 1955. I was about ten years old, and one morning when I got up, my mother gave me the astounding news that I would not be able to go to school as the streets were impassable. A few hours later, when the snow had stopped falling, all of us kids went out to play. That day I enjoyed a particularly spectacular battle with the other gang in my neighbourhood. (In those days we children formed opposing groups and fought each other constantly.) The snow reached above the height of my shoulders.

The ice, a nightmare for the city council, was the other present offered up to us children. While we amused ourselves by skating on the frozen surface of the River Manzanares and the lakes in the Retiro park or around the Casa de Campo, gangs of fire-fighters worked around the clock to repair the water pipes that, because of the frost, had burst all across the city. While we played at being explorers at the North Pole, caught between this intense ice and snow, the adults swore against this plague of a near-biblical character.

There was an enormous shortage of coal and firewood (for heating and cooking) in the city. In the 1940s and the early 50s, coal was hauled into the city on carts drawn by mules, and later on, in ancient lorries. The coal heavers were heavily muscled men, covered in coal dust, in sleeveless shirts; their arms, chest and eyes all glistened; they would heave shovelfuls of coal from boxes on the back of their lorries directly into the sacks and metal bins lined up by the residents beside the trucks. For several days, the whole street was covered in a filthy black carpet, but the smoke that emerged from the chimney stacks held out the promise of warm lodgings.

Very few houses had radiators at that time, and stoves provided nearly all their heat. School classrooms, too, had stoves installed in them: the teacher would draw the heater close to his desk, and as children we competed to get closer to him. Yet the corridors in every school felt like the frozen wastes of the Alaskan tundra. As we went from lesson to lesson, our breath emerged white and heavy from our mouths and nostrils, as if we were little inuit.

At night, adults made up the beds to keep out the cold. Between the sheets they would place a 'bedwarmer': a small round brazier, made out of copper, flat and filled with live coals. The warmer was moved from bed to bed; it left traces of soft warmth in the sheets behind it. As soon as the warmer was removed, you had to get into bed immediately, in order to conserve the heat it had left behind.

Children used to sleep in the same bed as adults. Families were far larger than those of today—not simply because the birth rate was much higher then but also because of a certain kind of family solidarity; even in the wealthiest homes, spinster aunts would be gathered in, along with widowed mothers-in-law and sickly siblings.

However many children there were in a family, there was always at least one adult, usually a spinster aunt, whose bed one could hope to share. We would hug her and rob her of her bodily warmth even as sleep overcame us.

Washing was complicated. The women would heat great buckets of water on the kitchen hearth and then transport them in equally large jugs to the bathroom. There the water, mingled with soap, would be poured into the washbasins in which you could wash your hair, your face and your armpits. As a rule, each house had only one basin. We children used to wash on a Saturday evening, all of us making use of the same water until it became cold. The running order was generally from youngest to oldest and in a large family the oldest child had to endure a bath in cold, grey water.

In the icy winter months, chilblains also threatened—a smarting and swelling of the skin which brought on an intense pain and severe itching of one's feet, hands and even ears. The cause of the discomfort was a combination of intense cold and vitamin deficiency. It is now years since I heard anyone in Madrid mention having chilblains.

Hot weather was regarded as a blessing by the poor and generally cold population. In the days before we had refrigerators, fresh water was kept in earthenware pitchers, and we bought bluish ice blocks from special factories or from the petrol station. The summer sun was not allowed to flood into our living rooms: windows were kept open during the night and when day came we closed the shutters and pulled down the Venetian blinds. We lived in twilight, but in a fresh atmosphere. In the Madrid of those days, there were quantities of mosquitoes, and to prevent them entering our rooms at night and devouring us in our sleep, we'd put pots of rosemary and basil on our window sills—the scent of the herbs seemed to keep the insects at bay.

We experienced the changes of season in the city with an intense and profound clarity; it affected all our senses. In February, there would always be a day on which you could discern a distant perfume, a subtle aroma that arrived on a wave of warm air. It was the first sign of spring, along with the white blossom on the almond trees, which flourished in the orchards to the west of Madrid. Then the season of birds and fruit began in earnest. Madrid filled up with thrushes and in lots of bars, there was a custom of serving a dish of fried birds by way of a canapé—or a tapa—to accompany a small tumbler of wine or a glass of beer. The markets would suddenly sport the first melons, watermelons and tomatoes among their wares; soon afterwards wild peaches, cherries and apricots would arrive. There were no hothouses in those days. You could eat an artichoke only in the spring, for example, and green beans at the height of summer. Tomatoes were not perfectly and regularly shaped, like those we now buy but they did give off an intense fragrance; their flavour was delicious and, unlike those we eat now, there was absolutely nothing insipid about them.

In the parks in spring, the air was full of the scents of every kind of flower: lilies, forsythia, broom, pinks, roses... The trees also provided us with sweet-scented flowers. Mulberry trees sprouted dark berries and we cut off the leaves to feed to our silkworms which we had bought in the market and kept covered in shoeboxes until they wove their white or yellow cocoons. There were butterflies on the streets of Madrid and caterpillars dropped from the trees—if you touched them they caused hives and other skin problems.

In summer, the birds went into hiding and the scents seemed to subside under the heat. During siesta hour, crickets sounding like the tuneless strumming of numerous guitars, maintained their noisy lament in the city parks. At the end of the summer, in September, honeyed figs would begin to crop, along with the first blackberries. Then the storms would also begin: loud and crude, bearing heavy thunder and flashes of lightning. The earth, sodden with water after three months of drought, gave off a powerful smell, as if it had a powerful and secret life. The storms also brought a degree of sadness to children as they announced a return to school imprisonment. Then at a stroke, one day in late October, the atrocious cold would again fall on the city, and the serious battle to protect ourselves from its depredations would come round again.

Throughout my childhood, adults would repeat ancient verses— all about the seasons—which, with remarkable frequency, would coincide with the actual forecasts made. 'In January, a dog seeks out the shade' (frequent sunny spells even in midwinter); 'February the crazy' (the unpredictable nature of the February climate); 'When March may, May marches' (if the weather is fine at the end of winter, spring will be cold); 'In April, waters mill' (a reference to the Spring rains); 'Water in May makes your hair and the grass grow' (Spring rains were particularly good for new growth); 'In August, with cold in your face' (the North wind got colder at the end of Summer); 'The air of Madrid never snuffed out either a candle or a man' (a reference, dating from the sixteenth century, to the iciness of the air in the sierra surrounding Madrid.)

In Madrid today, the four seasons exist only on a calendar. It hardly ever snows, the lakes and the river never freeze over and we eat fruit that tastes of nothing all year round. If March may, May calls up siroccos from the deserts of Africa. In April, it scarcely ever rains, and the ground cracks open. The birds have fled the asphalt, no caterpillars tumble from their cocoons in the trees, the crickets no longer thrum, the flowers barely smell and storms grow rare. The cold, happily, remains nestling only in the corners of my childhood memories. But a hard heat rolls in on weary, sticky waves, right into our brains where it lodges for months on end. It is a new kind of heat, wearisome and defeating, which still seems somehow unbelievable to those of us who happened to be born sixty years ago.

*Translated from the Spanish by Amanda Hopkinson*

# Rodrigo Rey Rosa
## Guatemala

*2015: A few words of advice for anyone considering taking a holiday or planning a move at any point during the coming decade to the shores of Lake Atitlan in Guatemala.*

**1.** Although this deep and recent lake formed in an extinct volcano was, until only a few years ago, a paradise for aquatic sports and one of the region's most popular tourist attractions, it is important to be aware that now it is wholly inadvisable to swim there from the beginning of May until the end of August. The lake has a catchment area of 348 square kilometres, including thirteen small towns, and huge quantities of rubbish and excrement accumulated during the dry periods of the year are now regularly swept down to the lake in rivers swollen by torrential rains. Even a few years ago one could observe, at the start of the rainy season, little floating islets of pumice stone and seaweed; nowadays these are joined by other islands of old rubber tyres, plastic bags and bottles, plates and straws, sweet wrappers and condoms. These agglomerations seem to be increasing every year and remain on the water surface for longer than they used to, making any nocturnal boat excursions—as well as those undertaken in speedboats during the day when the weather is either foggy or rainy—a dangerous activity.

2. The continual changes in the water level—though this inland lake has no tide—is a real headache to local architects, landscape gardeners, and the engineers responsible for the construction of wharves and jetties. On the most steep and canyonesque shorelines, the fashionable solution in recent times has been to build a moveable gangway of the kind seen on the sides of warships, to be raised or lowered according to the level of the lake. This aquatic fluctuation can be explained by the subterranean drainage system on the south side, the seismic shifts characteristic of the region, and the precipitous rainfall. Landing stages are either high and dry or suddenly submerged, and motor boats either drowned or strewn upon the beaches. There are some benefits. The inhabitants of the flat zones at the base of the ravines may note with sadness that the water is retreating from their gardens, year after year, but the most inventive of them have used the space to build tennis courts or football pitches. The bad news for this particular sector of our lakeside population is that they cannot forget the extent to which their lifestyles now revolve around an incessant war on flying insects, of which we have only time to single out the terrifying *Aedis aegypti* and the extraordinary 'come-backer', known to us as 'anopheles'. Among this landscape of green mountains and blue volcanoes with its temperate climate, where both dengue and malaria had become the near-forgotten diseases of the past, the quantity of such species has increased either seven or tenfold, according to which sources you refer to, between the year 2010 and today. Once again, the most go-ahead dwellers around Lake Atitlan have figured out how to snatch victory from the jaws of such a defeat and today there are families, particularly in the areas between Santiago and Cerro de Oro, rushing to develop a whole new industry: the refining of an oil extracted from mosquitoes which can be used as a sunscreen ointment or to create more new regional dishes in the fashionable cooking tradition that local people have recently adopted.

3. It is advisable to add to the existing list of 'things to bring' a pair of sunglasses which are guaranteed proof against UV-B rays. If you

happen to be the owner of any kind of pet, or if you have children, please remember that they should wear them too—at any time of day, from sunrise to sunset—and so avoid damage to their eyes in the shape of cataracts and other types of blindness. And should it already to be too late for you to take this type of preventive measure, there are branches of the distinguished 'Atitlan Club for the Seeing Blind' in Panajachel, in Santa Catarina and in San Pedro. 4. Should you or your relatives happen to live in the zone of the canyons located on the north side of the lake, or among the skirts of the volcanoes flanking the lake on its southern shore, you should always bear in mind the possibility that landslides of larger stones or boulders can occur—whether because of the rains, which fall for a shorter period of each year but more intensely, or because of the dry and violent winds that whip the volcanic crater at the year's end and make its waves of crystalline water turn black. To this prognosis one should also add the possibility, even the probability, of earthquakes or at least of tremors. A year or two ago a new custom began to spread, that of using the scrap iron left behind by the mining companies who used to extract gold and silver ore to the north of Solola during the previous decades. The idea of a house constructed from metal planks and cylinders might not appear overly attractive, yet some of our youngest and most promising architects have taken up the challenge, and come out of it with flying colours. Already, particularly in the zones around Tzununá and Santa Cruz, there are many examples of this type of dwelling. 5. If, disregarding all the above notes of warning, you have nonetheless installed yourself in the region under conditions that are beginning to appear increasingly unbearable to you—a response we find entirely natural in itself, of course—we have a piece of news which we sincerely hope may renew your spirits: thanks to the vast reserves of cyanide and other chemicals left behind here by mining and other related companies (whose names I shall omit in order to avoid repercussions), our local doctors and traditional healers have experimented for the first time with substances that, for mainly economic reasons, were previously beyond their reach. Not without an element of national pride, we boast that today we can meet every demand for our new and improved version of the tablets we call simply 'Adios'. These have a cyanide base, infused with a secret compound of special mushrooms, herbs and petals to make a swift, infallible and pleasurable concoction—even though none of our tasters have, at least until now, been able to advise us of quite how pleasurable. 'Adios' allows me to put at your disposal the culmination of the modern age working in tandem with the wisdom of our most distant ancestors. And it comes to you entirely free of charge.

*Signed by the President of the Association of the Friends of Atitlan.*

*Translated from the Spanish by Amanda Hopkinson*

# Subscribe!

Each quarterly paperback issue of *Granta* features new fiction, reportage, memoir and history by writers drawn from around the world. Usually, each issue has a theme—recent ones have included *What We Think of America*, *Film*, *Music*, *This Overheating World* and *Mothers*. Each issue is at least 256 pages, and costs £9.99 in bookshops. But when you subscribe—or give *Granta* to a friend who shares your love of reading—you get a large discount:

➤ **SAVE 30%** (£12) with a one-year (4-issue) subscription for £27.95.
➤ **SAVE 35%** (£27) with a two-year (8-issue) subscription for £51.95.
➤ **SAVE 40%** (£47) with a three-year (12-issue) subscription for £71.95.

SEE THE TEAR-OUT CARD IN THE ISSUE FOR MORE DETAILS AND AN ORDER FORM.

'I've grown up as a writer with Granta and it's impossible to think of literary life without it. There are other literary magazines and then there is Granta—unique, enduring and indispensable.'
Graham Swift, 2004

G R A N T A

# NOTES ON CONTRIBUTORS

**Margaret Atwood**'s *The Blind Assassin* won the Booker Prize in 2000. Her latest novel is *Oryx and Crake* (Bloomsbury/Doubleday).

**Karen E. Bender** is the author of *Like Normal People* (Picador/Houghton Mifflin) and is working on a collection of short stories.

**John Borneman** teaches anthropology at Princeton. His most recent book is *The Case of Ariel Sharon and the Fate of Universal Jurisdiction* (Princeton).

**Urvashi Butalia**'s books include *The Other Side of Silence: Voices from the Partition of India* (C. Hurst & Co/Duke University Press). She lives in Delhi.

**Geoff Dyer**'s book about photography, *The Ongoing Moment*, has just been published by Little Brown in the UK and by Pantheon in the US.

**Gilad Evron** writes for the theatre, film and television and has been awarded numerous prizes for his plays and screenplays. He lives in Tel Aviv.

**Simon Garfield** is a feature writer for the London *Observer* and the author of seven books of non-fiction. *We Are At War*, his second compilation of Mass Observation diaries, will be published by Ebury Press in October 2005.

**Simon Gray**'s plays include *Butley* and *Otherwise Engaged*. 'Wish You Were Here' is taken from the second volume of his diaries, *The Year of the Jouncer*, which is forthcoming from Granta Books in January 2006. An extract from the first volume, *The Smoking Diaries*, appeared in *Granta* 82.

**Robin Grierson** was included in *Family: Photographers Photograph Their Families* (Phaidon), and is working on a book of his family photographs.

**James Hamilton-Paterson**'s novels include *Loving Monsters* (Granta Books) and his latest, *Cooking with Fernet Branca* (Faber). He lives in Tuscany.

**Ismail Kadaré** was born in 1936 in Gjirokaster, Albania. His novel *The Successor* will be published next year by Canongate in the UK and by Arcade in the US. In 2005 he won the first Man Booker International Prize.

**Thomas Keneally**'s *Schindler's Ark* won the Booker Prize in 1982. *The Tyrant's Novel*, his latest novel, is published by Sceptre/Nan A. Talese.

**James Lasdun**'s new novel, *Seven Lies*, will be published by W. W. Norton in the US in October 2005 and by Jonathan Cape in the UK in January 2006.

**Javier Reverte** was born in Madrid in 1944. His most recent novel, *El médico de Ifni*, is forthcoming from Areté in October 2005.

**Rodrigo Rey Rosa** lives in Guatemala. His books include *The Good Cripple* (W. W. Norton) and a short-story collection, *Otto Zoo* (Seix Barral).

**Saïd Sayrafiezadeh** is at work on a memoir about the Socialist Workers Party and a play about the New York City draft riots of 1863.

**Maarten 't Hart** trained in zoology and ethnology and is the best-selling author of thirteen novels, most recently *The Sun Dial* (Arcadia/Toby Press).

**Frederic Tuten**'s novels include *The Green Hour*, published by W. W. Norton.